# Ministerial Life
## and Work

# Ministerial Life and Work

*By*

## W. H. GRIFFITH THOMAS, D.D.

*An Abridgement of*

## The Work of the Ministry

*By*

## HIS WIFE

BAKER BOOK HOUSE
Grand Rapids, Michigan

Reprinted 1974 by
Baker Book House
with the permission of the copyright owner
Winifred G. T. Gillespie
ISBN: 0-8010-8764-3

PHOTOLITHOPRINTED BY CUSHING - MALLOY, INC.
ANN ARBOR, MICHIGAN, UNITED STATES OF AMERICA
1 9 7 3

# INTRODUCTION

## WILLIAM HENRY GRIFFITH THOMAS
## (1861-1925)

W. H. Griffith Thomas was ordained into the Anglican ministry at age twenty-four. He served at St. Paul's Portman Square, London (1896-1905), became Principal of Wycliffe College, Oxford (1905-1910), and then served as Professor of Old Testament at Wycliffe College, Toronto (1910-1919). The main purpose of these Anglican colleges was to prepare men for the ministry. In 1919 he moved to Philadelphia and began a worldwide ministry of conference work, Bible lectures, preaching, teaching, and writing.

Previous training and experience in business gave W. H. Griffith Thomas the discipline of accuracy and clarity in statement and purpose. He was a prodigious worker and writer and excelled as a teacher and preacher. His careful outlines and expository contents were blended by a homiletical skill seldom matched. He was clear and concise, fresh and invigorating. Mr. Thomas followed closely the English Bible and John Bunyan as models for the work of the ministry. The well-stored mind, the simplicity of illustration, and the clear running style mark his writings and sermons as classics in naturalness and appeal.

*Ministerial Life and Work* originally was narrow in scope, intended for those in the Anglican communion. It has been edited to give it wider appeal. The work reflects a background of diligent study and research in Biblical and Systematic Theology. From a master we can study and learn.

RALPH G. TURNBULL

# FOREWORD

SEVERAL months before his death, it was suggested to my husband that he should revise and re-arrange *The Work of the Ministry* in order to make it more serviceable to ministers of different denominations. It was his intention, not only to delete all material belonging strictly to the Church of England formularies but also to rewrite the book in part, make additions to the subject matter and incorporate in it the results of his more recent reading. While the work is still available in its original form, it has been thought by many that my husband's aim should be carried out—even in a necessarily inadequate manner—by me. The preparation of this volume has been a labor of love, in which I have been assisted by my daughter. We send it forth with the earnest prayer that he, being dead, may yet speak to his brethren in the ministry.

*Philadelphia, 1926.*         ALICE GRIFFITH THOMAS.

# CONTENTS

## PART I

## THE MAN

## PART II

## THE WORK

# PREFACE

DURING my five years at Wycliffe Hall, Oxford, it fell to my lot to deal with the various aspects of ministerial life and service which are usually included in the term Pastoral. This involved regular addresses in Chapel on Saturday evenings, weekly lectures on Pastoral work, addresses at the openings of Terms, and occasional informal 'Conferences' on some of the more outstanding ministerial and pastoral problems.

This book embodies the substance of what was then given, and it is reproduced in the hope that those to whom it was originally delivered may like to have a record of what I have reason to know were occasions not without interest; and also that other brethren in the ministry may find it of some service.

If some readers should feel surprise at observing that several aspects of ministerial life are not dealt with in these pages, they may perhaps be reminded that my opportunity for treating Pastoral life and work extended at most to only thirty weeks each year, and that therefore with (as a rule) but one address and one lecture a week, it was impossible to cover more of the ground.

If, too, any brother in the ministry should be surprised at the comparative absence of reference to problems of Biblical Criticism and of scepticism, and to ways of meeting them, it ought to be said that these were dealt with in the Wycliffe Hall work by means of other courses of lectures.

Occasional repetitions may also provoke comment. The explanation is that the entire substance of the book was not given every year and, so, certain subjects were discussed under two or three different headings. But it is hoped that the prime importance of such topics will be sufficient justification of any such repeated treatment.

The book is intended primarily for clergy, and brevity with a view to the reader's own meditation, study, and elaboration appeared in every way best fitted to further the work of the ministry.

Ever since my thoughts were first turned in the direction of the ministry, I have felt a great attraction for all questions dealing with preaching, methods of ministerial work, and problems of teaching and service; and I have read as widely as opportunity has permitted various volumes of Lectures on Preaching and Pastoral work. These chapters are therefore indebted directly and indirectly to very many writers whom it is now impossible to recall and name.

It only remains for me to say with what joy (and I hope profit to myself) I have recalled in writing these pages the happy occasions on which I met the Students in the delivery of the addresses and lectures here recorded. The earnest attention of those Saturday evenings in Chapel, and the keen interest and animated discussions of the Friday evenings in the Library will never be forgotten by me, and will be cherished among the happiest times of my life at Wycliffe Hall. May both writer and readers of this book make "full proof of their ministry.'

*1911.*                    W. H. GRIFFITH THOMAS.

PART I

# THE MAN

$S$T. PAUL *points out in one single chapter
(Col. 1) that the ministry is related at once to
Christ ( v. 7); to the Gospel (v. 23); and to the
Church ( v. 25); to Christ as the Source, to the
Gospel as the Message, and to the Church as the
Sphere. All considerations of the Christian ministry must take account of these three aspects, and in
the various parts of Holy Scripture where the ministry is dealt with, it will be seen that this threefold
relationship in one or other of its phases is kept
in view.*

*The Biblical idea of the ministry may be con-
sidered in a number of ways. We will now look
at it as suggested for us by the Old Testament
Prophet, by the New Testament Apostle, by the
personal experiences of St. Paul, and by the counsels he gave to one of his younger ministerial
brethren.*

*Then follows a consideration of the ministerial
call and its subsequent obligations.*

CHAPTER I

# THE MINISTRY OF THE PROPHET[1]

THERE is a close analogy between the Old Testament and the New Testament prophet. The Greek word προφήτης gives a very fair idea of the meaning of the Hebrew word *Nabi*.[2] The prophet is a 'spokesman,' one who represents another, and Exodus 7: 1 is the best definition or description of what a prophet is, whether in the Old Testament or the New Testament.

Modern scholarship has rendered great service to the cause of Biblical truth by making these prophets much more definite, clear, and intelligible to us. We can now see pretty clearly what they were and did.

## SECTION 1. THE PROPHET'S CALL (*Isa.* 6)

The first thing that strikes us is that each prophet had a call to the work. This came in different ways and was associated with a variety of circumstances, but the fact was the same in every case, and was essential and fundamental. Prophets and prophetic men like Abraham, Moses, Gideon, and many others were all 'called of God.' No man took this honour to himself. What this call meant may perhaps be best understood by giving attention to one of whom we know most and whom we may regard as essentially typical of all; the prophet Isaiah (ch. 6). Taking the story as it stands, we observe the four stages of his call, and in it the analogous experiences which should be true of every minister of the Gospel who is really called of God.

---

[1] This section was suggested by, and is deeply indebted to, that valuable and suggestive book, *The Preacher and His Models*, by Dr. Stalker, one of the best of its kind for guidance in preaching and teaching.

[2] W. J. Beecher, *The Prophets and the Promise*.

I. *A Consciousness of God followed by a Conviction of Sin* (*vs.* 1-5).

Isaiah had a vision of God in His Sovereignty, His Majesty, and His Holiness (*vs.* 1-4). This sight of God was at the foundation of all that he became. God as 'infinitely great,' 'infinitely high,' and 'infinitely holy' possessed and dominated the soul of the young Isaiah, and it is only by such a sight of God that any man can become a prophet.

This vision, this consciousness of God, at once led to the result intended by God in giving it; conviction of sin. 'Then said I, Woe is me!' In God's light Isaiah saw light on himself, his life, his ways in the sight of the high and holy God. Conviction of sin based on a consciousness of God is fundamental to the life and work of a prophet of God, a minister of Christ.

II. *Confession of Sin followed by Cleansing from Sin* (*vs.* 5-7).

To be conscious was to confess, and Isaiah at once ('*Then* said I') poured out his soul in confession. He was conscious of failure in himself and in his nation in regard to uncleanness of utterance, and the vision of God as 'the King, the Lord of Hosts' had brought this out as never before.

But to confess was to be cleansed ('*Then* flew'). Cleansing immediate, perfect, assured, was his experience. The Divine fire did its work at once and thoroughly, and with the Divine assurance of absolute cleansing the prophet entered into the second, and was ready for the third stage of his experience.

III. *The Call of God followed by Consecration to God* (*v.* 8).

The prophet thus convicted and cleansed was now spiritually fit for further revelations from God, and it was not long before the Divine voice inquired, 'Whom shall I send, and who will go for us?' There was work to be done. The national life was at a crisis (*v.* 1), and the sin of the people called for Divine action (*v.* 5). Only as we see God, see our sin, receive God's forgiveness and know it, can we realize and answer the call, and so with whole-hearted consecration came the response; 'Here am I; send me.' To the man for whom God had done so much, consecration was the necessary, prompt and thorough rejoinder, and the man whom God had so prepared was ready for service ('*Then* said I'). Before, it was, 'Then said I, Woe is me!' Now, it is, 'Then said I; Here am I.'

IV.  *The Commission of God followed by Communion with God* (*vs.* 9-11).

The human readiness to be sent is quickly followed by the Divine authorization. 'Go, and tell.' The work to be done would mean plain speaking, and would need courage, persistence, and even severity of dealing. The ills of the people were not superficial and would not be met without drastic remedies. But when a man is conscious of a definite Divine commission: 'Go, and tell,' he can go because he knows that 'God's biddings are enablings.'

Not only so, but the prophet is now able to enter into fellowship with God, to seek to know more of His will, and to endeavour to understand His purposes. Faced with a difficult task, Isaiah approached God; 'Then said I, Lord, how long?' This is the privilege of the man who has seen God and received God's cleansing and commission. The Lord does not hide from such a man that which He will do. 'The Lord God will do nothing, but He revealeth His secret unto His servants the prophets' (Amos 3: 7). And thus the prophet, called, cleansed, and commissioned, is enabled to enter into the secret of his Divine Lord's will. 'The secret of the Lord is with them that fear him; and He will show them His covenant' (Psa. 25: 14).

This call and consciousness of God is essential to a man at the outset of his ministry. Unless he has it, he had better not start out. The ministry is a vocation, not a profession. 'How wilt thou run, seeing thou hast no tidings ready?'

But it is also essential when the man is actually at his work. The Church can only echo and authenticate the call

and unless the minister is ever conscious that he is where and
what he is, because God has called, placed, and equipped him,
his ministry must necessarily suffer in power and blessing.

And, not least of all, this consciousness of a Divine vocation is essential all through a minister's life. We must keep
in touch with God. People are quick to see both the presence
and the absence of this Divine consciousness in their clergyman's life.

Some years ago a well-known poet suddenly disappeared,
and there seems no doubt that he committed suicide. He was
the son of a minister, and he not only threw over his father's
faith, but set himself with intense violence and virulence to
overthrow Christianity. This is how *The Times* (London)
closed its review of his last work:—

'He had well nigh all that goes to make a great poet, except the
upward-seeing vision that is fixed on the Eternal.'

'Except the upward-seeing vision that is fixed on the Eternal.'
How true, how searching are these words when applied to
the minister. We may have all else, education, capacity, opportunity, but the one thing needful is the 'upward-seeing
vision.' As Dr. A. J. Gordon of Boston once said: 'It is
the look that saves, but it is the *gaze* that sanctifies.' It is
only as we see God, keep our gaze fixed on the Eternal, that
our life and service will bring glory to God, blessing to others,
and restful satisfaction to our own souls.

SECTION 2.    THE PROPHET'S WORK (*Isa.* 61: 1-3).

It has often been pointed out that there is a great and
fundamental difference between the Old Testament prophet
and the New Testament minister: the former addressed the
community; the latter the individual. Dr. G. A. Smith
argues with his own characteristic force that Isaiah had a
message for the individual, based on his own individual experience and inspired by his personal ideal for Israel.[1] But
probably most students of Old Testament prophecy will be
inclined to agree with Dr. Stalker in making individuality and

[1] Dr. G. A. Smith, *Isaiah*, Vol. 1, p. 289.

preaching to individuals essentially Christian ideas.[1]  Yet this
difference of opinion need not prevent us from endeavouring
to discover what was the prophet's work, and to apply the
truths to our own day and needs.  We shall find that
whenever we address individuals or communities the work of
the prophet of the Old Testament has much to teach us.

## I.  The Prophet was a Messenger.

He was sent from God, he declared the message of God,
and he spoke for God.  He has been well described as 'a
citizen with a message.'  This message was directed primarily
against the evils of his own day, but it also included the announcement of that great Day to which the Jews and the
Old Testament ever looked forward.  Today the minister
is pre-eminently a Messenger of Redemption, and undoubtedly
his primary message is and must be individual and personal.
Whatever results may accrue to the community through the
preaching of the Gospel, the needs of the soul in relation to
God must come first.  'The soul of all improvement is the improvement of the soul.'  But this is no reason why we should
not rigidly and fearlessly apply the principles of Redemption
to the facts of our social life and endeavour to let people
see that all such questions as Drink, Housing, Land, Unem-
ployment, Gambling, have their moral aspects which can only
be dealt with by the truths and grace of Christianity.

## II.  The Prophet was a Witness.

He was a 'Truth-Teller.'  'Cry aloud, and spare not,' was
his Divinely-given motto.  In ordinary appearance he differed
nothing from other citizens, but in attitude, bearing, conviction, he had the accent of one who had seen and therefore
could speak.  Coming from the presence of God, and judging
all things in the light of Eternity, he could deal with such
sins as idolatry, hypocrisy, selfishness, and oppression fearlessly
and fully.  For was he not the Divine witness against un-
righteousness, and in favour of truth, equity, and purity?
Even if the message is not heeded, the very presence in our
churches of a witness for God must and will tell.

--------
[1]Dr. Stalker, *The Preacher and His Models*, p. 62 f.

III.   *The Prophet was a Pleader.*

We greatly err if we think of the Old Testament prophet simply as one who warned, denounced, and threatened. There was another side to his message. He also appealed, and no one can read a passage like Isaiah 61: 1-3, or study the life of Jeremiah without seeing how strong and constant was this note of pleading. This is one of the chief characteristics of a New Testament minister. He must plead, he must appeal, he must 'woo,' he must deal tenderly, and must never forget the apostolic tone which said 'We *pray* you in Christ's stead.'

IV.   *The Prophet was a Comforter.*

Not only a pleader; a comforter. The Jewish remnant, that faithful few among the faithless, needed all the cheer they could obtain as they endeavoured to live for God amid the idolatry and iniquity of the nation. 'To comfort them that mourn' was therefore a prominent feature of the prophet's work, and the key-note of the entire section of Isaiah 40-66 seems to be found in 'Comfort ye my people, saith your God,' addressed not to the people but to the prophets, as they set about their work for God.

To-day the need for comfort is equally great. There are few congregations and few lives which are not burdened with some sorrow or discouragement. If the preacher omits this 'note' from his preaching he will fail at a vital point, but if he takes care to 'comfort' in the old sense of encourage, strengthen, hearten, cheer, he will find his ministry blessed to many needy, burdened, thirsty souls.

V.   *The Prophet was a Herald.*

This note was never long absent from the prophetic message. A good time was coming, a great Day, and a glorious King, and these constituted the heart of the prophet's word. On the strength of this he bade them lift up their hearts and find cheer, strength, inspiration in the promise and hope of redemption. To-day the dominant note of all preaching must be the evangelical note. The Gospel is *Good News*, and this in no narrow sense, but in the fullest, widest acceptation of the term. Above all applications to social problems, and beyond all intellectual questions, the substance of the Gospel, the Good News must be proclaimed. 'I delivered unto you *first of all* that which I also received, how that Christ *died for our sins.*' 'What must I do to be saved?' is still the primary question, and the Good News of Redemption is still the primary answer.

Messenger, Witness, Pleader, Comforter, Herald. Such was the prophet; such, still more, is the Minister. 'Difficult,' do we say? Yes, of course it is, it has never been anything else and never will be. How can a man be all this to his fellows without realizing the difficulty? Everything of value in life is difficult. To be a painter is difficult, to be a musician is difficult, to be a scientist is difficult. And to depict Christ, to bring out the music of the Gospel, to reveal truth for life must also be difficult. We need and must have the fulness of life both as to intellect and to experience. The fuller our experience of life and manhood the richer our life will ever be. 'As a preacher grows up intellectually he should grow down in simplicity and sympathy, like the weeping trees that rise with their stem but touch the ground with their branches, the strength never lessening the softness.' But though difficult it is *possible*. We have the same source of power as the prophet. 'The Spirit of the Lord God is upon me; He hath anointed me.' The Spirit is still ready, still available, still powerful, and in the presence of Christ, in fellowship with Him, we shall receive the anointing which teaches, which equips, which upholds, which uses, which blesses. Like Moses in the Mount, we shall learn the pattern and receive the power and then do the work God has for us to do.

## SECTION 3. THE PROPHET'S POWER

The great instrument of the prophet's work was the Word of God. A 'Word!' Only a Word! How light, how slight, and yet how mighty! Words have always had great influence and power in history. 'Where the word of a king is, there is power.' But the Word of God is the greatest power in the universe. 'He spake, and it was done; He commanded, and it stood fast.' All through Scripture the Word of the Lord stands out prominently as the greatest force in the world, and at all times His word through His servants has been the one supreme power over men. 'He hath made my mouth like a sharp sword' (Isa. 49: 2). The power of the Word in the prophet's own life needs careful consideration.

### I. *The Word Commissioning* (Jer. 1: 4, 9).

One phrase marks the prophetic commission. 'The Word of the Lord came' (Jer. 1: 4, 9). From the first occurrence of this term in connexion with Abraham (Gen. 15: 1) to the last occurrence in connexion with the greatest of all prophets (John the Baptist, Luke 3: 2), it stands out as the basis of all proper and authorized service for God.

1. It meant first of all a *personal commission*. It meant a definite call to work and constituted the man to whom it came a genuine, authoritative servant of his Lord and God. What a strength and inspiration it gave a man to know and feel that 'the word of the Lord came' to him. So it is, so it must be still. If in a very real way the word does not 'come' to a man for ministry, he had better not set out, for it will be embarking on a hopeless enterprise. But if he is assured of the 'Word of the Lord' commissioning him, how strong, how safe, how satisfied he is.

2. For it meant also a *personal communication*. Not only a definite call but a definite message, and the latter indicated and proved the former. By the message the call was demonstrated, by the communication the commission. This too, has a direct application to the ministry to-day, for in a very real sense we must get our texts from God; our message must be from Him if we are to speak in demonstration of the Spirit and power.

### II. *The Word Communing* (Jer. 15: 16).

The Word which calls and commissions must be that by which the soul of the prophet continues to keep in touch with his Divine Lord. So it was with Jeremiah. 'Thy words were found, and I did eat them; and Thy word was unto

me the joy and rejoicing of mine heart: for I am **called**
by Thy Name, O Lord God of Hosts.'

1. The Word must be received. 'I did eat.' The Word
as food is a suggestion often found in Scripture. Job says,
'I have esteemed Thy Word more than my necessary food'
(ch. 23: 12). Ezekiel was commanded to 'eat' the book
God gave him (ch. 3:1). The Psalmist rejoices in God's
Word as sweet to his taste, and sweeter than the honeycomb
(Psa. 21: 10; 119: 103). The Apostle urges the young
converts to desire the sincere milk of the Word that they
may grow thereby (1 Pet. 2: 2), and the truth of God is more
than once mentioned as the strong meat for the spiritually
mature (1 Cor. 3: 2; Heb. 5: 12). What food is to the
body God's truth is to the soul. It satisfies the cravings of
hunger; it invigorates the soul; it builds up the life. Meditation is the spiritual analogue of that process of appropriation,
digestion and assimilation by means of which food becomes
the nourishment of our bodily life. We must 'read, mark,
learn and inwardly digest.' 'He that eateth Me (τρώγω).'

2. The Word must be experienced. 'A joy and the rejoicing.' The joy of the Word in the prophet's life is a
suggestive and striking fact. Jeremiah is not usually thought
of as a man of joy, and yet here he expresses his joy in God's
Word in no measured terms. There will always be joy in
every true ministry in proportion as God's Word is 'found'
and 'eaten.' The knowledge of the truth brings joy; the
experience of its power causes joy; and the consciousness of
possessing a definite message from God is a never-ending
source of rejoicing. This is much more than a mere intellectual
understanding of the contents of the Word. It is the trans-
fusion of it into our emotional life, the influence of it on
our spiritual life, and the inspiration of it on our will for
consecration and service.

III. *The Word Constraining* (Jer. 20: 9).

The next step in the prophet's inner life in relation to the
Word naturally follows from the two preceding. The Word
that commissions and communicates begins to constrain.

1.   There is the consciousness of a great temptation.  'I will not make mention of Him, nor speak any more in His Name.'   It is an encouragement to find that the prophets were men like ourselves.   They were tempted to desist from speaking, to be silent and never again to testify for God. How often this temptation comes to a minister.   The strain of work is great; physical, mental, and spiritual!   The results of work are so slow, so few, so disappointing!   So he is tempted to silence.   'I will not make mention of Him.'

2.   But there is the consciousness of a great power.   If I say 'I will not . . . then there is in my heart a burning fire.'   The Word in the prophet's heart as a fire kindles afresh the strong convictions of his relation to God and his duty.   And so to-day the minister, when tempted to desist, to give up, to be silent, finds the pressure of the Word within like a fire stirring him to renewed consecration.   Like St. Paul, he becomes conscious once again of his profound spiritual debt, of his ministerial commission, of his duty of service, of the world's need, and of the unique power of the Gospel, and there comes again into his heart 'as it were a burning fire.'

3.   And then there is the consciousness of great results. 'I cannot contain.'   The fire begins to work and the prophet *must* speak.   Like Peter, he says, I 'cannot but speak' (Acts 4: 20).   The pressure of the Word overcomes all hostility, all danger, all difficulty, all distrust of self, all fear, all cowardice, all unwillingness.

'Thy Word have I hid in my heart.'   The 'heart' in Scripture means the center of the moral being, and includes intellect, feeling, and will.   So that the Word in the heart, means in the mind for thought, in the emotion for feeling, and in the will for action.   This is the prime essential in the inner life of the prophet; the Word of God.   The Word convicting; the Word commissioning; the Word communing; and the Word constraining.   And if only the minister will take care to get alone with God and His Bible, and seek the light and grace of Him Who inspired that Word, the spiritual results in the soul will be great, blessed, and powerful.   The Word will so transform, energize, and inspire him in his inner

life that when he comes forth to his people it will be quite
evident that he has seen a vision (Luke 1:), that God has
spoken to him, and that he is indeed the prophet of the Lord,
the messenger of the Lord of Hosts.

### SECTION 4.   THE PROPHET'S MESSAGE (*Jer.* 23: 28f.)

The Word thus received into the heart is intended to be
reproduced in life and work.    After Commission, Communion, and Constraint by the Word, comes the Communication of it to others.

### I.   *The Word Possessed.*

'He that hath My Word, let him speak that word faithfully.    What is the chaff to the wheat?'   God's word is the
expression of His mind and is therefore wheat, not chaff,
and the prophet is here described as the man that 'hath' it,
that possesses it.    This is essential to all service, the definite
possession of the Word of God.    As St. Paul says, 'We have
the mind of Christ,' and more than once he speaks of 'my
gospel,' rejoicing in the conscious possession of a message
from God.    No ministry can ever be of service to men which
does not start here, in the definite, conscious, blessed possession
of the Word of God.

### II.   *The Word Proclaimed.*

'Let him proclaim My word faithfully.' 'Faithfully.' We
must beware lest we mix the chaff with the wheat.   Some
men are tempted to indulge in mere eloquence without much
regard to the substance of the message; others are tempted
to prophesy 'smooth' or 'pleasant' things in order to attract
their people; others are tempted to be content and to keep
their people content with a low standard of life and deprecate
being righteous over-much; others are tempted to take up
themes of passing interest of a popular and even sensational
type in order to 'draw.'   But all such preaching will be as

'chaff' to the 'wheat,' and if yielded to will bring their own terrible Nemesis to minister and people.

The Rev. J. R. Wood, a well-known Baptist minister in London, once told of a Congregational minister who said he had been long enough at his church, because his people knew all that he could tell them. 'How long have you been there?' asked Mr. Wood. 'Eight years.' 'What kind of sermons do you preach? Topical sermons?' 'Yes.' 'You mean you have come to the end of your topics?' 'Yes.' 'Do you do much in your Greek Testament?' inquired Mr. Wood. 'No, not much.' 'Well,' said Mr. Wood, 'go into your study and spend an hour with your Greek Testament every morning, and then take to your people on Sunday what you get out of your Greek Testament during the week, and you will never want for subjects.'

III.   *The Word Powerful.*

'Is not My word like a fire . . . and like a hammer?' When the Word possessed is faithfully proclaimed it always has the effect suggested by the figures of 'fire' and 'hammer.' The Word, as fire, does its threefold work of burning, warming, and cheering. It consumes the things to be consumed, and for this there is no power to compare with the Word in its destructive influence. It warms the coldness of hearts and lives and makes them glow with life and love. It cheers the despondent, the sorrowful, the weary, and inspires with joy and courage. The Word, as a hammer, does its twofold work of breaking down and building up. The resistance of the sinful heart is met by the power of the Divine Word. The truth of God is concentrated on the life of man, and by the blessing of the Spirit hard hearts are broken, rebellious hearts are softened, resisting hearts are led to yield. 'Is not My word like a hammer?'

But the hammer is used to build up as well. Its work is constructive as well as destructive. It builds up, it edifies, it produces character, strengthens and holds together the elements of human life as they are fastened together by Divine Grace.

These are the results that should be seen in the ministry. The Word is to be mighty in hearts and lives, mighty to the pulling down of sinful strongholds, mighty to the erection of spiritual structures, mighty to the transformation of character and the inspiration of conduct.

To accomplish this we must *make much* of the Word, We must honour it, believe in it, and show in our proclamation of it that it is to us the very word of the living God.

And to make much of it we must *be much with it.* We must live in it. The Apostles said, 'We will give ourselves to the ministry of the word' (προσκαρτερήσομεν); i. e., adhere closely, keep ourselves firmly fixed, and never allow anything to divert us from putting this Word in the foremost place of our life.

Nothing can make up for this devotion to the Bible in our ministerial life. It is the secret, the source, and the spring of everything that is vital, useful, blessed, and powerful in Christian character and service.

### SECTION 5. THE PROPHET'S PERIL

There is one fact in the account of the Old Testament prophet which startles and even shocks us. It is the presence and even prominence given to the false prophet almost all through the history. At nearly every stage the curious phenomena are in evidence. The false prophet was arrayed against the true, and it is probably correct to say that the greatest conflict the true prophet had to wage was against the false prophet, and not even against the irreligious element in Israel. The lessons are many, serious, and searching, because *corruptio optimi pessima.* Let us heed them as we contemplate our own ministry.

I. *Who the False Prophets were.*

There seem to have been two classes of them. One consisted of counterfeit prophets (1 Kings 22.), men who for one reason or another found it useful to imitate a good thing. The other class evidently consisted of backsliders (I Kings

13), men who had been genuine prophets and had fallen away from their high estate.

We may well hope and believe that not many (one would like to say with certainty not any) of the former class are to be found in the ministry to-day. It is difficult, if not impossible, to conceive of men entering the ministry who are 'counterfeit,' who find it serviceable to imitate the real minister. But we pass from these by simply admitting the possibility of their existence. The other class is, we fear, much more likely to be found in the ranks of the clergy, men who started well, with high hopes, earnest spirit, and full determination, but whose fires have gone down, whose ideals have perished, and whose ministry is but a name. The awful, hideous possibility, and even probability, must assuredly be faced. 'Ye did run well; who did hinder you?'

## II.   *What the False Prophets did.*

Several charges are made against them. They prophesied 'smooth things' rather than 'right things' (Isa. 30: 10). They yielded to the temptation of saying only what the people liked and desired to hear. They cried 'Peace' when there was no peace, and their work was like that of building a wall with untempered mortar (Ezek. 13: 10-16). Thus they pandered to the prejudices of their hearers instead of proclaiming the truth of God without fear or favour. They prophesied falsely because the people 'loved to have it so' (Jer. 5: 31). Further than this, they indulged in flattery and pleased their hearers with personal praise which tended only to self-deceit (Ezek. 12: 24). Deepest degradation of all, they did not hesitate to speak falsehood. It is a short and easy step from the preaching of pleasant things to flattery, and from flattery to falsehood. The flatterer is essentially a 'liar,' and the terrible charge is made against these false prophets that they spoke lies in the Name of the Lord (Zech. 13: 3).

The temptation is a real one to the minister to speak 'pleasant things,' to pander to the prejudices of his people, whether rich or poor. It is as possible to do it to one class as to the other, for both poor and rich naturally like to have their own particular ideas emphasized and their partialities approved. But from the moment a minister allows himself to depart from the strict line of truth, he is in danger of ending where the false prophets ended. The awfulness of conscious, and still more of unconscious hypocrisy and unreality in the ministry is unspeakable.

III.    *What the False Prophets were.*

Since work is but the expression of life, and conduct the outcome of character, it is a natural and necessary question as to what these prophets really were. Can anything be known of their character and disposition? Several significant hints are found. In some cases they were men given to drink (Isa. 28: 7). In other cases they were impure (Jer. 23: 11), in still others, covetous (Isa. 56: 10, 12; Mic. 3: 11). Yet again, some were light and trivial (Zeph. 3: 4), while others were insincere and guilty of what we should call plagiarism; 'that steal my words from his neighbour' (Jer. 23: 30).

This catalogue is serious and solemn. Drunkenness, Impurity, Covetousness, Triviality, Insincerity. But are they impossible in the ministry to-day? Have we not known, or at any rate heard, of men of whom some of these things are true? Character inevitably expresses itself in conduct and service, and if our work is wrong our life must be wrong also.

IV.    *Why the False Prophets were what they were.*

The explanation was as simple as it was searching. It was due to one cause only; 'That prophesy out of their own hearts' (Ezek. 13: 2). This, and this only, was the reason, their vision came from within, not from above. And when once they began to 'prophesy out of their own hearts,' the time of the end was not far off. So is it always, and herein lies our greatest danger. Our messages must not be self-made, but God-made; must come from above, not from within; must be the result of listening to the Lord and not to the people. If the Word of God is not pre-eminent in

our ministerial life, there will always be the danger of proclaiming that which comes from below instead of above.
The Word is at once the substance of our message and the
standard of our own life, and the man who keeps in touch
with it will never lack something to say, or want power
and guidance in saying it. But we must go one step further
and deeper, and ask—

V. *How did the False Prophets become what they were?*

Is it possible to trace the line, or lines, of aberration?
Authorities generally tend to trace their declension to the
condition and life of the schools of the prophets. They
became formal, conventional, accustomed to sacred things
and words, and thus became spiritually deteriorated, until at
length disaster accrued. This may, or may not be the actual
explanation, but it certainly indicates a possibility, if not a
strong probability. It has been a proverb that 'the shoemaker's
wife is the worst shod,' and every one knows the danger of
the deadening influence of constant association with religious
and spiritual things. If the schools of the prophets were the
main cause of the decay and deadness of the life of these
men, it points with unerring and forceful meaning to the
necessity of the greatest and most prayerful thought in connexion with Theological Schools, and all similar places where
types of ministry are decided.

But the same dangers face us all through our ministry.
Constant use of Bible phrases, constant association with religious people, constant service in Church affairs tend to
spiritual formality, dryness, and even deadness which must
assuredly affect the spiritual quality of our ministry if not at
once and wholly altered. And herein lies the solemnity for
students and ministers of the Psalmist's words which call us
to face these issues with ourselves, and never to rest until
we can look up to God and feel perfectly sure that we are
not among the false prophets, or even in danger of travelling
on the way thither. 'Search me, O God, and know my heart:
try me, and know my thoughts: and see if there be any
wicked way in me, and lead me in the way everlasting' (Psa.
139: 23, 24).

## Section 6.  the prophet's life

There is one title frequently used of the prophet and probably of no one else: 'Man of God.' Eight are mentioned by name to whom this is given. Moses, Samuel, David, Shemaiah, Elijah, Elisha (thirteen passages), Igdaliah (Jer. 35), Timothy. Once an angel is called by this name, and several men unnamed are described by it. 'Man of God.' What does it mean? Just two things. Manliness and Godliness.

### I.  *Manliness.*

The prophet was just an ordinary man, one among his fellow-citizens, not of a separate caste, but raised up of God for the special work (Duet. 18: 18). The chief points which marked him were two. (*a*) He was a man with a message. When God gave him this he delivered it faithfully (1 Sam. 9: 6; 1 Kings 13: 1) and fearlessly. Nothing was allowed to hinder the complete and courageous delivery of the Divine Word. With absolute boldness he witnessed to God and His truth. (*b*) He was a man with a blessing. Not merely a man of words, but deeds. Moses, the Man of God, was able to bless as well as teach (Deut. 33: 1), and in like manner Elijah and Elisha carried blessing wherever they went. It is the greatest honour in a man's life that people come to him in their difficulties and trials because they feel that his character is stronger than theirs, his experience riper as a Man of God.

From all this it is clear that a manly man is the truest channel of communication between man and God. It was the uniqueness of Israel as a religion that it exalted manhood in the truest sense of that idea of exaltation. And so to-day true Christianity conserves and uses the truest, purest, and best in human nature. People will not respect the 'cloth' unless there is a man in it, nor the office unless a man fills it. There is no incompatibility, but, quite the contrary, the most perfect congruity between manliness and the ministry. A layman once said that of three ministers he had known, the first was a man, not a minister; the second a minister, not a man; the

third was neither man nor minister.[1]  A real minister will
be honoured and loved for his manliness and will therefore be
surrounded by numerous friends in his congregation who will
value, trust, love, and follow him.

## II.  *Godliness.*

This is the real foundation of all true manliness, the
power of a godly life (1 Tim. 6: 11).  Such a life will
convince of sin (1 Kings 17: 24).  People will soon find out
whether we are in earnest.  If we are hypocrites they will
know it; they may not tell anybody, they may not even
grumble or complain, but they will use us less, come to us less,
and value us less in the things of God.  As Emerson says,
'I cannot hear what you say; what you are thunders so loud.'
Character is all-powerful.

What is its secret?  Very simple, but very searching.  (*a*)
It means a true relation to God's Word (2 Tim. 3: 16, 17).
'That the man of God may be perfect, throughly furnished
unto all good works.'  No one will ever be a Man of God
unless he 'continues in those things he has learned.'  (*b*)  It
means a true relation to obedience.  The Man of God must
practise what he preaches.  Disobedience is fatal (1 Kings
13: 26 (*c*)  It means a true relation to prayer.  The Man
of God will be a man of prayer (Psa. 90: title).  Elijah
was a Man of God, and prayer was the prevailing characteristic of his life (1 Kings 18: 36, 37).  Prayer brings us
into that fellowship with God (1 Kings 17: 1) from which
all character springs.  Character is power, character is everything.  Character makes the man, and as Christ makes the
character, the minister as a Man of God is the prime fundamental secret of service.  It is only as he is a Man of God
that he can have power with men and become a blessing
(Gen. 22: 28).

And thus 'Man of God' is the highest title, the noblest
description, the finest testimony.  Manly and Godly.  Manly
because Godly, and Godliness expressing itself in Manliness.
Given these two elements, the life and work of the ministry
glorifies God and blesses Man.

[1] Stalker, p. 165.

## Chapter II

# THE MINISTRY OF THE TWELVE

THERE were three great aspects of our Lord's earthly ministry: His Teaching, His Miracles, and His Training of the Twelve Apostles. Of these the last was in some respects the most important, because it had special reference to the future and to the permanent life and work of the Church of Christ. Indeed, we may almost say that His Teaching and His Miracles had their primary and fundamental value in the influence they made on the Twelve. At least they formed no small part of the training of the Apostles for their work in the Church. The best part of three years was given to this, and we can see how, as the public ministry became less and less fruitful, this work occupied more and more of our Lord's attention. Among the many aspects of the subject the following portions of the Gospel story will enable us to realize some characteristics of the ministry, as seen in our Lord's relation to the Twelve.

SECTION 1. THE CHOICE (*Mark* 3: 13-15; *Luke* 6: 12f.).

Out of the larger number of His disciples it was necessary for our Lord to select some to be His especial followers and ministers. The occasion and circumstances of His choice of the Twelve are significantly brought before us in the Gospels.

I. *When the Choice was made.*

It was after a time of fellowship with God that Christ made the selection of the Twelve. On the mountain top, away from all earthly influences. His decision, as always, was the result of consultation with the Father, and of oneness with the Father's Will. 'The Son can do nothing of Himself,' and the time and circumstances of the choice of the Twelve show clearly the importance attached to it by our Lord and by the writers of the Gospels.

## II.  *How the Choice was made.*

Selection for the ministry must always come from Christ Himself, and must be due to his personal relation to the soul. It is only as this association is real, that any genuine choice can be made.

And it was a *definite* choice. 'He ordained.'  He gave authority and abilty (ἐξουσία, δύναμις).  Christ never calls without equipping, never commissions without providing, never authorizes without empowering.  'God's biddings are enablings.'

## III.  *Why the Choice was made.*

The primary reason was *Fellowship*; 'that they might be with Him.'  This is, and must be first.  'With' comes before 'for.'  'They dwelt *with* the King *for* his work' (1 Chron. 4: 23).  What we are, conditions what we do, and to be what we ought to be we must abide in and with Christ.  And all through their ministry the Twelve had this as their choicest privilege, they were 'with Him,' including all that this meant of wonderful instruction, holy influence and constant inspiration.  Instruction, Influence, Inspiration; these ever come as the result of being 'with Christ.'

The second reason for the choice was *Apostleship;* 'and send them forth.'  An Apostle is one 'sent forth,' and all through their ministry this was their privilege, duty and responsibility.  Mission!  What a thought!  'Sent' by Christ, as He was sent by the Father (John 20: 21).  Mission always implies commission.  It is the Master's Commission that gives our Mission its blessing and guarantees its success.  Every true minister is an 'Apostle,' one who is sent forth.  'Ministers of His to do His pleasure.'

The third reason of the choice was *Stewardship;* 'To preach, and to have power to heal sickness, and to cast out devils.'  The stewardship of preaching is the first function of the ministry. The minister is a 'herald,' one who proclaims the Gospel, i. e. the Good News.  And this the Gospel always is, not good advice but good news, or rather, good advice as the outcome of Good News.  'Any news?' said Tennyson to an old woman friend of his in Lincolnshire. 'No news, Mr. Tennyson, except that Christ died on the Cross! 'Well,' replied the poet, 'that is old news, and new news, and good news.'

The Stewardship of healing is included. We may not now have power to heal bodily sickness, but we are nevertheless to be healers in a very real sense, lifting burdens of soul, lightening pain of heart, and leading men into the presence of the Great Healer.

The stewardship of deliverance is also always our work. We have to cast out the demons of sin, of sorrow, of doubt, of despair, by the marvellous expulsive power of the new affection of the Gospel of Christ.

This constitutes true ministry; Fellowship, Apostleship, Stewardship. To this Christ calls us; for this He chooses and equips us. And amid the multifarious duties that crowd into our life, and tend to distract our thought, and dissipate our energies, we must never forget these primary functions of ministry. Fellowship, Apostleship, Stewardship. Nothing must rob us of our position 'with' Christ. Nothing must hinder us from exercising our Apostolic 'Mission.' Nothing must divert us from the stewardship of preaching, of healing, of deliverance. Then only shall we realize Christ's purpose in selecting us and sending us into His vineyard.

SECTION 2. THE PREPARATION (*Luke* 5: 1-11).

Character is a most important study, whether in the pages of a biography, or in the life of any one with whom we may be brought in contact. To discover in a child or youth the characteristics of his nature, to notice his weakness and strength, to watch the gradual growth and expansion even amid slips and falls, and to see the character deepen and ripen until at length it reaches the vigour, balance, and mellowness of maturity; all this is at once extremely interesting and very valuable.

Among the many lives which are available for study in this way, few lend themselves more readily to consideration and scrutiny than that of the Apostle Peter, for from the first notice of him in the New Testament he is seen to be a man of

clearly marked individuality, and almost every reference to
him enables us to note some salient feature in his character.
The incident associated with the text was a most important
step in his life, and one largely instrumental in making him
what he afterwards became. It is essential to remember that
this was not the first occasion on which our Lord met Simon.
The fact of Christ's entrance unforbidden into the boat seems
to imply familiarity. The story in St. John (ch. 1.) is the
record of the enrolment of Simon as a disciple with the promise and prophecy of something different and higher in the future. What that was, how and when it was to be realized,
were not then mentioned, but we can see the development by
comparing the passage with our present one. 'Thou shalt be
*called*' (John 1: 42). 'Thou shalt *catch*' (Luke 5: 10). The
former suggested his future character, the latter his future
work; and we see that this incident in St. Luke is the second
link in the chain of our Lord's purpose with Simon. It is the
call to Apostleship from Discipleship, and when we consider it
in this light, as a preparatory call to higher office and more
definite work, we find in it distinct though connected steps, by
which the disciple was led up to Apostleship.

I.    *The Revelation of the Master to the Disciple.*

Before Simon could be and do what Christ desired, he must
know more of his Master, and so we have a revelation with
two clearly marked characteristics.

The gradualness of the revelation is very evident from
the Greek and the Revised Version. At first Jesus said, '*Put
out* a little from the land,' in order that He might preach to
the multitude from the boat. But this was not all, it was but
secondary, for when He had finished speaking, He added,
'*Put out* into the deep.' Now we begin to see the object of
the Master, Who at once adds, 'And let down your nets for a
draught.' This Peter does, though not before telling Him of
their night of fruitless toil.

We now see the second characteristic of this revelation;
it was definite. The immediate result of the letting down of
the net was the miraculous draught of fishes, and by that

miracle Simon Peter realized that Jesus was some one out of the ordinary run of mankind, some one unique. This was our Lord's object; Peter was to see that His Messiahship involved His Divinity. The man's view of the Messiah was to a great extent the formal Jewish conception, and before he could become an Apostle he must have this erroneous idea removed. If our Lord was to gather round Him a band of disciples through whom He could work, it was necessary that they should first be quite assured concerning their Master Himself. They must know Him not simply as a Teacher, they must know Him in Himself as the Son of God, and this was His object in performing the miracle. For the moment Simon could only wonder in astonishment, but by means of that wonder Christ entered more fully into and possessed more of His disciple's heart. This was the first revelation, that of the Master to the disciple and it at once led to another.

II.   *The Revelation of the Disciple to Himself.*

The next requirement of the Lord Jesus was with reference to Peter himself, and we must see how it was brought about. For this purpose let us consider the immediate cause of the revelation. Peter saw the miracle and cried out, 'Depart from me, for I am a sinful man, O Lord.' Now let us inquire carefully what there was in the miracle that should make Simon realize his *sin*. What was the connexion between the miraculous draught of *fishes* and *sin?* How is it we do not hear of any such connexion with regard to other miracles? This question deserves very careful notice. It is generally supposed that somehow or other the disciple realized our Lord's marvellous holiness contrasted with his own lack of holiness, but is this certain? Why holiness in particular? On another occasion, very similar to this, as recorded in the last chapter of St. John, we read of Peter *hurrying to meet* our Lord immediately on recognizing Him after another miraculous draught of fishes, and yet at that time our Lord was none the less holy and Peter none the less sinful. Indeed, coming so closely after the denial, one would have imagined the very opposite of Peter's eagerness to meet Christ. We must therefore seek the cause elsewhere, namely, in Simon's first reply to Jesus, 'Master,' we have toiled all the night and have taken

nothing, nevertheless at Thy word I will let down the net.'
Are we quite sure we rightly understand the meaning of this
answer?   Is it possible that we do not catch the real tone of
it?   Very frequently it is put forward as a beautiful answer
of reverent obedience, but is it so?   The men had been toiling
all the night in the most suitable time for fishing, and the
idea of telling fishermen to go and try again in the morning
was almost too much for Peter, and his reply seems to say, 'I
will do what you say, but I am sure it will not be of any use.'
This may be seen more clearly in another fact not always
considered.   Our Lord said, 'Let down your nets' (plural);
Peter replied, 'I will let down the net' (singular) as though
feeling quite certain it would be of no avail and that it was
unnecessary to let down more than one net.[1]   The answer,
therefore, was an untrusting yielding to Christ, and indicated
a partial obedience only, as if to say, 'I know more than you
do.'   Then came the marvellous success and with it the vivid
realization of the unworthy and sinful spirit he had been in-
dulging.   He now saw that Jesus knew better than he himself
did, experienced fisherman though he was, and feeling how
wrong he had been he cried out, 'Depart from me, for I am
a sinful man, O Lord.'   Thus he saw himself as he really
was, and the disciple was revealed to himself.

Thus Peter, while he saw the power of Christ, had at the
same time a vision of himself such as he had never had before.
This is the second revelation, that of the disciple to himself.

Now we can understand the meaning of the text and appreciate the third revelation.

III.   *The Revelation of the Master's Purpose concerning
His Disciple.*

'Fear not, from henceforth thou shalt catch men.'   Notice
the assuring call: 'Fear not.'   Thus our Lord encouraged the
sin-stricken disciple.   'Depart'?   Surely not; his sin was the
very reason why Jesus should stay.   'Depart'?   Surely not;
the Lord could see the man through the sin.   Not only was the

---

[1] The text of the A.V. seems more intrinsically probable, even
apart from the interpretation now suggested.

Master not to depart, but the disciple should henceforth have a very different work. He was no longer to catch fish, he should 'catch men,' should 'take them alive' (R. V. margin). And so the disciple learned the purpose of his Master and gained an insight into the reason of that wonderful change of name. Thereby he experienced that which would very effectively tend towards the change of nature and of work, the rock-like character and the Christian Apostleship.

Then we have the prompt response. 'They left all and followed him.' No more returning to their boats; now they were to be Apostles as well as disciples, from henceforth the intimate friends and trusted followers of their Lord, to be taught, guided, strengthened, blessed, and used by Him for His glory in the manifestation and realization of His Divine purpose and love.

Such were the three revelations whereby Peter was called to the Apostleship, and now it is only right to consider what these truths have to do with us. We may see this by retracing our steps by way of application.

1. Christ has a purpose with every disciple. To become an 'Apostle,' one *sent forth* by Him to others. Not, of course, in the unique sense of the Twelve, but nevertheless to become with a very real meaning, 'fishers of men.' This is the supreme object of our Christian life and discipleship, to bless others. We are saved in order to serve, helped to help, redeemed to restore, delivered to declare. And to accomplish this Christ tests us, coming to us in ordinary every-day life to prove our capacity for higher service. There is a sad possibility of failure in partial obedience like Peter's, against which we need to be on our guard.

2. To fulfill this purpose we must know ourselves. We are sent to men who are sinners by nature and by practice, who show their sin in many different ways and degrees. It is only by a knowledge of the human heart and conscience, mind and will, that we shall be able to deal with them. Just as the fisherman needs knowledge, tact and experience in his work, so do we in our dealings with others on behalf of Christ, and these are only possible through a knowledge of our heart and its plague.

3. To know ourselves we must know Christ. Not by mere introspection and self-examination shall we see ourselves; we can only truly see ourselves by looking at Christ. In Him we see ourselves as in a mirror, and in His light of perfect holiness we really and truly see our own need of holiness. Thus by 'looking off unto Jesus' we gain a true knowledge of ourselves, and a true knowledge of Him. There will be a lower idea of self and a higher conception of Him (cf. *v.* 5, 'Master'; c *v.* 8, 'Lord'). In the possession of Him as our Saviour, in the surrender to Him as our Lord, and in the occupation of minds and hearts with Him as our Friend, we shall derive, as Peter did, the self-knowledge necessary for our effectual work for Him, and not only so, but 'beholding as in a glass the glory of the Lord we shall be changed into the same image' by the power of His Holy Spirit.

SECTION 3.  THE PRINCIPLES.  (*John* 6: 1-13).

The miracle of the five thousand is in all four Gospels, the only one found in all. There must be some good reason for this prominence. The moment was critical, pivotal in our Lord's ministry. The feelings of the people for Him were such that as the immediate result of this miracle they endeavoured to make Him a King. But He escaped out of their power, and on His reappearance next day delivered those discourses in Capernaum which so startled and shocked His hearers that His popularity suddenly began to wane, and for the rest of His ministry He was virtually left alone with the Twelve, for the special work He had come to do. The miracle was therefore at once a crisis and a symbol of our Lord's higher spiritual work. He had not come to be King, but to give Himself as the Bread of Life, the Bread of God for the world.

But the miracle can also be taken symbolically in another way; it may be regarded as a parable for workers. Christ and 'his disciples here indicate what Christ still desires to do through His workers, and the miracle reveals several of the deepest principles of Christian service.

## I.  *Co-workers with Christ.*

He took counsel with them; 'Whence'; and associated them with Himself; 'We.' This is what He always desires to do. 'Shall I hide from Abraham that thing which I do?' (Gen. 18: 17). 'The Lord God will do nothing, but He re vealeth His secrets unto His servants' (Amos 3: 7). 'We, then, as workers together with Him' (2 Cor. 6: 1). This is the joy, the honour, the inspiration of all service; our association with Christ, our fellowship with Him in the accomplishment of His purposes for the world. He might have done the work without us, but He has been pleased to permit us to be His ministers, carrying His Bread to the world.

## II.  *An Apparently Impossible Task.*

What a startling call! 'Give ye them to eat.' How could they? And yet the Master said, 'They need not depart.' The strong confidence of this word is evident. What does it mean? This, that Christians have what the world needs. The Master's word rings out: 'They need not go; you provide,' and in saying this He called His disciples to a task apparently impossible, but really practicable, because He Himself was behind every word He said.

## III.  *The Use of Natural Means.*

To feed the multitude Christ utilized the five loaves and two fishes as the foundation of the supply. He might and could have done without them, but He used them as far as they would go. Herein lies one of the deepest principles of the Bible and of God's method. He uses means. The miracles of the Old and New Testaments are usually wrought with existing agencies. Natural means are employed to the full extent of their possibility, and then supernatural power is added to them. There was no new creation, but simply the use of what was available as the means or channel of manifesting Divine supernatural power. In a similar way Christ uses the natural characteristics of His disciples as far as they will go and makes them of service in His vineyard. He takes us as we are and utilizes what we have, for His Glory.

## IV.   *The Secret of Blessing.*

The disciples were commanded to bring what they possessed to the Master, and then He blessed them and made them
sufficient for the need of the multitude.   The same principle
obtains to-day.   'Bring to Me.'   Let us bring to Him whatever we have, for 'loaves unblessed are loaves unmultiplied.'
We must have His blessing if we are to be of service to others.

## V.   *The Divine Employment of Moderate Means.*

Through the blessing of Christ on the five loaves and two
fishes the men, women, and children were 'filled,' and through
the blessing of Christ on our lives, poor and insignificant
though we are, the multitudes will be 'filled.'   Moses was
commanded to cast down his rod, and it became a serpent.   His
rod was just the ordinary shepherd's crook of his daily calling,
and yet by the power of God it could become transformed.
Our ordinary life, sinful though it be; our natural capacities,
few though they be, can be employed by God and produce
wonderful results in His service.   It is a great fundamental
and well known principle that size never determines power.
When Zinzendorf was at school he founded the 'Guild of the
Grain of Mustard Seed,' and we know the result in the Mora-
vian Church.   Be it ours, therefore, to surrender everything
to Christ, to trust Him with everything, to obey Him in everything, and then He will send us forth to fill and satisfy hungry,
fainting souls; blessed to be a blessing.

### Section 4.   the secret   (*Matt.* 14: 17).

As the Christian life is not complex, but simple; so also it
is with Christian service.   It can be reduced to a few great but
simple truths.   It really means nothing more, as it can mean
nothing less, than the full and constant contact of the soul
with Christ.   In these two passages now before us we find
the disciples in the one case face to face with a great work, and
in the other with a great failure.   The lesson in both was the
need of personal contact with Christ; 'Bring to Me.'

I. *Work.*

The miracle of the feeding of the five thousand, as we have seen, may be regarded as a parable of Christian service. There are three great pictures.

1. The perishing world. The people were in great need. Hunger had produced want and weakness.

2. The powerless disciples. Their store was small, limited, insufficient, and in face of the multitude they were powerless. 'Whence?'

3. The Perfect Saviour. 'He Himself knew what He would do,' and when once the disciples had brought their little He blessed, and gave, and fed the crowds.

To-day's *task* is great, almost beyond compare. The world is in need of Christ, whether it knows it or not. Sin ever produces want and weakness. The hunger of the soul is seen everywhere to-day.

To-day's means are also scanty. The Church knows not what to do. 'Whence?' The multitudes at home, in palace, castle, house and slum; the heathen abroad in China, Japan, India, Africa, all tell of apparent powerlessness on the part of the Church to cope with the situation.

But, thank God, to-day's *secret* is the same as of yore. 'Bring.' As Bushnell in one of his spiritual paradoxes says, 'Duty is not measured by our ability.' Duty is measured by His ability, and 'responsibility' is really *our* response to *His* ability. So, for work let us ever remember the secret of perpetual sufficiency. 'Bring.'

But it is to the other passage that we specially desire to turn.

II   *Failure* (Matt. 17: 17).

The circumstances of the healing of the demoniac boy are full of spiritual meaning for workers. Again there are three pictures.

1. The People. At the foot of the hill the crowd awaited, surrounding the disciples and feeling disappointed and distressed. The youth had been brought with high hopes of a

perfect cure, and the result had been failure.  The disciples could not cast out the evil spirit.

2. The Disciples.  What a humiliation for them!  The failure was as complete as it was unwarranted .  They had received the power, and yet they had not cast out the demon.

3. The Master.  When He learnt what it was He at once took the matter in hand and dealt with it satisfactorily.  He overruled the error, told them to bring the youth to Him, and soon the boy and his father were rejoicing in complete deliverance.  When the disciples asked Him privately the secret of their failure He told them frankly that it was due to their lack of prayer (and fasting).

To-day's *task* is equally great.  There are demons to be cast out and spiritual maladies to be healed.

To-day's *means* are equally ample.  Christ never commands us to 'Go,' without first assuring us that He has all power (Matt. 28: 18).  There is grace sufficient in Christ to meet every need, and we need not, ought not to fail.

To-day's *secret* is equally clear.  It lies in faithfulness to Christ, the faithful use of the power He gives, faithful obedience to the truth He teaches.

Our great danger to-day as workers is spiritual leakage.  There is no need of failure, for Christ has all power and has provided grace.  As Dr. Jowett says: 'We do not get close enough to men because we do not get near enough to God.  (1) We are drawn away by the gravitation of the world; its manner, thought, feeling, purpose.  (2) by the fascination of the glittering; the praise of men, not honour of God.  (3) By the stupefying influences of our 'office.'[1]  And the result is utter, disastrous, heart-breaking failure.

How then is this danger to be avoided?  In a very simple way.  We must maintain an attitude of constant dependence on God.  'This kind goeth not out but by prayer and fasting.'  We retain the word 'fasting' here, in spite of the reading of the R.V., because of its essential truthfulness.  Prayer and Fasting represent the two sides, the positive and negative, of the one attitude of the soul.  Prayer is the *attachment* of

---

[1] Notes of an address to ministers at Northfield, Mass., U.S.A., reported in the *Christian Workers' Magazine* (Chicago), 1909.

the soul to God.  Fasting is the *detachment* of the soul from the world.

There are two methods of progress to-day in connexion with motors and street-cars.  'The one is by the storage principle, by means of which so much gasoline or electricity is provided and used, and then a fresh supply given.  The other is by the contact principle, by which the car keeps in touch with the electric power above it or below it, and moves or stands still as it is, or is not, in contact.  There are many Christians who seem to think that the storage principle is the true way of living, but it is not.  God does not give so much grace for use until exhausted.  He requires us to keep in touch with Himself and find therein our sole and our sufficient means of supply.

We lose power and blessing because we do not realize the profound truth that Christ does not give *inherent* ability to any worker.  He does not expect grace to be used apart from Himself and then to be replenished when exhausted.  Grace is nothing so material as this.  Grace is relationship, and its power depends on the maintenance of that relationship by a constant attitude of faith and obedience.  Discontinue the attitude, and grace fails to work. Maintain the attitude, keep up the contact, and grace works in and through us to will and to do of God's pleasure.

How may this contact be maintained?  By prayer, by the Word, by the Spirit, 'Bring to Me.'  Keep 'in touch' with Christ, the Source of prayer.  By prayer we speak to God; by the Bible God speaks to us, and when these two are made real by the Spirit Who is 'the Spirit of grace and supplication,' we find the contact maintained, and the life kept, blessed, energized, used to the glory of God.

### SECTION 5.   THE TEST (*Matt.* 16: 13-19).

The Galilean ministry was over.  The Master and His disciples had withdrawn to Caesarea to prepare for the end. They had been with Him some time now, and in view of the future it was essential to know what had been the results of the teaching and fellowship they had enjoyed.  After a period of training and teaching comes the examination, and now the Twelve were to undergo an inquiry as to the precise spiritual value of their experience of their Master.

## I.  *The Inquiry.*

The Lord's first question was: 'Who do men say that I the Son of Man am?' i.e. 'What do men say of Me?' This in itself is of small account and involved no spiritual insight on their part. It was probably only asked to lead up to the next question: 'But you, what do you say of Me?' The final question was their own personal view of Christ. As Professor W. M. Clow aptly says, there is a world of difference between a verdict and a confession. The former question involved the verdict of their contemporaries; the latter demanded a personal acknowledgment from themselves. The one thing essential was a true personal attitude to Christ, and then right ideas of Christ. The Master's first message was, 'Follow Me,' and they had done so. Now it is, 'What *think* ye of Me?' Right ideas arise, and always will arise, out of a right attitude to Christ. It is only the follower who thinks rightly.

Herein lies the final question of the ministry. What is our attitude to Jesus Christ? Everything depends on this. Failure here means failure everywhere.

## II.  *The Confession.*

Peter's reply expressed what he and they had come to think concerning Christ. 'Thou art the Christ, the Son of the living God.' His Messiahship and His Divinity; these two were everything. In relation to the Old Testament hopes he was 'the Christ,' the Anointed One. In relation to God, 'the Son of the living God.'

The Divinity of Christ! Or, rather, as we are compelled to put it to-day, the Deity of Christ. This constitutes the fundamental confession because the final need of every soul. And of course it must ever be a life, and not merely a Creed. The confession of Peter was the result of personal contact with Christ. They had 'companied with Him,' and the experience of those hallowed, unforgettable days had created

and deepened in them the conviction that their Master was
none other than the Anointed One, the Son of the Living
God. This, and nothing less, is still the foundation of all
ministry. For salvation, for sanctification, for service, we
must have an Anointed One, a Divine Saviour and Lord. As
Bishop Moule says: 'A Saviour *not quite God* is a bridge
broken at the farther end.'

III.  *The Acknowledgment.*

The disciple was pronounced 'blessed' for making so definite a confession. It is always so. The possession and confession of a living Divine Lord always necessarily bring
'blessing.'

And the source of it is spiritual discernment: 'For flesh
and blood hath not revealed it unto thee, but My Father which
is in heaven.' From fellowship had come faith; from experience, conviction. Personal experience is essential to all
true service. We must have seen and heard and felt in order
to be able to speak, and a ministry that is not based on personal
conviction and personal experience will be useless and even
dangerous. Flesh and blood cannot reveal the secrets of
ministerial spiritual blessing; they must come from the Father
in heaven.

IV.  *The Assurance.*

To such a confession was added a twofold revelation of
assurance. A new character was declared to be his. In the
old days (John 1: 42) at the outset the word was, 'Thou *art*
Simon . . . thou *shalt be called*.' Now the 'shalt be called'
is changed into the 'art,' the future into the present. He
was now the Rock-like man as the outcome of personal experience of Christ.

And a new work was given. Christ would build His
Church on Peter thus confessing Him. Not on the man
alone; that would be too weak. Not on the confession alone;
that would be too abstract. But on both man and confession
together, on the man confessing.[1] It is as though
[1] Lindsay, *The Church and Ministry in the Early Centuries.* p. 25ff.

the Master said, 'Give Me a man who believes as the outcome of personal confession, and My Church shall stand on that as on a sure foundation.' And the man is to hold and use the keys. He is given authority and his work shall be that of opening and shutting the gates of the Kingdom (not the Church). Such a man with such an experience is alone qualified to wield his authority. Gehazi may be nominally in the service of Elisha, but the personal power had long gone. The man was an undeveloped hypocrite before the *dénouement* came. It is personal experience that gives authority to word and deed, and personal experience is the only basis of service.

Thus the Master tested His disciples, put them through their examination, and subjected them to the severest possible proof. The question remains for us: What is our attitude to Him? Have these months, or years, wrought in us a personal experience of Him? If they have, we are blessed, and we cannot help being useful in His vineyard. If they have not, then whatever else we may have and know, we shall be of no service in the ministry, for the ministry is absolutely dependent on men who by personal contact with Christ have arrived at a personal experience, and can tell out that experience by lip and life, and thus witness and win for the Master.

## SECTION 6. THE WORK (*Luke* 10: 1-24).

Two Missions were sent forth by Christ during His earthly ministry; that of the Twelve (Mark 3: 13, 14), and that of the Seventy (Luke 10: 1). The record of our Lord's instructions reveals both similarities and differences, but they are both alike in being concerned with principles of work. So after looking at some of the aspects of ministerial character it is necessary and appropriate to consider some of the elements of ministerial service. Our Lord's words embody principles for guidance in doing His work.

### I. *Preparation* (*vs.* 1-4).

The true minister will be Divinely appointed (*v.* 1): 'The Lord appointed.' This must ever be the foundation

of all work. 'How shall they preach, except they be sent?'
(Rom. 10: 15).

The true minister will be Divinely encouraged (*v.* 2).
What a picture our Lord draws of broad fields, abundant
crops, ripened grain, and few labourers. What is the meaning of this reference to the abundant harvest? It is not the
only time He alluded to it (John 4: 35). Are we quite
sure we have grasped the true and full import of the term
'harvest'? The Lord did not speak of the opportunities for
seed-sowing, but for *harvest.* He thought that men were
ready to be *reaped.* Would it not be well now if we thought
less of the seed sowing and more of the harvest, less of the
future and more of the present? We expect that some day
we, or some one else, will reap what now we sow. But the
Lord speaks of a present *harvest.* When Paul was in Corinth
the Lord told him He had *much people there* when as yet
only a handful were gathered (Acts 18: 10). And in every
congregation many are just waiting to be gathered and gar-
nered. Let this be our encouragement and let us endeavor to
reap as well as sow.

The true minister will be Divinely instructed (*v.* 24).
*Prayer* is the first element of instruction. 'Pray ye.' Prayer
must always be a powerful feature in every true ministry. Intercessory prayer prepares the way for our message, and the
more we pray the more successful our labours will be. Action
must follow prayer: 'Go.' They must work as well as
pray. They were to go confidently: 'I send you forth.' They
were to go unencumbered: 'Carry neither purse, nor scrip,
nor shoes'; and unanxious: 'Salute no man by the way.' Time
was fleeting. There was no opportunity for the elaborate
politeness of the Eastern salutation. So is it ever. In spite
of the dangers, we may go without fear, and our soul must
be in earnest as we drop what might be an encumbrance, or
set aside what might be a hindrance to our work. Time presses, souls are passing from us, we must have our eye on the
clock of opportunity, and while courteous, kind and thoughtful, we must spend no time or strength on things that are
meaningless and empty. Consecration must be seen in Concentration if our ministry is to be what God desires.

## II. *Plans* (*vs.* 5-11).

The salutation to be given is noteworthy (*v.* 5f.). The opening word was characteristic of their message: 'Peace.' The Gospel of Peace is the essential characteristic of the message of Redemption. So also the God of Peace is the most frequently found title of God in the New Testament. Peace on earth was the angels' song. 'Preaching peace by Jesus Christ' was the Apostolic message. 'Be ye reconciled to God' is our call to-day, for 'He is our peace.' No one will ever preach the Gospel aright who does not make very prominent, perhaps predominant, this message of Peace. Peace between God and man through Redemption; and then peace between man and man; peace between the elements of man's own nature as the result of peace with God, for 'being justified by faith we have peace.'

Their ministration followed their salutation (*vs.* 7-9). Their behaviour is first of all indicated (*v.* 7f.). It is our life that tells. It must ever be Christ, not self. We must accept what we find in the spirit of these instructions. Their work was to be healing (v. 9), and their testimony the nearness and imminence of the Kingdom of God (*v.* 9). If they were not received they were to leave and bear witness, rebuking them in the name of their God (*v.* 10f.). Along these lines we have still to travel, labouring, preaching, witnessing, warning, and rebuking. He is the true minister who lives and works according to these plans.

## III. *Protection* (*vs.* 12-16).

But there is another side. They are not to go alone, or at their own charges. He Who sends, supplies; He Who commands, controls; He Who commissions, keeps.

Their opponents are to be condemned (*vs.* 12-15). Those who will not heed shall be brought into judgment. We need have no fear if after faithful preaching there are no results. Results are God's; processes ours; and if we fulfill our part we can leave the rest to Him.

Their hearers are to be honoured (v. 16). What a privilege, to be assured that 'He that heareth you, heareth Me.'

Could anything be more inspiring and encouraging to the faithful preacher?

Their rejectors are to be dishonoured; 'He that despiseth you despiseth Me.' This is also true. If our message is God's, not our own, the rejection of it is a rejection of Him, not of us. This, too, however sad in consequences, should encourage the preacher amid difficulties.

IV. *Proofs* (*vs.* 17-24).

The joyful return resulted (*v.* 17). The men set out according to the instructions given and in due course returned with joy, bearing witness to the effects (*v.* 17). It is always so. God's Word never returns void, and the man who proclaims it will have results which will afford him what is perhaps the most exquisite joy on earth, the joy of soul-winning.

The wise warning followed (*vs.* 18-20). The Master told them that He had been noting their work ('I saw,' *v.* 18). He also explained the success as due to His own gift (*v.* 19). And He bade them guard against spiritual pride, lest they fell into the snare of the devil (*v.* 20). How necessary these words are for all earnest soul-winners, experience abundantly shows. The successful minister is tempted to think that his success is due to his own powers, and he 'burns incense' to his own net. Spurgeon said a wise word when he remarked that the reason why God does not allow us to see more fruit from our labours is that on the top of the harvest load we should probably feel giddy and fall down. Everywhere and always when success crowns our efforts we must sing our *Non nobis, Domine*; 'Not unto us, O Lord, not unto us' (Psalm 115: 1).

And so we find in this varied work three great aspects of ministry.

1. The Call to Service. It comes from Christ as 'Lord of the Harvest.' It is due to the great need, 'fields white'; and it is pointed by the sad fact that there are so very few to engage on it; 'the labourers are few.'

2. The Character of the Worker. Summing up all that we find here we observe the elements of Simplicity, Earnest-

ness, Winsomeness, and Faithfulness.    Let us ever test ourselves by these.

3. The Consequence of Labour.    We see what the Lord
told His disciples to expect; Blessing, Knowledge, Fellowship,
Satisfaction.

The ministry is therefore at once arduous and glorious;
the noblest and the most difficult of tasks; the highest and the
holiest of enterprises.

CHAPTER III

THE MINISTRY OF ST. PAUL

THERE is one Epistle in which more than in any other St. Paul lays bare his heart and soul. It is 2 Corinthians, which is his Apologia in the face of opposition, animosity, and calumny. Stung to the quick by the charges, taunts, and actions of his enemies, he reveals himself as he does nowhere else, and in so doing he lets us see some of the outstanding qualifications of all true ministry. A few of these, out of the many references to his life and work, call for special meditation.

SECTION 1. SINCERITY (2 *Cor.* 1: 12; 2: 17; 4: 2).

I. *The Apostle's Statements.*

1. He had evidently been charged with insincerity, especially in writing (*v.* 13), and he replies by challenging attention to the boasting of which he was never tired. 'For our rejoicing is this, the testimony of our conscience, that in simplicity and godly sincerity, not with fleshly wisdom, but by the grace of God, we have had our conversation in the world, and more abundantly to youward.'

(a) First, he speaks of his life in the world, and especially in relation to them. It was 'a walk up and down' (ἀναστροφή) and was as public as it could well be as they in particular knew (περισσοτέρως δὲ πρὸς ὑμᾶς). How fearless was the challenge.

(b) Next, he names the positive elements of his life. 'In holiness (or 'singleness,' A. V.), and godly sincerity.'

(c) Then, he mentions the secret of it all: 'Not in fleshly wisdom, but by the grace of God.' It was this complete and utter fearlessness of conscience that could make him free-

49

ly ask their prayers (*v.* 11), especially as his letters (*v.* 13), and also his life, had been unambiguous, straight, and true.

2.   But his work as well as his character had been questioned (ch. 2: 17), and to this he now turns his attention.   He repels the charge with scorn and makes it recoil on the head of his enemies.

(a) 'We are not as the many corrupting the Word of God.' The word 'corrupting' is vivid and arresting.   It refers to the huckster who gave bad measure, and to the dishonest tavern-keeper who adulterated his goods.   We, says the great Apostle, are not men of this sort, 'making merchandise of the Word of God.'

(b) On the contrary, 'as of sincerity,' yea more 'as of God,' 'in God's presence' and 'in Christ' he spoke his Master's message.   It is a terrible thing for a man to qualify or modify the Gospel in any way, tempering its severity, compromising its righteousness, or lowering its standard.   To insert our own ideas is to 'play the huckster' with the Word of the living God.

3. Once again St. Paul refers to his sincerity (ch. 4: 2). 'But have renounced the hidden things of dishonesty, not walking in craftiness, nor handling the Word of God deceitfully; but by manifestation of the truth commending ourselves to every man's conscience in the sight of God.' Another charge had probably been made, this time of deceit and cunning.   It is an awful thing to impute motives, for of necessity it tends to destroy confidence.

(a) He had 'foresworn the hidden things of baseness.'

(b) He was not walking in craft or unprincipled trickery.

(c) He had not proclaimed the Word with guile or deceit.

(d) But by manifestation of the truth he was continally recommending himself to every man's conscience in the sight of God.

The one and only end and object of preaching is to proclaim and manifest the truth in such a way as that it shall have its due effect on human hearts in the sight of God, and the preacher must take special care that no hindrance to the full manifestation comes from himself.   As Denney finely says:

'One great hindrance to its manifestation may easily be its treatment by the preacher himself. If he wishes to do anything else at the same time, the manifestation will not take effect. If he wishes in the very act of preaching, to conciliate a class, or an interest, to create an opinion in favour of his own learning, ability or eloquence; to enlist sympathy for a cause or an institution which is only accidentally connected with the Gospel—the truth will not be seen, and it will not tell.'[1]

And this is only possible as the preacher applies the truth to his own conscience (ch. 1: 12), and commends it to the conscience of others (ch. 4: 2). To quote Denney again:—

'Conscience is not the abstract logical faculty in man, and the preacher's business is therefore not to prove, but to proclaim, the Gospel. All he has to do is to let it be seen, and the more nakedly visible it is the better. His object is not to frame an irrefragable argument, but to produce an irresistible impression. There is no such thing as an argument to which it is impossible for a wilful man to make objections. But there is such a thing as an irresistible impression—an impression made upon the moral nature against which it is vain to attempt any protest; an impression which subdues and holds the soul for ever.'[2]

## II. The Present Application.

As we ponder the Apostle's hot, burning repudiation, what do we learn for the ministry?

1. Sincerity of Motive. If we are seeking the ministry, or if we are exercising our ministry for anything short of the highest motives, we shall fail and suffer untold trouble. Simplicity versus duplicity is the prime essential, no arrière pensée, but a single eye to the glory of God. The word rendered 'sincerity' in chapter 2: 17, is said by Trench to mean transparency, that which is judged in the sunlight, and found to be free from speck, or spot, or stain.

2. Sincerity of Speech. This is as important as sincerity of motive. There must be no exaggerations, no flattery, no withholding of the truth, but absolute frankness in declaring the message, whether men hear or whether they forbear.

3. Sincerity of Action. The possibilities of danger here are various. Sometimes avarice is the temptation; at others the desire for popularity at the expense of faithfulness; at

[1] The Expositor's Bible, p. 146.
[2] The Expositor's Bible, p. 147

others, again, the use of unlawful means to bring about spiritual results; and, yet again, the personal ambition which thinks of self only in the ministry.

This solemn question of 'adulterating' the Word of God needs the most careful attention from all who are, or intend to be, ministers of the Gospel.    Adulteration is practised in trade for various reasons.    (a) To increase the bulk of the goods, and thereby to increase the seller's gain. (b) To cater to particular tastes.    (c) To beat competitors.    But the results invariably are to (a) depreciate the real value of food; (b) degrade the business (c) deceive the customer, and (d) deprave the seller.

The application of this to the ministry is as evident as it is searching.

'There are two separable ideas here.  One is that of men qualifying the gospel, infiltrating their own ideas into the Word of God, tempering its severity, or perhaps its goodness, veiling its inexorableness, dealing in compromise.  The other is that all such proceedings are faithless and dishonest, because some private interest underlies them. It need not be avarice, though it is as likely to be this as anything else. A man corrupts the Word of God, makes it the stock-in-trade of a paltry business of his own in many other ways than by subordinating it to the need of a livelihood.  When he exercises his calling as a minister for the gratification of his vanity, he does so.  When he preaches not that awful message in which life and death are bound up, but himself, his cleverness, his learning, his humour, his fine voice even, or fine gestures, he does so.  He makes the Word minister to him, instead of being a minister of the Word; and that is the essence of the sin.  It is the same if ambition be his motive, if he preaches to win disciples to himself, to gain an ascendency over souls, to become the head of a party which will bear the impress of his mind.  There was something of this at Corinth; and not only there, but wherever it is found, such a spirit and such interests will change the character of the Gospel.  It will not be preserved in that integrity, in that simple, uncompromising, absolute character which it has as revealed in Christ. Have another interest in it than that of God, and that interest will inevitably colour it.  You will make it what it was not, and the virtue will depart from it.'[1]

Bishop Moule tells of a Cambridge clergyman who had an empty church, but even men who seldom attended would
[1] Denny, *The Expositor's Bible*, 2 Corinthians, p. 97 f.

have sent for him if they were dying. Men inevitably detect the spurious and the genuine in the long run. The majority may not, but the spiritual few will, for 'he that is spiritual discerneth all things.' And woe be to the minister who has been 'found out' by the spiritually-minded among his people.

Thus a man must be right all around; right with his message, right with himself, right with his Master. Nothing can make up for simple sincerity in the ministry.

III. *The Simple Secret.*

How is this to be accomplished? How is so high an ideal to be realized? As everything else in the Christian life, in a very simple way.

1. Live in the searchlight of truth. Listen to the Apostle; 'before God,' 'of God,' 'in Christ.' He lived 'under the Great Task-Master's eye,' and in that scrutiny he had no fear of man's words or deeds. 'They say. What do they say? Let them say.' The man who prays, 'Search me, O God,' will add, 'Thou hast searched me,' and the result will be satisfaction unspeakable even amid slanders otherwise unbearable.

2. Live in the safeguard of prayer. 'If,' says the Psalmist, 'I regard iniquity in my heart, the Lord will not hear me,' but when iniquity is not regarded and the soul is uplifted to God in prayer, the evil of insincerity not only cannot enter, but is effectually displaced by that spirit of sincerity which is one of the essential features of a minstry of power and blessing. He is thereby united to Christ and is enabled to speak and live 'in Christ,' safe, secure, and satisfied in the exercise of his calling.

### SECTION 2. CERTITUDE (2 *Cor.* 1: 19).

Among the charges laid against the Apostle was that of vacillation (see *vs.* 15-20), and he replies and vindicates himself. But in so doing he characteristically goes much farther than a mere reference to himself. He brings in his Master and his message, and says that his message to them had not been unstable (v. 18), because it concerned the Son of God who was by no means vacillating and unstable (v. 19). The text is abrupt and expressive of the Apostle's intense feeling, but the general meaning is clear. Weymouth's Version brings out the ideas very forcibly and suggestively.

> 'Did I display any vacillation or caprice in this? Or the purposes which I form—do I form them on worldly principles, now crying, "Yes, yes," and now, "No, no?" As certainly as God is faithful, our language to you is not now "Yes" and now "No." For Jesus Christ the Son of God—He Who was proclaimed among you by us, that is by Silas and Timothy and myself—did not show Himself a waverer between "Yes" and "No," but it was and always is "Yes" with Him.'

This is man's deepest need, certitude. Carlyle's 'Everlasting Yea' is expressive of an universal yearning.

## I.  *Certitude in Christ.*

The Gospel of Christ is 'a mighty affirmation,' it has no ambiguities.

1. There is the 'Yea' of a Divine Assurance. The Gospel is the 'Good News' of God's love. In the Person of His Son God's love is assured to the whole world. There is nothing hesitating or vacillating in this; it has all the power of a Divine fact.

2. There is the 'Yea' of a Divine Welcome. God is ready to receive all who will respond to His love. His welcome is at once hearty and lasting, and nothing is more certain than the assurance that 'God is not willing that any should perish, but that all should come to repentance.'

3. There is the 'Yea' of a Divine Security. One of the great foundation words of the Bible is the word 'Covenant,' as expressive of God's relations to man, and it is 'an everlasting covenant ordered in all things and sure.' This Covenant is expressed in the Atonement, the Blood of the new Covenant, and manifested in the grace of God. The Covenant of Grace is the great foundation fact which assures men of every security in Christ.

So that Christ is not an Uncertainty but a Certainty, not a mere Ideal, but a Redeemer, and this assurance is absolute, decisive, complete, and unchangeable.

II. *Certitude in the Preacher.*

If the message is certain surely the messenger ought to be, and can be.

'It is in this positive, definite, unmistakable character that the strength of the Gospel lies. What a man cannot know, cannot seize, cannot tell, he cannot preach.' [1]

1. The Need of Certitude is great and constant. The underlying thought is that life and character are determined by the interest that predominates in them, that occupation re-acts on the spiritual life and fashions it. Paul's life was per-meated and influenced by the Gospel he preached. As there was nothing shifting in that, so there was nothing shifty in him. Our message should be definite, positive, and unchang-ing. The unrest to-day has effected so many that, as Dr. Forsyth has aptly said, instead of crying out, as of old, 'Here am I,' they ask 'Where am I?' It must not be 'Yea' and 'Nay,' now one thing and now another, it must come from the deep convictions of one who can say 'I know.' If we do not know we cannot preach, for there is no real message apart from convictions, as people only too easily see and feel. Dr. Forysth said some time ago:—

'The difficulty that caused most of the ills that afflicted them in their Churches at the present moment was not that men were wrong, but that they were in a cloud and did not know where they were. The thing most necessary and the thing they must lay their foundations on was that men should be turned out, not knowing a whole theology, but at least knowing the trend which theology should follow, and which would give them a foothold from which they would not be removed, however widely their vision might be enlarged.'

2. The Elements of Certitude are obvious. We must preach a threefold Christ. Christ as a Saviour for Pardon; Christ as Sanctification for Power; Christ as Satisfaction for Peace. These are the deepest and most constant needs, Par-don, Power, Peace, and the man who proclaims them posi-tively, definitely and whole-heartedly will never lack hearers or blessing.

[1] Denney, *The Expositor's Bible*, 2 Corinthians, p. 41.

3. **The Secret of Certitude is not far to seek.** It means that our own soul should be at anchorage in union and communion with Christ. The anchorage of trust; relying on, and receiving from Him. The anchorage of fellowship; through prayer and the Bible. The anchorage of testimony; telling out our experience thereby confirming it. If only we live in the abundant wealth of Scripture we shall never have a poor or faltering message. Spirituality is our greatest guarantee of certitude, as secularity is our greatest foe. The man to whom Christ is real, vital, precious, is the man who speaks with unfaltering tongue because he 'knows Whom he has believed' (2 Tim. 1: 12.)

## SECTION 3. LIMITATIONS (2 *Cor*. 1: 24).

The Apostle has been defending himself against the charge of fickleness, and here he digresses to say a word about his ministry. Denney says that, like Plato's, Paul's digressions are sometimes more attractive than arguments. He tells the Corinthians that it was to spare them he had not come, and that if he really wished to lord it over them he would have come sooner. And if after verse 23 they should be tempted to say, 'And who, pray, is he who speaks like this?' the answer is given by anticipation in verse 24. 'Not for that we have dominion over your faith, but are helpers of your joy.' Like Peter, he would not 'lord it over God's heritage' (1 Pet. 5: 3), and as he himself said to Roman Christians, he is just as ready to receive as to give a blessing (Rom. 1: 11). So we have here St. Paul's plain statement about the limitations of a spiritual ministry exercised through human agency.

I.   *What the Ministry is not.*

'Not for that we have dominion over your faith.'
1. The realm of personal faith is a realm between the soul and God into which the ministry cannot enter. A minister cannot create faith in God in another. 'Faith cometh by hearing, and hearing by the Word of God,' and all the minister can do is to provide the materials and opportunity for faith by the proclamation of the Gospel. Nor can the

minister compel or coerce faith; the most he can do is to
persuade to it. Above all, the minister cannot kill faith. If
faith dies it will be by suicide, not by murder. What the
minister can do is either to strengthen or to shake faith. He
can confirm it, or cause it to waver. A serious position enough,
but that is as far as he can go.

2. When this is realized it is at once evident that the minister is not a Director. We must beware lest the ministry
ever becomes a Directorate of the soul. This is the *esse* of
the Roman Catholic view of the ministry, and it can easily
become the *esse* of many a Protestant ministry. But it is
futile and fatal in both. In the Roman Catholic Church the
Minister as a Director is really a source of spiritual weakness
rather than of strength. It is not possible for any but the
morbid to tell everything thoroughly to a human being. As
some one says, speaking from personal experience:—

'Confession at the fullest is only partial, and the unconfessed sins
vastly outnumber the confessed, leaving the very uncomfortable result of a work imperfectly done. The only escape for the sinner is
in coming face to face with the Cross. It is just at this point where
confession breaks down.' [1]

And a Roman Catholic priest of wide experience not long
ago said that during his many years of experience in the con-
fessional he had never once received a confession of the sin
of covetousness. And yet perhaps there is no sin so prevalent
as covetousness in its various forms. The same thing is true
of anything like a Protestant Ministerial Directorate. It weak-
ens the individuality, tends to lead the soul to use the minister
as a crutch, keeps the soul an invalid instead of sending it
forth to walk in newness of life. Whether therefore in its
Roman Catholic or in its Protestant form, "Clericalism is
the enemy." We must carefully distinguish between ministerial *direction* and ministerial *guidance*. By all means let
us teach, and lead, and guide, but never, never let us control.
The ministry is a medium, not a mediation. Faith is a personal matter between the soul and God, and is intended to
grow towards maturity, and grow it will, if it is not inter-
fered with.

[1] Cauldwell, *The Cross in Dark Places*, p. 110.

II.  *What the Ministry is.*

'Helpers of your joy.'

1.  Helpers.  What a fine, suggestive, and satisfying idea of ministry!  Nothing could be more inspiring.  A Helper. What more could man wish to be?  Teaching with authority is not dictating to the conscience, or forcing your personality on another, or compelling another to reproduce you.  A helper of others will endeavour to develop their personality and make them as far as possible independent of himself.  It is sometimes charged against Theological Colleges that they tend to make men into machines, all of one pattern, echoes of their teachers, and unable to deviate from certain lines of action. I am not so sure from my own experience whether this is actually the case or not, but we can at least heed the warning and follow the counsel given by the Lambeth Conferenece to Theological Colleges to encourage men to think for themselves and to form their own conclusions.  We must beware of accepting without testing, of assimilating without verifying.  We must collect facts, grasp principles, and then draw deductions for ourselves, and in proportion as we are thus truly individualistic ourselves we shall be 'helpers' to our people to become the same.

2.  But in particular we are to be 'Helpers of Joy.'  Joy is the ideal of the Christian life.  'Rejoice in the Lord always.'  Is this so to-day in ourselves and in our Churches? Pensiveness is not a New Testament note; wistfulness finds no place in the Christian life of the New Testament.  Joy is the supreme fact and factor of the Gospel of Christianity. The joy of Salvation, of Truth, of Holiness, of Fellowship, of Service, of Hope.  'Joy unspeakable and full of glory.' And it is the minister's duty to help this joy in every possible way.  How?  By possessing it himself, by preaching it, and by living it .  There is nothing so inspiring, uplifting, strengthening as Christian joy.  'The joy of the Lord is your strength.' Suffering often hardens; joy never does.  Suffering often saddens; joy always gladdens, and as 'good news' is the essence of the Gospel, so 'glad tidings' should be the substance of the preacher's message.

III.  *What the Ministry requires.*

If this work is to be done two things are needed.

1. We must cultivate our own individuality. This is the fundamental requirement of all who would lead and guide their fellows. What a fine testimony Mr. Asquith gave to his old Head Master, Dr. Abbott, of the City of London School. After praising his scholarship and its effect on his pupils in 'those stimulating and vivifying lessons,' he said:—

'But, my old schoolfellows, *behind and beyond all that there was something more.* There was the force, the influence, the personality of a man cultured, disinterested, austere, but, at the same time, with a vivid interest in the affairs of mankind, and in everything that concerned the boys who came under his charge. I am perfectly certain there is not a full-grown man here who in those days—the days of the '60's and the '70's—was under Dr. Abbott's tuition and guidance who will not agree with me that the most precious possession we took away with us from the City of London School, whether to Oxford or Cambridge, or to the works of business and to the avocations of life, was the sense of that strong, self-sufficing, but, at the same time, widespread, vivifying, many-sided personality to which many of us have looked back in the stress and strain of life as the best example and the best influence.'

So must it be with the true minister. He must be a whole-hearted, manly personality if he is to instruct and inspire his people.

2. And the minister must also cultivate self-effacement. This is no contradiction of the foregoing, but the most perfect complement. Individuality and yet self-effacement, and the greater the personality the more thorough the self-effacement. We must ever guard against the danger of the strong will dominating the weak; we must ever watch against forgetfulness of our limitations. Like the Baptist, while we must take care to be a voice, that is, a real sound and not a mere echo, we must also take care to be only a voice, that is, the expression of a personality which is summed up in the words, 'Not I, but Christ.'

And the one secret of all this is to make Christ real in our own experiences. Only thereby shall we avoid the dangers and fulfill the duties of the ministry. If like the Baptist we say, 'He must increase, but I must decrease,' we shall find to our joy that souls will be helped and blessed by our ministry, led to Christ, kept near to Him, growing up in Him, used by Him in His service and for His glory. And this is the end of all ministry.

## SECTION 4. RESPONSIBILITY (2 *Cor*. 2: 14, 15).

We have here a characteristic outburst of the Apostle. He had been narrating purely personal matters (*vs.* 12, 13), and especially his suspense through the absence of Titus. When he could bear it no longer he went forth to meet him in Macedonia. He met him and received a full account of Church matters at Corinth (ch. 7: 5, 6), but his heart is so full that he cannot stay to say anything further of these personal concerns; he bursts out into thanksgiving at the thought of his ministry. Let us ponder what he says.

## I. *The Splendour of the Ministry.*

1. It was a Triumph. 'Thanks be unto God, which always causeth us to triumph in Christ.' How are we to read this? With the A.V., 'which always causeth us to triumph'? Or with the R.V., 'which always leadeth us in triumph'? Etymological considerations alone would lead to the rendering of the R.V., especially in the light of the same word in Colossians 2: 15. But the idea of the context is not that of God's triumph in Paul, but of Paul's triumph through the Gospel. The thought of Paul as a 'conquered enemy', is not in the passage, and the word should probably be rendered quite generally as meaning to make a show, or spectacle, indicating glory, not disgrace.[1] Even those who, like Denney, adhere to the etymology, and render with the R.V., are compelled to admit 'a certain air of irrelevance' in the interpretation (p. 87), and seem unable to give a satisfying meaning in the

---

[1] So that acute scholar, Dr. Field, in his *Notes on the Translation of the New Testament* (p. 181). Cf. Denney, 2 *Corinthians* (p. 86). Schmeidel, Bruce, *St. Paul's Conception of Christianity* (p. 79), and McClellan, *Expositor*, Series 6, Col. x. p. 192, are ample authorities for preferring the A.V.

light of the context. And so without hesitation we retain the A.V., and render it so as to refer to Paul's own truimph in Christ. The Corinthians, or a section of them, had been bitterly opposing him and his Gospel, but the good tidings received from Titus showed that the devil had not been allowed to have the victory. God had enabled His servant to triumph in Christ, and this was his invariable experience, for 'God *always* causeth us to triumph.'

2. It was also a Testimony. 'And maketh manifest the savour of His knowledge by us in every place.' Wherever he went God used him to reveal His will, His grace, His love, Himself. The 'fragrance' of God was evident everywhere through the Apostle's testimony. The triumph was granted for the sole purpose of making known the Gospel of Divine Grace. It was God's will that His Gospel should be victorious, and this was actually brought about by the instrumentality of the Apostle. Wherever he went the self-righteous, the despairing, the hardhearted, the indifferent were led to Christ, and to the knowledge and acceptance of His Gospel. This was the glory, the splendour of the ministry. So it is always, the triumph and testimony of the Gospel of Grace and Peace.

II. *The Solemnity of the Ministry.*

But there is another side to be noticed and emphasized. Although there were triumphs, there were also rejections of the Gospel. God does not compel assent and insist on adhesion. And so. while in them that were being saved St. Paul could say that he was 'a sweet savour of Christ to God,' it is not at first easy to realize how he could say that he was the same 'in them that were perishing.' What can this mean? It should be carefully noted that in both cases the recipient of the fragrance is God, not man. 'We are unto God.' It is not that the sweet savour is received by the hearers of the Gospel of both classes, but that in both cases the incense ascends to God, the 'sweet savour' of grace in one case and of justice in the other. It means that God is glorified in the saved and vindicated in the lost, and that if a minister does his duty, God regards his work with satisfaction whatever be the outcome. Even if there are no results God is pleased with a faithful ministry. How solemn and searching this is, no words are needed to point out.

### III.  *The Satisfaction of the Ministry.*

1.  The Apostle's outburst of thanksgiving shows that his heart rejoiced at the results of the ministry.  To be 'a fragrance of Christ,' and that 'to God,' was the highest possible joy of his life, and he could not but express his joy in thankfulness.  Wherever he went he had more or less of success, but beyond this, in all cases, among saved and perishing alike, a fragrance of Christ was ever ascending to God, though not of the same nature; and it was in this view of all the consequences that the Apostle breaks forth in a strain of praise.

2.  But he was not unconscious of the awful seriousness of the other side.  His ministry was 'a savour of death unto death' to those who were unwilling to receive Christ, and that the Apostle keenly felt this is evident from his concluding words, 'Who is sufficient for these things?'  The minister has to realize and preach these alternatives; the greater the mercy, the greater the condemnation.  Susceptibility decreases in proportion to resistance, and moral sufficiency increases as men become conscious of opportunities lost.

Well may St. Paul cry out, 'Who is sufficient for these things?'  The Christian ministry is not to be taken up lightly, or prosecuted without the profoundest thought, the deepest feeling, and the tenderest sympathies for the wandering, the lost, and the perishing.

### SECTION 5.  ASPECT (2 *Cor.* 2: 17; 4: 5; 5: 11; 5: 20).

The ministry, as exercised by St. Paul, had several aspects according to the work required, and the various words used by him to describe what he did are full of suggestion for the ministry to-day.

### I.  *Speaking* (ch. 2: 17).

1.  The message was God's Word and nothing else.  A word from God.  And to be delivered intact, unadulterated.

And to be declared 'as of sincerity'; 'as of God'; 'in the sight of God'; 'in Christ'!

2.    The manner of delivery was simply 'speaking'; natural, ordinary conversation, talking.    'Talk ye of all His wondrous works' (1 Chron. 16: 9).    'Let the redeemed of the Lord say so' (Psa. 107: 2).    The earliest extension of Christianity to the Gentiles went along this natural line.    Certain men came to Antioch and 'spake' to the Greeks (Acts 11: 20).    We should cultivate this ordinary, natural way of declaring God's truth.    While there is of course necessary and ample place for the more set and elaborate discourse, there is equal call, perhaps a greater call, for simple, natural testimony to God and His Word in our ordinary speech.    Our message should not be far away at any time, with perfect naturalness we should be ready to give it in ordinary speech and conversation.

## II.    *Heralding.* (ch. 4: 5).

1. The Manner here is noteworthy.    'We herald.'    This is an important aspect of the Christian ministry.    There is no 'bated breath and whispered humbleness' about the announcement of a herald.    The attitude and tone indicate confidence and fearlessness.    He knows his Master, his Master's position, authority, and power, and he declares his message accordingly.    What an illustration of the Christian minister as he declares his message.

2. The Message.    'We herald not ourselves, but Christ Jesus the Lord; and ourselves your servants for Jesus' sake.'    Not ourselves, but Him.    Observe the force of the three titles: *Christ, Jesus, Lord.*    His threefold relation (a) to God (Christ), (b) to the sinner (Jesus), (c) to the believer (Lord).    This is the substance of our message; the proclamation of a personal, Divine, redeeming Lord.    Not ourselves, but Him.    A friend of mine, himself a notable preacher, went once to hear two very great preachers, and when I asked him his impressions, he said, 'In the one case I could not see the man for the Master.    In the other I could not see the Master for the man.'    'Not ourselves, but Christ Jesus

the Lord.' And yet, 'ourselves as your slaves for the sake of Jesus.' Not I, but Christ, be honored, loved, exalted.' This is a theme worthy of all the heralding we can give to it.

III.    *Persuading* (ch. 5: 11).

1. The method is to be carefully noted. 'We persuade.' We impel, though we cannot compel. Persuasion is the one element of Christian preaching which keeps a sermon from being a mere essay. The truth is to be applied and acted on, not merely to be placed before people. It is for acceptance as well as consideration. We do not simply preach *before* men, we preach *to* them with a view to immediate and definite action. No sermon is worthy of the name that does not contain this essential element of persuasion.

2. The reason of such a method is seen in the Apostle's words. 'Knowing, therefore, the fear of the Lord.' It is this element of fear that constitutes the supreme reason for persuasion. Fear is a note far too seldom heard to-day in preaching and teaching. By an apparently inevitable rebound we have gone to the other extreme of dwelling on the element of love to the omission of fear. But we must find room for both if we would be true to the New Testament revelation. Modern teaching about the universal Fatherhood of God tends to rob the Gospel of its solemn and even severe element. God is regarded as a benign, gentle Father, Who will not be too severe with His wayward children. But the New Testament idea of Fatherhood always includes the elements of righteousness and fear. 'If ye call on the *Father*, Who without respect of persons *judgeth* according to every man's work, pass the time of your sojourning here in fear' (1 Pet. 1: 17). It is a serious and fatal error to omit the note of fear from our preaching. There is reason for Dr. Dale's remark to a friend; 'No one fears God nowadays.' But there are signs of return to a better mind. Men are finding out that the moral and spiritual results of preaching love and avoiding fear are not satisfactory, and as a consequence the old note of fear is coming once again into the messages. A well known Cambridge scholar, Dr. Bethune

Baker, has voiced this need in a little work in which he pleads for the return of the element of fear in preaching.

'We have almost ceased to teach what has been called "the Gospel of Fear." . . . We have quietly dropped the word "damned" altogether. A new school of theology arose that made the Incarnation and the Love of God the Gospel, in place of the Atonement and the Fear of God. . . . But surely the reaction has gone too far. . . . And surely the Love of God—the Everlasting Arms ever open to receive His children—is not the whole of the Gospel. . . . But did He not also hate evil, were He not wounded by every failure and lapse of His child, were He not also Judge to "make inquisition for sin"—the less were He Love and Father. We must preach this part of the Gospel too. Welcome always awaiting the prodigal; but he must set his face homewards first. Healing for every transgression; but we must first turn away from it unto the Lord.' [1]

IV. *Representing* (ch. 5: 20).

1. The Christian minister is an ambassador on behalf of Christ, and his message as such is noteworthy and striking. It is nothing less than the announcement that 'God was in Christ, reconciling the world unto Himself, not imputing their trespasses unto them,' and that based on this, it is the work of the minister to beseech men to be reconciled to God (*v.* 21). This is the very heart of the Christian Gospel, the message of Reconciliation. Estrangement in St. Paul's teaching is two-sided, not one-sided only (Denney, p. 211). Something in God as well as in man had to be dealt with if there was to be reconciliation, and it is this 'something' which constitutes the centre and core of the Christian message.

'"Reconciliation" in the New Testament sense is not something which *we accomplish* when we lay aside our enmity to God; it is something which God *accomplished* when in the death of Christ He put away everything that on His side meant estrangement, so that He might come and preach peace.' [2]

Canon Simpson well says that 'Luther was only stating in the form of a brilliant paradox the very essence of the Pauline doctrine of Justification when he exclaimed, *Ego sum Tuum*

[1] *The Old Faith and the New Learning*, pp. 48-51.
[2] Denney, *The Expositor's Bible.* 2 Corinthians, p. 212.

*peccatum, tu es justitia mea.*[1] The fuller quotation from the great Reformer is worthy of reproduction:—

'Thou, Lord Jesus Christ, art my Righteousness, I am Thy sin. Thou hast taken what was mine, and hast given me what was Thine. What Thou wast not Thou dost become, that I might become what I was not.' And this is pre-eminently the message of the Gospel.

' When St. Paul says that God has given him the ministry of reconciliation, he means that he is a preacher of this peace. He ministers reconciliation to the world. His work has no doubt a hortatory side, as we shall see, but that side is secondary. It is not the main part of his vocation to tell men to make their peace with God, but to tell them that God has made peace with the world. At bottom, the Gospel is not good advice, but good news. All the good advice is summed up in this—Receive the good news. But if the good news be taken away; if we cannot say, God has made peace, God has dealt seriously with His condemnation of sin, so that it no longer stands in the way of your return to Him; if we cannot say, Here *is* the reconciliation, receive it, then for man's actual state we have no Gospel at all.' [2]

The man who knows this by blessed, personal experience is the man who alone can properly perform the functions of an ambassador for Christ.

2. But the methods of the ambassador must not be overlooked. 'As though God were entreating you also' (ch. 6: 1). The ambassador 'exhorting' and 'beseeching' is a striking contrast. He comes in his Master's Name and begs the acceptance of the Divine reconciliation.

'Most expositors notice the amazing contrast between πρεσβεύομεν ("we are ambassadors") and δεόμεθα ("we beseech you"). The ambassador, as a rule, stands upon his dignity; he maintains the greatness of the person whom he represents. But Paul in this lowly passionate entreaty is not false to his Master; he is preaching the Gospel in the spirit of the Gospel; he shows that he has really learned of Christ; the very conception of the ambassador descending to entreaty is, as Calvin says, an incomparable commendation of the grace of Christ . . . in his dignity as Christ's ambassador and as the mouthpiece of God, in his humility, in his passionate earnestness, in the

---

[1] Simpson, *Fact and Faith*, p. 57.
[2] Denney, *The Expositor's Bible*, 2 Corinthians, p. 213.

urgency and directness of his appeal, St. Paul is the supreme type and example of the Christian minister.' [1]

As we review these four aspects of the Christian ministry do we not see something of its greatness, its grandeur, its intensity, its applicability?  Be it ours to enter into these elements and realize them in our service in the power of the Spirit of God.

### SECTION 6.   THE FOUNDATION (2 Cor. 6: 3f).

The highest aspect of the Christian minister is that of an ambassador with the ministry of reconciliation (*ch.* 5: 19-21). The chief requirement of the minister is character, and without this all ideas of office or work go for naught.

## I.   *The Possible Evil.*

1. The minister must not give any occasion of stumbling, lest the ministry be blamed.  Our Lord laid great stress on the possibility and danger of occasions of stumbling (σκανδάλά), and of the consequent need of watchful caution.  The application of this to the ministry is particularly pressing, for some people seem to be only too ready to use anything as an excuse against a clergyman.

2. This danger may take various forms.  A minister may be marked by ignorance and shallowness while occupied with the highest possible themes.  He may be full of conceit and pride while proclaiming humility.  He may be actuated by worldliness and self-advantage while warning against ambition.  He may be dominated by indolence and ease while urging self-sacrifice.  He may be influenced by selfishness and avarice while extolling liberality.  He may be guilty of unspirituality while insisting on the highest spirituality.  There is no greater danger, no more serious peril, than that of a gulf between word and deed, between message and character, between preaching and practice.

3. This peril comes to the minister by various channels, as to which he needs to be on guard.  Sometimes it is due to

---

[1] Denney, *The Expositor's Bible*, 2 Corinthians, p. 216.

bodily strain.  The pressure upon body and nerves leads to a breakdown which reflects on consistency and character. At other times the intellectual demands of the ministry may lead to the same sad result.  The pressure upon his intellectual life to provide material for his people may easily lead him to forget the application to himself.  He may preach an ideal which he not only does not realize, but shows no sign of doing so.  And he will fail to 'lure to brighter worlds' unless he himself 'leads the way.'  Again, trying circumstances may lead to failure in Christian living.  People are exacting, irritating, annoying, and in his impatience he gives way to some outbreak of peevishness, or perhaps even of temper, which at once spoils his ministry and leads people to reflect on the difference between his preaching and his practice. And so, whatever be the cause, we lose by our life what we say by our lips, and the ministry is blamed because we have given occasion of stumbling.

## II.  *The Definite Duty.*

1.  We must 'commend' the ministry by our life (*v.* 4). 'In all things approving ourselves as the ministers of God.' In chapter 4: 2, St. Paul had spoken similarly of 'commending ourselves to every man's conscience in the sight of God.' There is no contradiction here to the apparent contrasts in chapter 3: 1 and chapter 5: 12, where he deprecates 'commending himself,' for the motive and purpose of the 'commendation' are quite different.  The minister commends himself as a minister, as a servant of God, and as representing his Master.

2.  But how is this to be done?  St. Paul tells us of several ways.

(a)  Sometimes it will be by suffering (*vs.* 4, 5).

(b)  Sometimes it will be by doing (*vs.* 6, 7, 8a).

(c)  Sometimes it will be by being (*vs.* 8b, 9, 10).

It is far easier to record and recount these various methods of commending the ministry than to reproduce them in natural life, and yet this is the ideal to be aimed at, and by the grace of God realized.

III. *The Simple Secret.*

How is this life to be lived? That is the supreme question for all ministers.

1. The first point to be remembered is that conduct is only truly based on character, and life can only be lived aright if it is the expression of what we are. No emphasis can be too great on ministerial character. We are too apt to think of ministerial reputation, but this is always erroneous and may prove disastrous. Let a man take care of his character and God will take care of his reputation. Never a thought need be given to reputation, which will be all that is essential if only our character is right with God.

2. And character in turn is based on communion with God. Faithfulness springs from fellowship, and the man who stands right with man is he who keeps right with God. Communion with God purifies, clarifies, solidifies the inner life and makes the man what he should be. And this communion is only possible through prayer and the Bible. In prayer we commune with God; in the Bible He communes with us. The two together provide all that we need for the protection, sanctification, and consecration of daily living. As with Joshua of old, the man who makes God's Word his daily meditation will find his way prosperous and will have good success.

# CHAPTER IV

## THE MINISTRY IN THE PASTORAL EPISTLES

I
T is in the Pastoral Epistles that naturally we find much about St. Paul's view of the ministry. And of these a special interest attaches to 2 Timothy, because it contains the Apostle's last words. They are personal revelations of himself given as counsels to Timothy. The position of the Apostle gives pathos to the writing. He was in prison, and yet is full of cheer and hope as he bids his timid young friend to look forward to life and work. The weakness (perhaps partly physical) of Timothy was ever in view, and Paul valued him highly because of his earnestness.

SECTION 1.   THE MINISTERIAL GIFT (2 *Tim.* 1: 6f).

I.   *A Reminder.*

1.   Of a gift bestowed. 'The gift of God which is in thee through the putting on of my hands.'

Dr. Hort (*Christian Ecclesia,* p. 186) distinguishes between this and the counsel in 1 Tim. 4: 14;  'Neglect not the gift that is in thee, which was given thee by prophecy, with the laying on of the hands of the presbytery'; and regards this as not referring to Ordination only, but to the whole life (*v.* 5). In any case, it means the Holy Spirit as a definite Divine gift.

2.   Of the need of using the bestowed gift. 'Stir up,' i.e. 'fan to a flame.' There was danger of the fire dying down, as there always is this peril in things spiritual. In medicine, the medicinal matter is on top and the water is at the bottom, and it must be shaken in order to give every particle the medicinal quality. So in science, there is a difference between latent and energetic power, the former has to be transmuted into the latter. And so also in regard

to human life, it is character that gives quality to action. When the excitation is withdrawn there is an inevitable tendency to precipitate itself. Hence the reason for 'stirring up' the gift, for fanning it into a flame.

## II.  *A Reason.*

1.  An actual gift had been bestowed, a gift which could be characterized in no uncertain terms, both negatively and positively. Negatively, it was 'not a spirit of fear,' or 'cowardice.' There was no fear in the Apostle. He neither cringed to the great nor was intimidated by the many. The ministry is in danger of being afraid. We may hide what we are, or have, or we may withhold what we possess. There may be simulation, or dissimulation, the pretence of what we are not, or the hiding of what we are. This is not the spirit of the Christian ministry. There must be no fear, no cowardice, nothing craven, or shrinking. But what precisely and positively does this spirit mean?

(*a*)  It is a Spirit of Power. The Spirit of God is an energy in the soul, and a capability in speech and action. There is nothing more characteristic of Christianity than δύναμις, power, and that is part of our gift for life and ministry.

(*b*)  It is a Spirit of Love. This is the method of the Spirit; overcoming opposition, rendering service, and suffering everything in an atmosphere of affection.

(*c*)  It is a Spirit of Discipline. Not as the A.V., 'sound mind' (which would be σωφροσύνη), but 'd i s c i p l i n e' (σωφρονισμός). It is the spirit of self-control, and the spirit which enables a man to control others.

These three elements of the gift show definitely what the Spirit is and does for the minister of Christ.

## III.  *A Remedy.*

How is the gift to be 'stirred up'?

1.  We must recognize its possession. 'I believe' in the Holy Ghost, and I must believe that the Holy Ghost is in me.

Let us take time to dwell on this; the Holy Spirit is actually dwelling in me.

2.   We must remove all hindrances.   As fire needs attention by the clearance of ashes, if the combustion is to have free course, so we must take care that no spiritual hindrance in us prevents the free movement of the Holy Spirit in and through us.

> ' The dearest idol I have known,
>    Whate'er that idol be,
> Help me to tear it from Thy throne,
>    And worship only Thee.'

3.   We must replenish the fuel.   Fire needs both clearance and a fresh supply of fuel, and the soul requires fresh additions of the 'fuel' of the Word if the Spirit is to do His work.   There is a close connexion between the Word and the Spirit; the Spirit uses and works through the Word, and it is only as the Spirit has the Word on which to work that He can fulfil God's will in us.   He is the Spirit of *Truth*, and if God's truth is in us He will make it mighty and cause it to prevail.

SECTION 2.   THE TWO DEPOSITS (2 *Tim.* 1: 12-14).

The Apostle speaks here to his friend Timothy of two 'deposits.'   In verse 12 'my deposit,' and in verse 14 'the beautiful deposit.'   In these two phrases we have the ministerial life summed up.

I.   *Our Deposit with Him* (*v.* 12.)

1.   What it is.   It must mean our lives.   'That which I have committed unto Him.'   This is the true attitude of the Christian, and especially of the Christian minister.   He is to 'yield' himself to God (Rom. 6: 13).   To 'present' his body as a sacrifice to God (Rom. 12: 1).   He 'commits' his soul to God (1 Pet. 2: 23).   He 'hands himself over' on behalf of Christ (Acts 15: 26).   This surrender must be definite. unreserved, irrevocable.   We must 'deposit' ourselves with Him and abide there.

2. What it obtains. He guards, preserves, keeps our 'deposit.' The need of this is only too obvious; we cannot keep ourselves. Our life is ever at the mercy of sin, temptation, weakness, until and unless it is deposited safely with Him Who is 'able to guard' it.

3. How long does this last? 'Against that day.' The deposit is permanent, never to be recalled by us, never to be returned by Him, and never to be plucked out of His hand (John 10: 28). Continuance is the main essential of the ministry. Our deposit is for ever.

4. What is involved in all this? It means deep conviction, and implies four steps in the spiritual life and attitude of the soul. Let us look carefully at the text and see how our experience travels. First, we *believe*: 'Whom I have believed.' Then, we *know*: 'I know Whom I have believed.' Then, we *commit*: 'that which I have committed unto Him.' Then, we are *persuaded*: 'and am persuaded that He is able to keep.' This means a ministry with an irrefragable conviction, and it is all essential. There can be no ministry, such as God intends, without this conviction. It is the only power against every form of materialism; against every phase of doubt; against every aspect of worldliness. Nothing can make up for the supreme assurance of conviction, and nothing can stand against it. The minister who possesses it has the pledge of everything that is worth having in Christian life and service.

II. *His Deposit with us* (*v.* 14).

1. What it is. Undoubtedly this must mean the Gospel. 'O Timothy, keep that which is committed to thy trust, avoiding profane and vain babblings, and oppositions of science falsely so called' (1 Tim. 6: 20). 'Hold fast the form of sound words, which thou hast heard of me, in faith and love which is in Christ Jesus' (2 Tim. 1: 13). This is the faith 'once delivered unto the saints' (Jude 3), of which the Apostle speaks of himself as a trustee (1 Tim. 1: 11). The Lord has handed over to us His glorious Gospel, His Divine message, and we are the trustees of so weighty a charge.

2. What it needs. Like our deposit with Him, so His with us needs 'guarding.' There are two acute dangers in ministerial work in relation to the Gospel. There is the danger of losing the truth of the Gospel by adulterating it, by mixing it with other ingredients, and so causing its purity and fulness to be lost. And there is the danger of losing the reality of the Gospel by weakening it in our life, through low standards, or inconsistencies. Whether by adulteration of truth, or by lowering the standards of life, we are only too apt to 'lose' the deposit of the Gospel.

3. How it is preserved. In a threefold way. (*a*) By pondering it. (*b*) By living it. (*c*) By spreading it. Thought, life, testimony. Meditation, obedience, witness. When these three are combined, then, and only then, can we expect to guard the beautiful deposit.

4. The Divine Secret. 'By the Holy Ghost.' Herein lies the possibility of so pondering, living, and spreading the truth that it shall be for ever preserved. The presence of the Holy Ghost in the soul is the secret of all power. He makes the Truth real to the soul, and keeps it vital in life and service. He keeps the life strong, and maintains it at the right standard. Therefore our ministry must be 'in the Holy Ghost,' for only thus can we be sure of power and blessing.

As we review these two deposits and contemplate the two sides of the ministerial life we may sum up all by saying; (1) We trust; (2) He entrusts. (1) He keeps what we trust; (2) We keep what He entrusts. In these two lie all things that pertain to life, godliness, and service.

SECTION 3. THE VARIED SERVICE (2 *Tim.* 2).

The whole of this chapter, taken up as it is with special exhortations to Timothy, may be said to refer to the ministry. There are at least seven aspects under so many words or phrases. The keynote is in verse 1; 'Be strong in the grace that is in Christ Jesus.' Timothy is exhorted to strength in Divine grace, and then is shown what the ministry is to be.

I. *The Teacher* (*v.* 2)

It is his work to pass on the deposit (*ch.* 1: 14), and the need of competent teachers is constant and great. Teaching is far too rare a characteristic in·the ministry; men can talk, or exhort, or appeal; but none of these must be confused with teaching. Teaching is causing another to learn, and nothing short of this will suffice. We must not only endeavour to cultivate the teaching gift ourselves, but we must also ever be on the look-out for such to train them. The deepest, strongest, and most lasting results in the ministry accrue from those who can *teach*.

## II.  *The Soldier* (*v.* 3).

The Christian man is here described as 'a beautiful soldier of Jesus Christ,' and he is exhorted to endure hardness, to regard himself as on campaign, and to be prepared to suffer accordingly. How is he to do this? By keeping himself free from all entanglements. 'No man that warreth entangleth himself with the affairs of this life; that he may please Him Who hath chosen him to be a soldier' (*v.* 4). As no soldier can possibly entertain the idea of any association with civil duties, so no Christian minister can allow himself to become entangled with anything that may hinder his work and warfare. Sometimes he is unduly given to society, sometimes he becomes a too constant frequenter of clubs. Well, every man must face these and other things for himself, but there can be no doubt of the absolute necessity of a genuine aloofness on the part of a Christian minister. If he is to 'please Him Who hath chosen him to be a soldier' he *must* keep himself free for active and strenuous service.

## III.  *The Wrestler* (*v.* 5).

Here we have the thought of life as an arena in which the Christian athlete is engaged. Christian life involves contest; Christian service requires struggle and effort. And it behooves the Christian man, and especially the Christian minister, to 'play the game.' He must 'strive lawfully.' His methods must be straight and true, and nothing must be said or done in our service for God which cannot bear the searching gaze and test of the Great Taskmaster.

## IV.   *A Husbandman* (*v.* 6).

The Christian worker is here described as one who tills
the ground, a metaphor which is as intelligible as it is appropriate.   Human hearts are the soil in which the seed of
the Word is cast, and this means labour on the part of the
husbandman.   And in this passage we have the additional
thought that the man who labours is to be the first partaker
of the fruit.   This is because he labours, and only on this account.

This simile, together with the two preceding (the soldier
and the wrestler) will be seen to have special reference to
the prize and how to win it.   Whether soldier or athlete or
husbandman, we must so live and work that we may rightly
win and claim the reward.

## V.   *A Workman* (*v.* 15).

Mark the threefold description of the true workman here.
(*a*) He is to be zealous to be approved unto God.   This is
the supreme object of all 'zeal.'   (*b*) He is to 'cut-aright'
the Word of Truth.   This may refer to the track of the
plough, or the knife of the butcher, but in either case it
means 'right-handling' (R. V.) of the Word of God, bringing out things new and old and giving to each his portion
in due season.   He is to be a labourer that 'feels no shame'
(Plummer, *Expositor's Bible*, p. 370).   No shame from God,
no shame from his fellows, is to come to him in his work.

## VI.   *A Vessel* (*v.* 21).

Here is another figure, full of vividness and suggestion
for the ministry.   A vessel!   That which will *hold* something   that which can be *used*.   That which may be an
*ornament.'*   Mark the fourfold description: (*a*) unto honor;
(*b*) sanctified; (*c*) meet; (*d*) prepared.   How glorious the
privilege of being a vessel of mercy (Rom. 9: 23) for service
in the Temple of the Lord.

But how is this possible?   Only by being cleansed.   'If
a man therefore purge himself.'   The vessel must be clean and

empty.    Empty to be filled, and clean to be used.    'Such honour have all His saints.'

VII.    *A Slave* (*v.* 24).

Once again the figure becomes personal, and the minister is regarded as a 'bondservant of the Lord.'    He is so in a threefold way.    (*a*) By purchase: 'Ye are not your own, for ye are bought.'    (*b*) By possession; 'He is thy lord.'    (*c*) By service; 'I love my Master, I will not go out free.'

As we contemplate these seven aspects of ministry we naturally ask, How can they become possible?    The answer is in verse 1: 'Be strong in the grace that is in Christ Jesus.'

1.    'In Grace.'    This is our *Position*.    A missionary remarked some time ago that the great feature of life in India is the strain due to the lack of those opportunities for recovery of physical elasticity and spiritual tone which are so valued in England.    The Indian climate, too, taxes to the uttermost man's power of endurance.    Not only so, but an alien race, with uncouth habits of life, caste rules which prevent freedom of social intercourse, the consciousness of the English civilian's deterioration when removed from the religious atmosphere of a Christian country—all these will test a man's spiritual life to the utmost.·    Then comes the question, What resources will meet such demands?    He answers as follows:—

'You must find them within yourselves.    Nothing suffices to meet the strain, the depression, the moral shock of life in India—nothing but the Christ within you.    "It pleased God to reveal His Son in me."    If that is your equipment, you may take up the life to which you are called in the fulness of hope and confidence.    There is no sufficient motive for missionary work but our personal relation to Christ, and it is in this relation, too, that you will find the grace that sustains, that carries you through the inevitable stage of disappointment and disillusion, and keeps fresh within you the devotion and enthusiasm which flows full-tide in your hearts to-night.'

This word has an application for us at home as well.    There is nothing to compare with the indwelling of Christ to enable us to rise superior to all surrounding difficulties.

2.    'Be strengthened.'    This is our *Power*.    The Greek word is noteworthy.    It is either Middle or Passive.    Not

'be strong,' but 'be strengthened.' And the word itself is noteworthy in its New Testament uses. Paul was strengthened (Acts 9: 22). Abraham was strengthened in his faith (Rom. 4: 20). We are to be strengthened in the Lord (Eph. 6: 10). We can do all things through Christ which strengtheneth us (Phil. 4: 13). Christ strengthens us for service (1 Tim. 1: 12). He stands by us and strengthens us (2 Tim. 4: 17). With our position in grace and our power in Christ assured, nothing need deter us or check us from rendering true and laudable service in our ministry.

section 4.   character and work (2 *Tim.* 2: 24-26).

In every ministerial, indeed, in every Christian life, character and work are inseparably connected and inextricably bound up. A careful consideration of each is therefore necessary, and both are brought before us in this passage.

I.  *The Work.*

The people with whom we have to do are described as 'those who oppose themselves.' Field (*Notes on the Translation of the New Testament,* p. 215) renders the Greek, 'those who think diversely.' In either case the fact of difference, and therefore of opposition, is clearly taught. The people will often oppose their clergyman as well as oppose themselves, even when their best interests are involved. Opposition is pretty certain in every genuine, earnest ministry.

1.  The first great need of such people is 'repentance to the full knowledge of the truth.' Repentance is God's gift, and 'in case God should' give them this, the minister is to work, and strive, and pray. Opposition must be changed, and this can only be by means of repentance.

2.  The second great need of the people who oppose themselves is 'that they may recover themselves out of the snare of the devil, who are taken captive by him at his will.' The wording of the original is very suggestive, and even startling. 'Recover,' i.e. 'wake up,' ' wake from fumes.' They have been 'drugged,' and are in the snare of the devil. St. Paul

had a profound sense of the reality of spiritual powers of wickedness. These people thus 'hypnotized,' or 'anaesthetized,' had been taken captive by the devil at his will. The A.V. here is far more likely to be correct than the R.V., and the American R.V. renders the passage like the A. V. The two pronouns refer to the same subject, just as in John 5: 39 and 19: 35. We are not to expect the purism of the classics here, though Field (p. 246) quotes Xenophon for the identity of αὐτοῦ and ἐκείνου.[1]

'Taken alive' by the devil! How sad, terrible, and startling. There are only two passages where the word ζωγρέω is used in the New Testament. Here, where it refers to the capture of man by the devil; and in Luke v. 10, where the Christian fisherman is to 'take men alive' for the Master. The 'capture' is very real and demands constant attention from the servant of God, if he is to recover men and take them alive for God.

## II.  The Way.

How is this work to be done? We are told, first, negatively, and, then, positively.

1.    Negatively; the servant of the Lord 'must not strive,' 'not fight.' Is it not deeply significant that μάχομαι is never once used of the Christian life, even in its warfare against sin? We must not be 'combative.' We must strive (ἀθλέω) but not fight (μάχομαι). There is a constant danger of a combatant's spirit. We sometimes stand up for the truth, but the 'old Adam' comes in and colours our testimony, and we do harm rather than good. Controversy is essential, and yet it must be waged in the right spirit. Like St. Paul, we may be called upon to withstand even a St. Peter, and yet we must be careful to 'speak the truth in love.' No one is ever recovered from the snare of the devil by contentiousness and a pugnacious spirit. 'The servant of the Lord must *not* fight.'

2.    Positively; the servant of the Lord must be 'gentle unto all men, apt to teach, patient, in meekness instructing

[1] See also *Homiletic Review*, vol. vii., p. 650.

those that oppose themselves.' Mark well these four elements of true service.

(a) Gentle, i.e. mild (1 Thess. 2: 7). Like the gentleness of Christ (2 Cor. 10: 1), we must produce the fruit of the Spirit, 'gentleness' (Gal. 5: 22), for 'gentleness allayeth great offence' (Eccl. 10: 4, R.V. margin). Gentleness is rare because it is not a natural gift, or an inherited grace. It comes from above, the result of the Divine action when the faculties are possessed by the Divine Spirit. It is to be carefully distinguished from weakness, for it is quite compatible with sturdiness of character. God's works are full of gentleness and yet of strength. Nor is gentleness for a favoured few only. Loudness and violence are not Christian, but are anti-Christian. Warmth can be gentle. Gentleness may often need the discipline of suffering to produce it. There is profound truth in the well known text, 'Thy gentleness hath made me great.'

(b)     'Apt to teach,' i.e. explaining, not contending.

(c)     'Patient,' i.e. ready to endure malice.

(d)     'In meekness instructing,' i.e. with gentle humility bring under true Christian discipline those who oppose themselves.

All this means character for the accomplishment of work, that is, we must *be* in order to *do*.

'Though no warning against an unspiritual, no exhortation to a holy life, may be tolerated, let your own pure, earnest, unworldly charter and bearing be to the careless soul a perpetual atmosphere of spirituality haunting and hovering around it. The moral influence of such a life cannot be lost.

III.  *The Secret.*

Such a work demanding such a character can only be accomplished by Divine grace, and this we must learn to obtain by the due use of means.

1.   For perception of the truth which is to be brought before 'those who oppose themselves,' we must study and become mighty in the Scriptures. In the Pastoral Epistles St. Paul lays great stress on 'sound doctrine,' i.e. doctrine which ministers to moral and spiritual soundness, or truth

(ὑγιαίνω).  This will mean a regular, steady, personal study
of our Bible in fellowship with God in Christ by the Spirit.
It is only in this way that we shall obtain that insight into
spiritual truths which will enable us to present those truths
in the right way to our people.  Nothing can compare with
this definite Bible knowledge in mind and soul, if we would
do the difficult work of recovering souls from the snare of
the devil.

2.  For power in using the truth thus obtained, prayer is
the supreme secret.  It must not be a mere appendix of our
spiritual life, but the central and dominant feature.  We
ought to have fixed times, and if possible, a fixed place.  The
essential principle is that habits of regularity tend to make
the spiritual life capable of constant, instructive action.  A
well-known novelist used to say that he had so habituated
himself to working at his novels at nine o'clock in the morning that, when that hour arrived, his mental powers were like
servants standing ready to do their master's bidding.  It is the
same in the supreme business of conscious relationship with
God.  If we have regular appointments with Him, we shall
find that, when the hour draws near, our souls will reveal a
certain bias and expectancy, and will be watchful for His
appearing.

And so long as this regularity of time is observed we can
vary our methods as much as we like, and perhaps the greater
the variety the better.  Posture of the body, while important,
is of course secondary to the attitude of the soul, and our
methods of prayer must be largely settled by our temperament and choice.  The Bishop of Durham (Dr. Moule)
once said:—

'As regards attitude, I very seldom venture to kneel at prayer in
secret.  At night it leads almost invariably and very speedily to sleep-
ing on my knees; and even in the morning hour, I know not how,
recollectiveness and concentration of heart and mind are usually
quickened in my case by a reverent standing attitude as before the
visible Master and Lord, or by walking up and down, either indoors,
or, as I love to do when possible, in the open air.  A garden may
prove a very truly hallowed oratory.'

And these times of prayer must be definitely, largely, and

increasingly times of intercession. Our horizon must be ever-widening, our prayers less and less self-centered, and our intercessions more intellectual, more systematic, more constant, more persistent, more believing.

And thus by the Scriptures and by Prayer we shall build up that character which will in turn affect our work with vital power and make it instinct with spiritual blessing.

SECTION 5. THE MINISTER AND THE SCRIPTURES

(2 Tim. 3: 14-17).

In all Christian work there are three elements absolutely indispensable: the Spirit of God as the power, the Word of God as the message, and the man of God as the instrument. The Spirit of God uses the message by means of the man. In that handbook for Christian workers, the Acts of the Apostles, we have these three elements in order brought before us. The first eleven chapters are full of the Spirit of God. The next nine chapters have less of the Spirit and more of the Word of God. The last eight chapters have very little about the Spirit, and very little about the Word, but a great deal about the man of God. Eleven, nine, eight: that is the order and the proportion. The Spirit first, the Word second, and the man third. The Spirit greatest and foremost, then the Word, and only last of all the man. It will be found, through a concordance, that the references to the Spirit, the Word and the man are exactly along this line. These three are indispensable, inseparable from all Christian work that is worthy of the name.

Two of these are very prominent in the present passage, and the other is at least implied in our word contained therein. The subject, therefore, is the Word of God in relation to the man of God for the purpose of the service of God.

I. *What the Scriptures are.*

1. They are *Divinely inspired.* We read in verse 16, 'Every Scripture inspired of God,' or 'all Scripture is given by inspiration of God.' We are all aware that the phrase, as thus rendered, is one word in the original: 'God-breathed.'

The A.V. is, 'All Scripture is given by inspiration of God, and is profitable.' The R.V. is, 'Every Scripture inspired of God is also profitable.' Some prefer the one and some the other. Yet I do not think there is very much in the difference, because in either case the reference must be to the Old Testament Scriptures. Either it is a statement that they are inspired and profitable; or else that, being inspired, they are also profitable. One reason that makes me prefer the old version in this case is that there are six or seven texts which in the Greek are exactly like this, with a noun and three adjectives connected by *and*; and this fact seems to suggest that we ought to translate this passage in the same way, which would be according to the A. V. rather than the R. V.

There are three reasons why we believe that the Scriptures are Divinely inspired, God-breathed. The first is, the testimony of the Lord Jesus Christ. Not only before, but after His resurrection, He bore His testimony to the Old Testament Scriptures in such a way that they were for Him the absolute and supreme authority. The second reason is the testimony of history. If there is one thing clear it is the testimony of all Christian history to the inspiration of Holy Scripture. And, of course, the third reason is the testimony of experience. There is that in this book which, as Coleridge says, 'finds us,' something unique, something inexplicable, fully inexpressible, and yet so real, so true, and so blessed that we can say, and say with all our hearts, This is from God. So that the Bible is the key to the lock of human nature. We can test these things for ourselves. When we put two and two together, we know by the certain principle of mathematics, that four will be the result. When we blend oxygen and hydrogen in the proper proportion we know the result will be water. When we bring human nature and the Bible together we find that one is the problem and the other is the solution. All Scripture, every Scripture, is God-breathed, Divinely inspired.

2. Then they are *Divinely powerful*. 'The sacred writings which are *able*.' Mark the precise force of the Greek phrase, 'which are continuously powerful,' implying the continuous process of power. We know what this is when we

contrast this Book with other books, these writings with other writings. They are continuously powerful, they are able, continuously able, to do everything that man needs for time and for eternity. Divinely inspired; Divinely powerful.

3. They are also *Divinely profitable.* 'Every Scripture inspired of God is also profitable.' It is a marvellous thing to realize that this book was written centuries ago and is living and fresh and profitable to-day. Think of the sermons that are composed and preached from this Book week by week. Take, again, the Commentaries; almost every month we read or hear of some work coming forth from the press. When we go through it, if the writer is a scholar and a Christian, we are certain to find something in it that we have found in no other. There is nothing more delightful than to study a commentary by a man who is worthy to write it, and to find in it marvellous proof of, and testimony to, the freshness and profitableness of the Word of God. Take Lightfoot, Westcott, Hort, or any other of the great grammatical exegetes, and allow yourself to be led step by step, from point to point, and you will find freshness after freshness, until it is true of you, as it was true of Alford, who said that in preparation for his Greek Testament he found something fresh every time he went over the passages for the new editions. The profitableness of the Scriptures is one of the marvels of the present day. Every man knows this in his own experience. You may come to the most familiar passage, and in the power of the Holy Spirit you may see something you have never seen before. As John Robinson of Leyden says, it is still true that

'The Lord hath yet more light and truth
To break forth from His Word.'

II. *What the Scriptures do.*

1. The first thing they do is to *save*; 'which are able to make thee wise unto salvation,' able to save. They bring into our minds, darkened by sin, the illumination of God's truth and will, and the result of that wisdom is that the Christian man is one who has not five but six senses. There is the

sixth sense of spiritual perception that come as the result of God's Word brought to bear upon the soul. We know the oft-quoted illustration of a lady who looked at one of Turner's master-pieces. She said to him, '*I* never saw such colours in nature.' 'No, madam,' he replied; 'don't you wish you could?' William Pitt was once taken by Wilberforce to hear Richard Cecil preach, and Wilberforce prayed that Pitt might get a blessing. Wilberforce was soon rejoicing in the message, and prayed that his friend might hear and heed. Pitt placed himself politely to listen, just as he would attend to a speech in the House of Commons. At the end Wilberforce was overflowing with joy and thankfulness for the message, and said to Pitt, 'What did you think of it?' 'Well,' said Pitt, 'I gave the gentleman my very best attention, but I really could not understand what he meant.' Why not? These things are spiritually discerned. 'The natural man receiveth not the things of the Spirit of God,' and we might go on to translate the Greek, 'neither can he recognize them.' He has not the faculty. It is the Holy Spirit, by the Scriptures, Who makes all men wise unto salvation—salvation in the widest, greatest, deepest of all senses. Salvation for the past; the Holy Scriptures assure us of justification. Salvation for the present; the Scriptures assure us of sanctification. Salvation for the future; the Scriptures assure us of glorification. There is nothing to compare with that spiritual perception which comes from personal reception in experience of the Holy Spirit in the Word. I never tire of quoting a phrase which I believe was uttered by James Hamilton, of Regent Square: 'A Christian on his knees sees further than a philosopher on his tip-toes.' It is because he has been made wise unto salvation. That is why St. James is able to say, 'Receive with meekness the implanted word, which is able to save your souls.'

2. Then the Holy Scriptures *guide* as well as save. Let us look very carefully at this passage. 'Profitable for teaching, for reproof, for correction, for instruction which is in righteousness.' I take these together, and include them in the word "guide." You will find four distinct ideas. The first is positive: profitable for 'teaching.' The second and

third are negative: for 'reproof' and 'correction.' The fourth
again is positive: 'for the instruction which is in righteousness.'
First of all, the Scriptures inculcate truth; they are profitable
for teaching.    How true this is every one of us knows as he
bows before the Scriptures and says, 'Lord, send out Thy
light and Thy truth.' They are profitable for 'rebuke', or
'conviction,' whatever it may be.   How true that is we also
well know.   When we come to this Book and there is something unconfessed and unforgiven in our soul the Scriptures
convict, confute, rebuke us.   If we regard iniquity in our
heart the Lord will not hear us.   Oh, the rebuking power of
the Bible!   Then, for 'correction'; that is, putting straight
things that are crooked in our lives.   That seems to be the
meaning of the word: setting right all that is wrong.   If
there is anything wrong or doubtful in our lives, the Bible
will meet us.   That is the value of the Scripture for the
deepening of the spiritual life.   Many a life has to be cor-
rected before it can be deepened.   You must have the channel
straight before you think of the depth of it.   The fourth
thing is positive: 'instruction'; but it is really much more
than that.   It means 'discipline,' 'making like a child,' making us real children of God.   It is for 'discipline which is
in righteousness,' everything that is included in the combined
ideas of the duties of parent and teacher.   There is no discipleship worth the name without discipline, and both ety-
mologically and spiritually there is a close connexion between
these two words.

That is what I mean by guidance, everything for our daily
life of sanctification in the fullest sense of that term; incul-
cation of truth, refutation of error, correction of our conduct and the exercise of our character and conduct.   All this
is in the Word of God.

3.   The third thing the Scriptures do is to *equip*.   'That
the man of God may be completely furnished, complete unto
every good work.'   The words 'complete,' and 'furnished'
mean jointed, adjusted, fitted; and the reference is either to
a piece of machinery fitted for its work or to the human
body with every joint and part adjusted ready for action.

'That the man of God may be complete, furnished, completely unto every good work.'

'The man of God.' This is the last book in the Bible where the phrase 'the man of God' occurs, and we are rather surprised to see it applied to Timothy. He is addressed twice by this title. In the Old Testament it was used for the prophets. Here in the New Testament it is actually given to a somewhat weak, nervous man. This is great encouragement for us, for it shows clearly that the weakest of us can have the highest of all titles, 'man of God,' one who is *manly* and *godly*; and when you have manliness and godliness you are 'God's man.'

III.  *What the Scriptures require.*

1.  The first thing the Scriptures require is *knowledge.* 'The things which thou hast learned and hast been assured of, knowing of whom thou hast learned them; and that from a babe thou hast known the sacred writings.' There were two generations behind this boy. He had been taught these sacred writings from a babe by his mother and by his grandmother. And he had also *seen* the Scriptures in their lives. The result was he knew them.

This is what you and I need. First of all, we must know the contents of the Bible. Then we must seek to know the meaning of these contents. Thirdly, we must get to know their application to our life and to our service. Knowledge, that is what we need above all things—intellectual, devotional, homiletical knowledge; but let us take care we do not put the homiletical first. Intellectual, or, what these books say and mean; devotional, what they mean to me; homiletical, what they mean to my people for next Sunday.

2.  The second thing these books require is *trust*: 'through faith which is in Christ Jesus.' That was St. Paul's view of the Old Testament. There are many people who do not seem to take much account of the Old Testament Scriptures to-day, but St. Paul thought so highly of them that he said they were able to make wise unto salvation through faith in Christ. They need trust. We all know how true that is. A promise comes to us; let us trust it. Let us trust Him Who

is the Promiser. In proportion to our faith in the truth of this Book we shall find the power of it in our daily life.

3. The third thing is *continuance*. 'Abide thou in the things which thou hast learned.' At least three times we have the idea of continuance connected with the Word. 'If ye abide in My Word, then ye are My disciples indeed.' We remember that it is said of Satan that he 'standeth not in the truth.' Conversion is not everything. We are thankful when we are able to count conversions and say that God has blessed the Word. But it is of much more importance to ask what about those people five years, ten years hence? 'Continue thou in the things which thou hast learned.' 'So Daniel continued.' 'Continue instant in prayer.' 'Continue ye in My love.' The secret of all growing life lies in knowledge and trust continued day by day to the very end.

So I ask you to notice that what I have been saying is, first of all, the secret of *personal power* in Christian life. The Scriptures known, trusted, obeyed, and continued in; these things are the secret of personal power. Daily meditation, not weekly, otherwise it will become 'weakly' in the other sense. If we live upon what we get elsewhere from men or books, our Christian life will be very poor, for it will only be a second-hand Christianity. But if day by day we come to God's Word for daily and definite meditation, we shall find in that the secret of personal power. Our mind will become saturated with truth, our heart will be inspired by the love of the Scriptures, our conscience will become ever-increasingly sensitive, our wills will be more and more subjected and submitted to the will and power of God.

This is also the secret of *ministerial power* in Christian service. Some one asked Hudson Taylor once how it was that he had such freshness in his messages as he delivered them day by day when on deputation work. He said he could only account for it in this way, that he was accustomed to spend time with the Lord in the morning and then pass on in the afternoon and evening what the Lord had told him. Some people wonder what they shall preach about next Sunday, and they fear they will very soon come to an end of their Bible. If we keep close to the Greek New Testament, or even to the

English Bible, the difficulty will be, not what we shall preach about, but what we must leave out. If a man has been in the ministry for thirty or forty years, and follows this plan, at the end even of that long time there will be any number of subjects that he has never been able to take, and never will be able to take, unless there are sermons up in heaven. The secret of ministerial freshness is the power of God's word.

This is also the secret of congregational power. This is so, positively, both in regard to expository preaching from the pulpit, and to Bible class work. It is also the secret of power, negatively, because it will set aside and render unnecessary all the more than doubtful methods which obtain in many Churches. Bible classes and expositions, teachers training classes and prayer meetings will shut out all other instrumentalities. The secret of congregational power is the prominence that we give to the Word of God. The source of everything fruitful and mighty in the life of God's people is to be found there. So let us determine that we will go to our Churches and congregations with the words of the Apostle on our lips: 'We will give ourselves to the ministry of the Word and prayer.'

## SECTION 6.   PARTING WORDS (2 *Tim.* 4: 5).

Just as the last Epistle of the great Apostle closes he gives his young friend and disciple four parting words as watchwords of his ministry.

### I.   *Soberness.*

'Be sober.' The minister must be fully awake and in a condition the very opposite of drowsiness. The contrast with verse 3 is clear. 'But.' There were those who were turning away from the truth, *but* Timothy was to be on his guard. The thought is much the same as in chapter 2: 26, the necessity of being fully aroused, spiritually alert, keen, watchful. No minister can afford to be drowsy, or other than awake and watching. As Simeon of Cambridge used to stand before the picture of Henry Martyn, the serious face seemed to say to him, 'Be earnest.'

## II. *Endurance.*

'Endure afflictions.' 'Suffer evil with me.' The call was to sacrifice and suffering as essential to the life and work of the ministry. It is an appeal against all self-indulgence, and for readiness to do strenuous service in the face of trial, persecution, and suffering.

## III. *Evangelization.*

'Do the work of an evangelist.' This means that a man must have a message, an evangel, an announcement of 'good news.' The minister is not a philosopher, though his Gospel has philosophy in it. The minister is not a moralist, though the Gospel has ethic in it. He is a proclaimer of Glad Tidings, or he is nothing, and without this all else will be worthless.

Fifteen years ago two American missionary students, occupying the same room, talked thus to one another: 'What message have we got for the heathen to whom we are going? Can we tell them of a Christ mighty in us, Who saves us day by day? If we cannot, it would be cheaper to send Bibles and tracts.' There and then they decided that their first work was to know God for themselves, and so from then, right on through the rest of their course, they rose regularly at 5 A. M. and had one unhurried hour with God and His Word, and another unhurried hour with God in prayer. Note the outcome—the fulness of the Spirit for the satisfaction of their life needs, and the promised 'rivers of water.' These two men became prominent workers at home and abroad. One of them was led to publish a tract made up mainly of extracts from President Finney's writings, and that tract led Mr. Goforth to seek and find the fulness of the Spirit. He in his turn became an instrument of revival in the East. All this because two young men sought God's best with all their hearts.

## IV. *Faithfulness.*

'Make full proof of thy ministry,' or 'fully discharge thy ministry.' Let the ministry 'fill' your life, with nothing left undone that ought to be done, and nothing done that does not minister to the service to which we are called. We must draw 'all our cares and studies this one way.' There must be a power of detachment and concentration if the ministry is to be fully discharged. We must do our own work and that alone.

From these four watchwords we readily recognize four things in connexion with the ministry: a Supreme Necessity; a Supreme Danger; a Supreme Problem, and a Supreme Secret.

1. The Supreme Necessity. This is spiritual life, and life in abundance. Without it there is, and can be, no ministry.

2. The Supreme Danger. This is spiritual death. By this I mean soul-death, what some one has called a lost soul in the pulpit. Not sinfulness, but uselessness; not badness, but soullessness. Sermons well prepared but without the electric spark of fellowship with God.

3. The Supreme Problem. This is to keep the soul alive. Not our sermon, nor our work, nor our organization; but *ourselves*; to keep our spiritual life keen in the face of professionalism. And to this end we must guard the fire and keep it burning. One of the foremost dangers of the ministerial life is intellectual indolence, and it is far more common than is generally supposed. Mental activity is not natural, but acquired; not congenital, but achieved. It requires and demands mental toil. A man may be "fussy" and busy and yet be an intellectual "dawdler." He may engage in work of all sorts, and yet not compel his mind to work. Intellectual interest must ever be strong; we must feed the fire of the mind; reading, thinking, storing.

And the spiritual enthusiasm must be maintained by a closer walk with God. As some one has acutely said, ninety-nine may tolerate our sermons, but the hundredth will find us out. Some men may be able to hide intellectual sloth, but the clergyman cannot. Some men may hide spiritual weakness, but the clergyman cannot.

4. The Supreme Secret. This is perpetual freshness of soul, due to the 'continual dew' of the Divine blessing, and

spiritual freshness can only come through prayer, the Bible, and the Holy Spirit. But when these are real all else is real, for the life grows strong and influential, and full of grace and glory. A recent book describes how, when riding in Wales, the author came upon a preacher's cottage, lonely among the hills and rain and miry roads. 'How does he stand the monotony?' he asked his companion. 'The Bible is to him the Word of God,' was the answer. 'He lives to preach it. There is no monotony when all life is one great desire.'

## Chapter V

# THE CALL AND ITS RESPONSIBILITIES.

**E**VERY Christian is called and expected to be a witness (Acts. 1: 8), but not every one is called to the ministry.

## Part I.  The Divine Call

### I. *Its Necessity.*

What are we to understand by a Divine call to the ministry? A friend of mine who has to interview candidates for the ministry once told me that many of the men who came before him were quite unable to adduce any definite proofs of a call from above. Indeed, they are without an idea on the subject, hopelessly confused about any such thing. And yet all true ministry must commence here. The call must come from God and not from man. It must be in some way the immediate appeal of God to the soul; 'Son, go work to-day in My vineyard.' This call will not be primarily through the Church or a particular denomination, but is the internal work of the Holy Spirit. And as such it will be an 'effectual call'; such a man will inevitably reach the ministry.

Why do we insist on this necessity of a Divine call? Scripture is full of it. Old Testament prophets were all called of God, as we see from the stories of Samuel, Isaiah, Jeremiah, Amos, and others. The New Testament Apostles were similarly called of God; the Twelve, St. Paul (Gal. 1: 1), and Timothy. Of the ministry we may say what is recorded of the Aaronic priesthood. 'And no man taketh this honour unto himself, but He that is called of God' (Heb. 5: 14). The very nature of the case suggests the same thing. The minister is called an 'ambassador.' He is said to have 'received' his ministry, and to have it 'committed' to him. Human governments illustrate this principle. A man must

be called to his office. And if it should be argued that the
Bible illustrations are special cases, it may be replied that
Church History bears testimony to the same profound principle. If we think of men like Ambrose, Augustine, Luther,
Latimer, Knox, Wesley, Whitefield, and many others, we
cannot help being conscious of the working of Divine grace.
God never calls without equipping, and the very fact of
equipment proves the call. The Lord ascended to give gifts,
and he still bestows the varied gifts of ministry. (Eph. 4: 11).

## II.  *Its Proofs.*

How may a man tell whether he has received a call from
above? The call may be proved in various ways; there is
no precise law of detail or method, but a few marks may be
confidently stated.

1.  An intense desire. This may come early in life, or
after conversion, or at some still later time. But it will
come. It will not be an unreasoning desire, but full of serious and earnest thought. It will be a disinterested desire,
and motives will be pure and true. And it will be a persistent desire. It will come again and again. The man will
say, 'I ought, I want; and please God, I will.'

2.  Converging circumstances. These are different in
different cases. Sometimes they may be expressed in the desire and prayer of our parents. At other times we may see the
hand of God in the provision of means and the opportunity
for training. But whatever they may be, and however they
may reveal themselves, circumstances will converge and indicate the will of God

3.  Some indications of qualifications. There ought to
be physical qualifications. A minister must be prepared to
'endure hardness.' A serious defect in the voice, or some
pronounced bodily infirmity, may well make a man question
seriously whether God is calling him to the ministry. It may
be going too far to insist on the old Aaronic requirement of
absence of physical blemish, as is done, we believe, in the
Church of Rome to-day, but the underlying general principle is sound, whatever may be the precise personal applica-

tion. Intellectual qualifications will necessarily be included. A man ought to have *brains* for the ministry, some mental aptitude, and no looseness of intellectual machinery. Greatest of all are the moral qualifications; steadfastness of character, stability, self-control, and some concentration of purpose. These are the qualifications essential to ministerial life, and the man who is really called of God must not be known to have failed in every other calling.

4. Approval of those who know us. The opinion of wise friends will be valuable on this point. Not merely the opinion of mother and sisters, nor necessarily of the opposite sex at all, but the judgment of men friends and acquaintances who really understand us, fellows of our school days, men of our University and College. And not least of all, the opinion of the best men of the Church which we attend and where we are known. 'A good report of them that are without' will be a further qualification to support the idea of a Divine call.

5. A measure of blessing on our work. If we have not already done something for our Master it is hardly likely that we are being called to the ministry. We ought to have endeavoured to win someone for Christ, or to have tried to help some weak young Christian to a firmer footing in discipleship.

When these five characteristics exist; desire to enter the ministry, providential circumstances pointing in that direction, some evidence of qualifications, the approving judgment of those we can trust, and some experience of Christian work, we may 'assuredly gather' that God is calling us to preach the Gospel.

III. *Its Assurance.*

Of the inward movement of the Holy Spirit there should be no doubt in the man's mind. He has faced the situation and he can confidently go forward.

But there should also be humility. His confidence is not baseless, but founded on a genuine Christian hopefulness and humility. While he does not venture to say, "I know I am called" because he might possibly be mistaking the Divine Voice and Providence, yet in the true spirit of Christian trust and self-distrust, he will be ready to say, "I trust I am called," and will wait to obtain further verification in actual experience.

This is the Divine call, and it is the foundation of all else. Let us face it before we enter the ministry lest we find out our mistake afterwards. Who shall dare to say he is called unless he has such definite personal dealings with God the Holy Ghost as will enable him to feel sure that he is in the pathway of God's will? The personal experience of the Holy Spirit in this call is at once the most solemn and the most blessed reality of the Christian life.

The spiritual element in a Divine call is further emphasized by a considering of the revealed will of God.

1.  The will of God may be deduced from Holy Scripture. In the various elements of the ministry and its purpose of serving God for the promoting of His glory and the edifying of His people we learn 'what the will of the Lord is.'

2.  The will of God may be learned from personal providences in life. As we review our pathway we should be able to see 'all things working together for good' in relation to our entrance upon the ministry.

3.  The will of God may be gathered from the marks of personal fitness we possess. Body, mind, and soul should combine to prove that we are ready for this 'office and ministration.'

4.  The will of God may be deduced from a consideration of our spiritual experience. The witness of the Spirit within, and our knowledge of and fellowship in things spiritual, ought to bear their culminating testimony to the other lines of evidence of a Divine call.

Let us therefore face this afresh and make sure of our call to the ministry of the Church.

A true call to the ministry will always be accompanied by the following characteristics:

1.  Definite Convictions. The mind must be made up on certain matters, and our position held with tenacity. Such subjects as the Deity of Christ, the Personality and Divinity of the Holy Spirit, the Redemptive Work of Christ, should

be settled, never to be re-opened. It is only by definite convictions that any minister worthy of the name can live and work.

2. Wide Sympathies. While definite we must not be narrow; although possessing preferences we must make room for other outlooks. While our convictions are part of ourselves and are founded firmly on the Rock of Ages, our sympathies should be as wide as they can be. It is the 'intensive' man who can safely be 'extensive,' it is only the shallow man who is in danger of losing everything definite by extending his sympathies.

3. Genuine Spirituality. This will give warmth to our convictions and strength to our sympathies. The men to be feared and avoided are (1) the man of convictions only, who is narrow, cold, hard and perhaps bitter, without the warmth of spiritual experience: and (2) the man of genial indifference to settled doctrine, and of easy-going acceptance of all types of thought and effort, without the safeguard that comes from a true spiritual life. But when convictions, sympathies, and spirituality meet and blend in reality and proportions, we have the true minister as contemplated by Holy Scripture.

Part II.  The Responsibilities of the Divine Call

Section 1.  the belief of the scriptures.

There are two important considerations as to the Bible: (a) Its place in the minister's life; (b) His use of it in his work. It is of the utmost importance that attention be directed to the relation of the ministry to the Holy Scriptures, for it is vital to all else.

The Authority and Sufficiency of Scripture were based on the conviction of its possession of a Divine Revelation guarded by Inspiration. This Revelation meant that God had spoken, and that His will had been made known and could be understood and followed in Holy Scripture. Inspiration was never defined or described, but was assumed, taken for granted. The Church in the sixteenth century was not engaged on the proof of Divine Inspiration. Inspiration was pre-supposed. It was assumed and taken for granted.  The use of Scripture, and the reference to it as authoritative, showed that the Church believed the Scriptures revealed the presence of the Spirit of God as the Spirit of Truth ('Thy Word is truth,' John 17: 17), and the Spirit of Holiness ('Thy Word is very pure,' Psa. 119: 140).  Revelation and Inspiration are best proved by the Gospel contained in Scripture, as it affects in transforming power our lives and the lives of others.  It is the uniqueness of Scripture which is the great thing, its authoritativeness or life as a revelation from God.  And whatever may be our precise theory of Inspiration, we shall be well advised if we adopt none that tends to diminish our reverence for the Bible as the work and instrument of the Holy Spirit. 'The sword of the Spirit, which is the Word of God.'  We are on a sure foundation when we accept, without attempting to explain, the two statements of God's Word: 'All Scripture is God-breathed' (or, 'Every Scripture is God-breathed,' 2 Tim. 3: 16), and 'Holy men of God spake as they were moved by the Holy Ghost' (2 Pet. 1: 21).

Are we prepared to accept its truth and acknowledge its authority?  It should never be forgotten, amid all the critical controversies of today, that the fundamental question is as to the historical trustworthiness of Holy Scripture.  It is not a question of any precise theory of Inspiration, but whether the account given in the Old and New Testament of God's revelation of Himself can be relied upon for its historical trustworthiness.  Some words of a modern scholar are worth quoting on this:—

' What is of vital concern to the Christian Church is not questions of literary analysis or minor points of literary history and criticism, but whether the story of Israel's history from the call of Abraham down to the preaching and writing of the last Apostle is, as to all its essential and characteristic features, correct; whether, in particular, what it tells us of the part God took in it, is as objectively true as what it tells us of the part men took in it.  We need not be troubled if an inaccuracy be found here and another there, whether of thought, or sentiment, or date, or name, or number, or any other subject; for neither a nation's nor an individual's whole history can be discredited because mistakes may have crept into the literature by means of which its life has found expression, and through which later generations have to learn what it was. What the Christian Church needs to be on its guard against, is the acceptance of a reconstruction of the history of Israel which eliminates the special Divine acts, revelations, and inspiration, whose purpose was the reconciliation of God and man; in a word, all that has constituted, and still constitutes, its distinctive value.' [1]

The minister must be clear here, or else he had better not think of the ministry. Error on this point is fatal to usefulness and power. 'How canst thou go, seeing thou hast no tidings ready?'

The question is searching. This is a call for sincerity, and if a man lacks that, he lacks the essential of all ministry. Sincerity leads inevitably to reverence, and no one will ever use the Bible aright unless he is reverent to it. All Bible problems should be approached from the point of view of spiritual religion. Literary study alone is useless. And reverence in turn will lead to spiritual power.

This confession of personal experience should be uttered without any hesitation or qualification. There should be a personal conviction, showing that the man knows by experience what the Scriptures are. His confidence, conviction and courage will thus be abundantly manifest.

From all this we see that the ministerial attitude to Scripture determines all else. It comes in at every point. The Bible must be our Fount of Doctrine. Its Authority must be our deciding factor. The Life of the Bible must be our ideal, and the Grace of the Bible our dynamic. Indeed, the first and most natural view of everything in the ministry ought to have a close relation to the Bible.

And this will of course mean a first-hand experience of the Bible as the Word of God. The mind must be saturated with its truth, the heart inspired by its love, the conscience made sensitive to its law, and the will submissive to its grace. Then, then only, then always, will our life be fragrant and our ministry fruitful to the glory of God.

[1] Principal Simon, *Some Bible Problems*, p. 284.

SECTION 2.   THE USE OF THE SCRIPTURES.

From the minister's own personal attitude to Holy Scripture we naturally pass to the consideration of his use of it in ministerial life and work.

1.   Reading.   The value of this part of Divine Worship cannot well be over-estimated.   Let us make the most of it, so that the hearing of God's Word may be a blessed means of grace.

2.   Preaching.   As the Bible is necessarily the source of our sermons, so it should be their substance and their inspiration.   We are to 'preach the word'; we are to be 'faithful dispensers of the Word'; our work is primarily a 'ministry of the Word.'   If our sermons are not Biblical they cannot properly be Christian; the Bible must enter into every part of our preaching work.

3.   Teaching.   In the various methods of instruction employed by all Churches; Bible Classes, Sunday schools, church services, the teaching must be above all things Biblical.   Our people need to be 'built up in their most holy faith,' and this faith is drawn primarily and pre-eminently from the Word of God.   No Church that is worthy of the name dare neglect the teaching of the Bible, nor fail to give it a prominent place.

4.   Pastoral.   The clergyman is pastor as well as preacher, shepherd as well as teacher, and the Bible must be as prominent in this as in other spheres of his work.   It is only by the ministry of God's Word that he will be able to heal the spiritual diseases of his people.   For the weary, the sorrowing, the despondent, the hardened, the fearing, the despairing, the Bible will naturally and necessarily be the minister's *vade mecum,* his indispensable help.   And the more he studies it with this practical pastoral end in view, the more effective and the more blessed will be his ministry.   Our minds and hearts should be so stored and saturated with the Bible that the Scripture view of things should instinctively be the first that occurs to us.   No time is too long, no trouble too great, that is spent with the Bible in relation to pastoral preaching, teaching, and service.

*4994/*

The minister must know his Bible, and his knowledge will
be threefold: Intellectual, Devotional, Homiletical.

1. He must first master its contents. Whatever may be
his methods of study he must know the contents of his Bible.
To this end a few suggestions may perhaps be given.

(*a*) Let us study the Bible itself first and chiefly, instead
of what is said about it. Dr. Campbell Morgan has said that
the weakness of preaching to-day is its uncertainty, the
absence of any clear note, and he attributes this to the lack of
Bible study on the part of the clergy.

> 'I feel very strongly that a great deal of this is due to their almost
> total neglect of study, prayerful study, of the Bible. Many have
> been so busy dealing with it as literature that they have entirely
> neglected its spiritual note. They can read it in Greek and Hebrew,
> but scores of them leave their theological college utterly unable to pass
> the simplest examination in the Bible. Many a humble old woman
> in their Church knows her Bible far better.'

Are there not many who could give the arguments, *pro* and
*con*, as to the criticism of Deuteronomy, the unity of Isaiah,
and the Apostolicity of the Fourth Gospel, who would find it
difficult to pass an examination on the actual contents of
Deuteronomy, Isaiah, and St. John? While we do not fail
to make ourselves acquainted with all the modern scholarship within our reach, we must first of all make ourselves
acquainted with the actual contents of the Bible. And another thing follows.

(b) Let us study the books as they are, before we concern
ourselves with their real or supposed sources. To resolve a
book into its sources is perfectly legitimate, but it is not everything and it is not the primary thing.

2. He must then consider how to apply the Bible to his
own life. The Bible is not only to be mastered, it is to be
assimilated. Meditation has been defined as 'attention with
intention,' and the Word of God is to be a mirror in which
we view ourselves (Jas. 1:23-25); the water which cleanses
(Eph. 5: 26); and the food which strengthens our spiritual
life (1 Pet. 2: 2; Heb. 5: 12-14; Psa. 19: 10). The message of the Bible must come home first of all to our own

hearts if it is to be of use to others. 'What saith my Lord to His servant?' (Josh. 5: 15); 'What wilt thou have me to do?' (Acts 9: 6), must be our constant, personal, definite inquiries.

3. He must then use the Bible, thus mastered and assimilated, in his ministerial work. For preaching, teaching and pastoral needs the Word of God is all important. All Scripture 'is profitable for doctrine, for reproof, for correction, for instruction in righteousness' (2 Tim. 3: 16). And it is just at this point that we see the force of studying and using the Book with a belief and confidence in the great truth of its contents. To be able to prove that three sources exist in Genesis, or two in St. Mark, is one thing, but to argue that these sources when analysed are contradictory is quite another. We ought to be able to assume in our ministerial use of the Bible that the history as a whole is correct, and that the Scripture account is a trustworthy record of Divine revelation. It is difficult to imagine ordinary men believing the truth of the Bible if it is proved inaccurate on matters of fact. The question at once arises whether inspiration is compatible with frequent inaccuracy or frequent incompetency. In all this we must be genuine, open-eyed students, determined to discover and possess the truth, not followers of any fashion in scholarship, whether ancient or modern. We must call no man master, but determine to go our way and settle these things for ourselves. We may depend upon one thing, that any view of the Bible which cannot be proved and taught, is pretty certain to be wrong, or at any rate so doubtful as to be practically useless for pastoral work. Sir William Robertson Nicoll once remarked of Old Testament questions that ordinary hearers cannot be expected to follow the intricate process of historical criticism, and that therefore in our preaching we must take the Old Testament as it is, or leave it alone.[1]

4. This threefold attitude of Scripture, intellectual knowledge, devotional experience, and ministerial use, will be at once the cause and the effect of a convinced and everdeepening belief in the Scriptures as the Word of God. We

---

[1] Index to *Expositor's Bible*, Introductory Essay.

shall believe in its power over men as we experience its power over ourselves, and we shall be convinced of its sufficiency for all ministerial needs without resorting to any methods of service in which the Bible finds little or no place. And so the minister will be 'mighty in the Scriptures,' and will find in them the supreme secret of ministerial joy and power.

Each day he must do something in regard to the intellectual knowledge, the devotional application, and the pastoral use of Scripture. Each day he must unite with these three methods the exercise of prayer for light, guidance, and blessing. 'We will give ourselves to the ministry of the word and prayer,' said the Apostle (Acts 6: 5), and it is only in this firm and constant waiting on God in His Word and prayer that we shall wax riper in our service and be 'throughly furnished unto all good works.'

## SECTION 3. THE WORK

After the consideration of the Minister's relation to God, to the Church, to the Holy Scriptures, the thought of his work naturally follows.

### I. *Strenuous Service.*

This service will not be light and easy. There will be plenty of work, and work, too, which will put a heavy strain on mind and body. If a man imagines that he will have 'an easy time' by entering the ministry he will find himself very much mistaken. He will soon experience calls upon his time, a pressure upon his strength, a demand upon his intellect, and, not least of all, a drain upon his sympathies.

And yet the service of the ministry is one of the most searching tests of character, because our time is our own in the sense that unlike men in professional or business life we are not subject to particular hours of duty which must be observed. A clergyman can easily fritter away his time between breakfast and lunch, and find by one o'clock very little done. It is essential for a man to make some definite rules for the use of his time, and keep to them. Thus, the avoidance of the newspapers and the easy chair until after lunch would often prove a help to genuine work between nine and one. But whether morning, afternoon or evening, it still remains true that the very fact of the clergyman having the control of so much of his own time offers a real temptation to waste it, and thereby to do himself and his ministry great and lasting harm. From the earliest days of our ministry, and indeed, before we enter it, we shall do well to form the habit of regularity and method in the employment of our time, or else our freedom may prove a spiritual snare to us.

Another difficulty and temptation will be found in the multifariousness of ministerial duties. So many things will arise that seem to clamour to be done that a man may utilize all his time and find nothing at the end to show for his efforts. A man can easily be busy and yet not industrious. The minister must soon learn to says 'no' to requests for his services and to demands on his time. He will have to limit his work and determine to do only those things that are nearest to and most directly in line with his sphere. Our Churches to-day are suffering from over-organization, and if they would do less they would accomplish more, less of the indirect and more of the direct, less of the secular and more of the spiritual. There is no problem to-day more pressing on the ministry than the best disposal of our time in order to accomplish the greatest possible work of the right kind, that which will be spiritually productive.

II. *Spiritual Service.*

The ministry is primarily and fundamentally spiritual. The clergyman is to conduct a Divine Service, to administer the Holy Communion, to read the Scriptures in Church, to instruct the youth in the faith, to baptize, and to preach. His paramount duties are therefore spiritual, and this element must ever predominate. The salvation of the sinner and the edification of the believer must always be in view. First things should be put first, and since this is so, no pressure of modern life ought to crowd out these primary spiritual realities for which the clergyman is ordained. The ministry of the New

Testament is a spiritual ministry, and nothing must ever be allowed to set this aside.

## III.   *Social Service.*

It is not to be supposed that what has been said about spiritual work excludes the true idea of social service. On the contrary, the spiritual may, and must, be expressed in the social. Christianity appeals to the whole man, and from the very first the care of the poor, the sick, and the aged has been part of Christian work. In the Incarnation the human body has been raised to its proper position and we are now enabled to understand what it means to 'glorify God in our body' (1 Cor. 6: 20). And yet even this work is not merely social, but in strict subordination to the spiritual. Whatever social efforts are attached to a Church must be the outcome of the spiritual efforts.

## IV.   *Satisfying Service.*

1.   The Ministry will be a *glad* service. This is a simple but searching test of the quality of our ministry. Are we enjoying it? Are we glad in it? We may be tired *in* it, but we ought not to be tired *of* it. There is no service on earth in which there is so much deep gladness.

2.   The ministry will be a *willing* service. Not forced labour, but spontaneous service out of a ready mind and willing heart. The moment the foot begins to drag and the service becomes a burden, it is a call to inquire as to our spiritual, or our mental, or, most likely of all, our bodily health.

3.   And the ministry will be a *trustful* service. Herein lies the supreme secret; 'Not by might, nor by power, but by My Spirit, saith the Lord of Hosts.' And hence, too is the fearless response; I can do all things through Christ which strengtheneth me.' In the face of all the problems, the demands, the temptations, the disappointments, the weariness, the failures, the word rings out beyond all question, 'My grace is sufficient for thee.' And the heart responds as it rests on the Word of our Heavenly Father; 'With God all things are possible.' 'All things are possible to him that believeth.'

## SECTION 4. THE PERSONAL LIFE

After the official duties comes the consideration of personal life. Character is the true source of service, and duties can only be efficiently performed by one whose life is true. 'They made me the keeper of the vineyards; but mine own vineyard have I not kept.'

### I. *The Call.*

The call of the ministry is to holy living and example.

1. *Personal life.* On the publication of a volume of sermons, someone said to the writer, "They will stir people strongly." "No," said he, "written sermons seldom do. It is the man behind the sermon that stirs." This is the case in every department of ministerial life and activity. It is "the man behind" that tells. What, then, is the life of the true minister of Christ?

(*a*) It should be marked by Sincerity. In everything said and done he should be straight and true. In the matter and manner of his sermons, in the substance and form of his teaching, in the conduct and guidance of parochial affairs, his life should be consistent. Not ability, but reality is what people earnestly desire and rightly demand.

(*b*) It should be marked by Seriousness. As we have seen, one of the key words of the Pastoral Epistles is "grave" (σεμνός), and it is the more striking in that it is pressed upon young men. But can we expect gravity from young men? Yes, if we remember that gravity is not gloom, and that brightness is not lightness. The minister is rightly expected to take a serious view of life and not to allow himself to degenerate into·a reputation for lightness, still less for flippancy.

2. *Home life.* A bachelor minister has a special opportunity for making or marring his reputation. In his use of time, in the books he reads, he can do much to glorify God and recommend his Master's service. It is a true test of a man to find out how he lives in the privacy of his home. These questions may seem small in themselves, but "straws show which way the wind blows,"

When the minister is married and a family is growing up around him, the call to be a wholesome example is ever more pressing. People will become aware whether the children are well disciplined, whether the minister's wife is concerned for the welfare of the congregation, and above all, whether the man who preaches such eloquent sermons is able to "show piety at home." It is one of the saddest and most deplorable things when a clergyman's house gets a reputation for the very opposite of these things. It is all the more terrible when the clergyman happens to preach the highest spiritual doctrine and yet fails in his own living. Who can wonder if spiritual religion is repellent in that parish by reason of the unwholesome example of its minister. His teaching will fall on deaf ears. And this is no fancy picture. Men soon take the measure of their clergy. Truth will out, and the average judgment of a congregation respecting the clergyman can usually be trusted with unerring certainty. A layman once judged a clergyman by a single test only; whether he would be the sort of man to send for when one is on a deathbed. A very fair, a very true, and a very searching test. 'Wholesome examples of the flock of Christ.' This, and this above all, is the secret of ministerial blessing and power over men. There is a way to Hell, says Bunyan, even from the gate of Heaven. 'He that endureth to the end, the same shall be saved.' 'Hold fast that which thou hast, that no man take thy crown.'

## II. *The Standard.*

We must live our life in constant view of Holy Scripture. The Word of God is to be the 'discerner,' the 'critic,' the criterion of our inner life (Heb. 4: 12). We must submit ourselves to it as to a search-light, as to a probing instrument, as to a plumbline. If our life does not ring true to Scripture it means that there is a flaw in the metal. No lower test will suffice. Our own view may easily be partial. 'I know nothing against myself, yet am I not hereby justified.' And the view of others will not always and necessarily be correct and complete. 'In Thy light shall we see light,' and it may be said without hesitation and without qualification that the man who allows himself to be tested and searched and guided day by day by the unerring Word of God will never backslide in any degree whatever.  On the other hand, if our lives are not lived ever in the light of Holy Scripture, 'according to the doctrine of Christ,' and in face of the mirror of truth (Jas. 1: 23-25), it is impossible to say how far a man may not go from the path of rectitude and holiness.

III.   *The Secret.*

But this reference to Holy Scripture inevitably suggests something more.

Scripture finds its fullest power over the life only when we are in fellowship with Christ.  The Persian parable tells of the clay being asked how it was that it was the possessor of such fragrance, and replying, 'I have been living near a rose.'  Henry Drummond tells of a young girl of exquisite beauty of character, and when after her death they opened a locket, expecting to find the portrait of some loved one, they saw nothing but the words, 'Whom having not seen, ye love.'  This was the secret of her loveliness of spirit.  It is there and thus that we shall assimilate such a spirit that we shall never fail to be 'wholesome examples of the flock of Christ.'

This fellowship comes in a simple way, by the twofold method of prayer and meditation.  In prayer we speak to God; in the Bible God speaks to us.  And prayer is the response of the soul to the Bible as the Word of God.  Private prayer, regular private prayer, definite regular private prayer, is the one prime secret of holy living.  There is a profound truth in these words:

'If you go into a minister's study and find that there is a bare place on the carpet in front of his chair, get him to pray for you; but if you find the bare place in front of his looking-glass you pray for him.'

The story is familiar, but well worth recalling, of Dean Hook of Chichester, that when a workman was going up a ladder early one morning at the Deanery, he saw through the window the Dean even then in his study and at prayer, and this made a deep and lasting impression on the man.  Be it ours to 'pray, always pray,' and then will assuredly come holiness of heart, acuteness of mind, insight of soul, resoluteness of will, and winsomeness of life.

## SECTION 5.   CONTROVERSY

### I.   *The Necessity for Controversy.*

We are not to seek it, and yet it will often be found to be a duty.  We shall doubtless shrink from it as trying to the flesh, and yet we must not be afraid of it.  St. Paul doubtless felt it to be one of the most testing times of his life to stand up against St. Peter at Antioch, and yet he did it.  But we have to take care that we are not mere controversialists, for this type of man is one of the most unlovely, unspiritual, and objectionable of beings.  We must not wage war for the love of it, but if we find it necessary to wage it, we must do so in love.

### II.   *The Aspects of Controversy.*

Erroneous and strange doctrines are of several sorts, and we must be ready to meet them all to the best of our ability.

1.   One controversy will be on the Deity of Christ. Whether we have to deal with Unitarianism or Scepticism, the Godhead of our Blessed Lord and His Virgin Birth will call for a defence and an advocacy which cannot be other than controversial.  And in this endeavour we are fighting for the very existence of our Christianity.

2.   The Atonement of Christ will also be to the forefront. And this especially, because of the controversies about Sin. Sin and Redemption go together, and a denial of one will often mean a denial of the other.  The facts of Sin and Atonement will need emphasis, and the views of modern thinkers will have to be faced, and since Christianity is pre-eminently the religion of Redemption, it will not be long before we are engaged on these vital and fundamental questions of our faith.

3.   The Divine Authority of Scripture will inevitably occupy our attention.   Rationalism of various kinds makes this
the center of attack, and we shall be compelled to take up an
attitude against the foe of truth.   Since we believe (on any
theory) in a unique element in Scripture which gives it its
authority, we must of necessity be prepared for warfare
against those who, if allowed freedom to spread their views
unchecked, would certainly injure the faith and life of unin-
structed believers.

4.   The Supreme Authority of Scripture will also engage
our efforts.   Roman Catholicism meets us here.   Indeed, it
may be truly said that practically all differences are somehow
concerned with the position and character of Scripture. From
the days of Celsus downwards the strongest opposition has
been directed against Holy Scripture, as containing the substance of Christian belief, and whether we like it or not we
shall have to 'contend earnestly for the faith which was once
delivered unto the saints' (Jude 3).

5.   And we shall pretty certainly have to face the practical question of the soul's direct relation to God.   From two
quite different quarters this truth is being assailed.   Rome in-
terposes the priest and the Church, and says that it is through
the Church to Christ.   We, maintaining the same position as
our Reformers, urge that it is through Christ to the Church,
and that no human intermediary can ever be allowed to come
between the direct approach of the spirit to God.   Justified by
faith the soul enters into the Holiest, abides there, rejoices in
the presence of God, and receives the grace of God for daily
living.

But in the present day a very serious attack is made on this
position by a form of intellectual scepticism which tells us
that knowledge of, and fellowship with Christ is impossible
because we know little or nothing of Him as an Historic
Figure.   And thus by destroying the supernatural element in
Christianity, by removing from us the unique Personality of
Christ, the souls of men are bereft of all that peace, and grace,
and love which Christian experience through the ages has
known and valued and spread.   Such a view robs the soul of
rest and hope, cutting at the very vitals of faith and godliness.

It is due, no doubt, to the overwhelming, and, it must be added, over-weening influence of critical studies which tend to dissolve everything that cannot be vindicated at the bar of reason and physical science. But there are deeper things in life than reason and science, and the heart will soon know its own bitterness if they take away the Lord.

III. *The Standard of Controversy.*

God's Word is our perfect and constant standard of truth. The Pastoral Epistles frequently remind us of teaching which is 'contrary to healthful doctrine.' Isaiah appeals to the law and to the testimony (8: 20). St. Paul speaks of doctrine which is 'according to godliness.' And the prophets were always asking, 'What saith the Lord?'

1. This means that the Scriptures must be known by us. Ignorance of Scripture will do more than anything else to play into the hands of opponents, and knowledge of Scripture will be our most powerful weapon against every form of error.

2. This means, too, that the Scriptures must be preached. Teaching and preaching the truth of Holy Scripture is our paramount duty. Like Philip with the Eunuch, we should be ready to take up Scripture at any point and preach Jesus as the Saviour and Friend of man.

3. But most of all, this means that Scriptures must be lived. Our lives must 'express the Holy Gospel we profess.' The man who preaches by his life will perhaps do more in that way than in any other to safeguard his people against error. And our teaching and preaching must be positive as well as negative. As Spurgeon once said, laying down the straight stick of truth is the best way of showing the crookedness of error. No knowledge of Scripture can be too great, too minute, too thorough, for use in our necessary but difficult work of 'banishing and driving away all erroneous and strange doctrines.'

A thoughtful writer has called attention to the solemn fact that the people of God are being attacked along three lines: sceptical, heretical, and fanatical. The sceptic endeavours to make us disbelieve the Divine authority of the Bible, to question God's love, and even His very existence. Then comes the heretic with his new doctrines, apparently supported with scattered passages from the Bible. He will tell us how we have been mistaken, and how God is revealing Himself to progressive minds in other ways. Last of all comes the fanatic, who does not doubt God's Word as the sceptic does, or attempt to elicit from it any new Gospel as the heretic does, but who pushes everything beyond the bounds of Scriptural authority and the limits of sober reason. Many good people are thus on the verge of a dangerous fanaticism, who are not in any way tempted to scepticism and heresy. How, then, are God's people to meet these errors? Against the sceptic, we ministers must teach them to hold fast to the absolute authority and Divine inspiration of Scripture. Against the heretic, we must insist upon the whole of Scripture in its various parts and progressive teaching. And against the fanatic, we must walk with God in the Spirit, and thus be able to discern between the true and the false. The closer we keep to the Word of God in spiritual study and practical, earnest meditation, the more thoroughly we shall be kept alive to these various errors, and have the spiritual perception to detect them, and the spiritual power to defeat them. Every error comes in some way or other from a neglect of God's Word, and every safeguard against error comes from the closest adherence thereto.

IV.  *The Spirit of Controversy.*

It is a necessary work, a hard work, and therefore one that requires the best of our powers. Such work is not to be done without very definite and sustained effort.

Pastoral anxiety for the well-being of the sheep must be the motive for the participation in controversy. This is the paramount consideration and must ever be the object of the shepherd. He does not wish to win any mere gladiatorial victory, but he desires so to fight and strive that his sheep may be protected and guarded. Or to change the figure, he must be careful that his flock enter no poisonous pastures, and to do this he must lead them in green pastures of Divine truth. If this positive spiritual view and purpose of controversy is ever kept in mind, the work of the shepherd will go forward with ever-increasing blessing.

And this will mean 'speaking (or living) the truth in love' (Eph. 4: 15). We shall endeavour to see the truth for which our opponents think they are contending, and we shall conduct our controversies in faith and love. Not victory, but edification will be our aim, and in meekness we shall endeavour to instruct those who 'oppose themselves; if God peradventure will give them repentance to the acknowledging of the truth; and that they may recover themselves out of the snare of the devil, who are taken captive by him at his will' (2 Tim. 2: 25, 26).

And so we shall ever keep in mind the great truth of 'Principles, not Party.' Whatever be our party we must never be partizan. No man worthy of the name of man can ever submit himself wholly to his party, however much he may be in general sympathy with its principles. 'My party right or wrong' is as vicious in religion as it is in politics. We must carefully distinguish between a partizan, an advocate, and a judge.

And it follows that in our work we shall emphasize principles and not attack men. Our opponents may be charming and our own side may repel, but in either case, in both cases, we are concerned for truth, and truth at all costs, under all circumstances.

And so the supreme need is for Consecrated Controversy. The one great object is to know the truth, and to get it known, loved, and lived. And if our lift is lived in the atmosphere and under the control of the Spirit of Christ we shall be at once fearless, loving, and righteous in our necessary warfare for Christ, His cause, and His Church. And then, neither we nor our people will be carried away by error, but rather established and settled in the truths of the Gospel.

## Section 6.  Maintaining Peace

The minister is to be ready to wage war, and yet to maintain peace. It is something like the twofold statement of the

Gospel concerning our Lord's mission: 'Peace on earth'; 'Not peace but a sword.'

Quietness, peace and love are the ideals to be maintained among all Christian people, and especially among the minister's own flock. The value of these things lies in their being an illustration of Christ-likeness. Their glory consists in their being an exemplifcation of the 'new' commandment of our Lord, and the 'brotherlove' of the Epistles. The 'newness' quite evidently lay in the new objects of affection consequent on the new relationship to 'one another' in Christ (John 13: 34, 35). And the prominence given in the New Testament to brotherlove, not brotherly love (love *because*, not *as* brethren), is another proof of the new Christian grace. 'See how these Christians love one another!' And the power of these things is seen in the blessing that inevitably attends Christian unity, wherever it is realized and manifested. 'Behold how good and how pleasant it is for brethren to dwell together in unity!' 'For there the Lord commanded the blessing' (Psa. 133: 1, 3). The opposite is always fatal to Christian life and work. There is scarcely any part of a clergyman's work which is so fruitful in spiritual results as this endeavour.

The clergyman's first work will be among his own people, and he will do his utmost to prevent or remove friction, jealousy, and misunderstandings in the Church of which he is the minister. If any 'root of bitterness' should spring up between members of a congregation, and especially between Communicants, the results may easily prove heart-breaking to the minister. It is no wonder that St. Paul urges Christians to show zeal in keeping the 'unity of the Spirit in the bond of peace' (Eph. 4: 3). If Satan can but drive in a wedge of discord between two members or two sections of a congregation, his work there can be left to produce its own dire results of spiritual barrenness.

In politics it is for the minister to proclaim principles and not the applications which those principles involve. Social feeling also tends to become acute as between rich and poor, a tendency that has become accentuated by that unfortunate phrase, 'the classes and the masses.' To the clergyman these distinctions will have to be faced with the greatest possible care: that the rich have duties as well as privileges, and that the poor have their responsibilities as well as their disadvantages.

The relations of denominations will provide yet another opportunity for fulfilling this Divine requirement. The minister should make friends as far as possible with believers of all denominations. It is one of the finest features of College life that men of different and differing views and Churches should meet and live together, and there is no reason why parochial life should be inferior in this respect to the College. The minister has a unique opportunity of doing the work of a peacemaker, and he will lose much if he fails to respond to it. The secret of maintaining and setting forward peace among Christians is the careful and constant distinction between principles and sympathies. Let the principles be firmly fixed on the unmistakable rock of Divine truth, but let the sympathies go out as widely as possible to all who are endeavouring to live and labour for Christ. Never shall I forget the words of the saintly and noble Bishop Whipple of Minnesota, the Apostle of the Indians, as I heard them in London on a memorable occasion: 'For thirty years I have tried to see the face of Christ in those who have differed from me.'

What sort of man must he be who is to maintain peace and love?

1. He must be filled with the Spirit of *Truth*. Unity must be based on Truth. Anything else will prove disastrous. First righteousness, then peace (Isa. 9: 7); first pure, then peaceable (Jas. 3: 17). As it has been well put, we must not work for compromise at the expense of truth, but for comprehension within the truth. 'In things essential unity, in things doubtful liberty, in all things charity.' Yes, but beneath all things fidelity.

2. He must be filled with the Spirit of *Love*. Love to Christ elicits and compels love to man. 'He who loveth God must love his brother also' (1 John 4: 21). Love will express itself in sympathy, for we shall be keen-sighted enough to see things from his standpoint. And Love will show itself in tenderness. Nor will true Love ever mean weakness, for

the stronger the convictions the greater the love. It is just because we are so convinced of our own position that we can
love others with a pure heart fervently.

3. And he must be filled with the Spirit of *Wisdom.*
Truth united with Love will lead to the threefold qualifications of Wisdom, Perception, and Tact. Love is not blind,
but keen and far-sighted, and when love is guided by truth,
and truth is inspired by love, the result is a spiritual wisdom
which is from above, and will do God's work in God's way.

But we must go still deeper.

How can this threefold spirit become ours? It can only
come from a deep, true, full, spiritual life. There must be
a rich experience of Christ and a real fellowship with Him.
It is only as the soul draws 'nearer still and nearer' to Him
Who is 'the Lord of Peace' that the work of ingeminating
peace can be done. It is only as 'the Spirit of Jesus' possesses
us that we bring forth fruit, the fruit which is 'love, joy, and
peace,' and produce 'the peaceable fruits of righteousness.'
And in the same way it will only be by a similar work of
grace in the hearts of others that they will be drawn nearer
together and help to bring that day in when the reign of everlasting peace will commence. It has often been pointed out
that when the tide is out there are little pools of water here
and there on the shore, separated from each other by vast
stretches of sand, and it is only when the great tide rolls in
and submerges them all in its vast embrace that they become
one and are united. So must it be, so will it be with our
severances of heart, 'our unhappy divisions,' the great tide
of God's love will flow deeper and fuller into each and all
of our lives, and in the ocean of that love we realize the
Divine ideal of love, joy, peace for evermore.

## Chapter VI

# SOME ASPECTS OF THE MINISTRY

THE essential idea of the ministry is not that of a paid official or administrator, or even only of a trained teacher or expert. The minister is first and foremost, and all the time, a man of God, a servant of God to His people.

## SECTION 1. THE GREATNESS OF THE MINISTRY.

### I. *The High Dignity.*

Ministers are Messengers, Watchmen, and Stewards.

1. In relation to God they are Messengers. This means that they are *sent* by Him and *taught* by Him. They are men with a message and men that possess both *authority* and *ability*. This is equivalent to the idea of Apostleship. 'Even so send I you.' There is the authority. And when He had said this He breathed on them and saith, 'Receive ye the Holy Ghost.' There is the ability.

2. In relation to the Word they are Watchmen. This is equivalent to the New Testament idea of an Evangelist. 'They that watch for your souls' (Heb. 13: 17). The Old Testament prophet was also a watchman (Isa. 52: 8; 56: 10), and the work includes watching against evil and for good; sleepless vigilance on behalf of the souls for whom Christ died is the essential work of a Watchman.

3. In relation to the Church they are Stewards. This may almost be said to be equivalent to the work of the Pastor. A steward is a trusted servant. He has to give food to the household. And similarly, the Christian minister as a steward is specially concerned with the household of faith.

## II.  *The Weighty Office.*

1.   As Stewards, Ministers have to teach, and to admonish, and to feed and provide for the Lord's family. To teach, he must know how. There is a vast difference between teaching and talking, between teaching and preaching. Many can preach or talk, while few can teach. And yet for Christian people teaching is absolutely essential and exceedingly important. To admonish he must be faithful. No one can admonish without incurring the possibility of hostility, or at any rate of some opposition and difficulty. And yet warning is as much a part of his work as teaching (Col. 1: 28). To feed and provide he must know where and how to obtain food for his flock. It is only too often true that 'the hungry sheep look up and are not fed' because the minister has not fed himself. Many are the complaints from time to time that the clergyman does not break the bread of life to his people. 'He does not feed me or my children,' said one earnest man, 'What am I to do?' Pastoral work is an absolute necessity and should be a prominent feature of ministerial service. If a man says he has not time for it, then it must be said with all love and faithfulness that he must *make* time for it. Fewer meetings of a secular, recreative, or entertaining class, and more teaching and visiting work. Less effort expended (often fruitlessly) in providing an institutional Church, and more endeavor to feed the flock of God in Church, class, and home. The New Testament has three epithets to describe the Steward. He is wise (Luke 12: 42); faithful (1 Cor. 4: 2); good (beautiful) (1 Pet. 4: 10). He will be 'wise' in his efforts to instruct and feed. He will be 'faithful' in the discharge of duties. And he will be 'good' both inwardly and outwardly (καλός) in that attractiveness which ministers and wins for Christ.

2.   As Watchmen, Ministers have to seek for Christ's sheep. This means evangelistic work, the work of 'catching men alive.' The work of a Watchman will therefore be intensely real and definitely personal. Individual work was a prominent feature of Christ's ministry, and it should be of ours also. The solemn responsibility is made very clear in

Scripture. 'But if the watchman sees the sword come, and blow not the trumpet, and the people be not warned; if the sword come, and take any person from among them, he is taken away in his iniquity; but his blood will I require at the watchman's hand (Ezek. 33: 6). 'Obey them that have the rule over you, and submit yourselves: for they watch for your souls, as they that must give account, that they may do it with joy, and not with grief: for that is unprofitable for you' (Heb. 13: 17).

3. As Messengers, Ministers have to receive and deliver their Master's message. This means that we have a message to deliver and that we mean to pass it on without addition or subtraction. 'How canst thou run, seeing thou hast no tidings ready?' And this in turn involves spiritual fellowship with God. The Holy Spirit is ever desirous of making disclosures to the soul. 'What I tell you in darkness, that speak ye in light.' Dr. R. W. Dale well said to students for the ministry:—

'Your generous impulses, your strenuous and exhausting labours, your eagerness to bless men, your natural powers, your learning, will achieve nothing in those higher regions of human life, in which alone the enduring results of our work are to be found, unless you have received the gift of the Holy Spirit.'

Herein lies the supreme secret of Christian ministry: a man who knows God, who knows God's truth, who knows by experience what Christianity is, and who intends at all costs to tell what he knows and give what he has received. The man who is in doubt can never be a messenger of the Lord of Hosts.

SECTION 2.   THE RESPONSIBILITY OF THE MINISTRY

After the consideration of the Dignity, it is natural to consider the Responsibility of the Ministry.

1. *The Greatness of the Treasure.*

Our people are described in a threefold way; as the Sheep, the Bride, and the Body. As Sheep, they are Christ's blood-bought possession (Acts 20: 28). As the Bride they are loved by Him Who 'gave Himself for' them. (Eph. 5: 25). As the Body of Christ they are one with Him in life and grace (Eph. 1: 19, 20). Nothing could well be more searching and solemn than this thought of the value of the people among whom we labour.

## II.  *The Possibility of Danger.*

Two dangers may be mentioned here: hurting and hindering. One refers to the wounding of conscience, the other to the prevention of spiritual progress. It will be admitted by all who have had experience of the ministry that the flock are in danger from the negligence of the shepherd.

Young beginners in the ministry are apt to take pleasure in 'shocking' older Christians. They think the old views are narrow and impossible, and they wish to let these Christians know how far advanced the younger generation is. But if this is done, as it is often, with a disregard to old-fashioned consciences, it will serve the very opposite of its purpose. It will not do the older people any good, and it will often do the younger man harm. When next he goes to God in prayer he will see for himself what he has done. The fact is that no air of superiority and certainly no ridicule has a place in Christian ministry. Ridicule is only another word for sneer, and some one has said that a 'sneer is an apology for an argument made by a man who does not understand.' Jesus Christ, though angry, never ridiculed the views and life of those who were opposed to Him.

Sometimes, too, the minister is tempted to introduce elements into his teaching which, if they do not 'hurt,' at least 'hinder' the spiritual life of his people. There is profound force in Dr. Torrey's testimony on this point. I make no apology for quoting it in full:—

'It is a great temptation to a minister of the Gospel who thinks or reads some view of things that strikes him as new and original and likely to prove interesting. He thinks it is true, but he did not think it through, and he gave out that view of things he supposed true, but which he has not thought through, and he awakens some day to the awful fact that he has been preaching error instead of truth and poisoning the flock of God. I ought to confess right here that I have had that bitter experience myself. In my earlier ministry I had certain views of things, I thought they were original. They were not, others had held them, though I did not know it at the time. I thought them fresh, and new, and original, and I was sure they were striking, and I was certain they would prove interesting. I knew they were not generally held in the Church in which I was an ordained minister, but I honestly told the people what I thought. Brethren, it is good to be honest, but it is safe to be sure, and I beseech you, out of a bitter experience, do not for honesty's sake preach anything until you have thought it through and way through upon your knees before God. Do not for honesty's sake preach anything in this position of responsibility until you have thought it way through in the white light of God's own presence. If somebody had said this to me when I began my ministry, and I had had sense enough to pay attention to it, it would have saved me one of the bitterest experiences of my life. I found out my error and renounced it, but that was not the bitterest part. The bitterest part was that I had led men and women into error, and I could not lead them back again to the truth when I had discovered my error. It is a great deal easier to lead people into error than to lead them back again, for the human heart loves error. I think to-day of a young man in my Theological Seminary who was in the class below me—the most brilliant man there, the man of greatest promise beyond question— but not a very clear thinker. He depended upon me, and what I thought he adopted rather than take the trouble of thinking it through for himself. And the result? I came back, but I have not been able to lead him back. And to-day that man, after a brief and brilliant ministry, from the human standpoint, is out of the ministry altogether. And the last conversation I had with him he said to me, "If I were to define my position to-day, I think the most correct definition I could give would be—I am a Christian Agnostic." And that magnificent man is lost to the Church, and lost to the ministry, I think largely through my influence. I have had the joy of leading many others into the truth, but I have never been able to lead that man back. So, brethren, I beseech you, out of an aching heart, don't, don't, don't, declare anything from your position of responsibility, opportunity, and influence in which God has put you, until you are absolutely sure it is true, before you have thought it through in the white light of God's presence.'

III.   *The Demands on the Ministry.*

The minister must never cease his labor, his care or diligence. He will therefore need:

1.   Constant thought.  He must consider the aim of his ministry.  With this in mind he cannot be negligent.

2.   Unceasing diligence.  The spiritual work of the ministry means work, unsparing work, unceasing work on behalf of the people.

3.   Whole-hearted effort.  This will mean effort that costs, for it must be according to all the power that lieth in the minister—nothing left undone, nothing disregarded, but everything used in furtherance of the one object.

IV.   *The Goal of the Ministry.*

The purpose of the ministry is to bring the flock of God into an agreement of faith and knowledge and to a ripeness and maturity in Christ, so that there will be no place for error or wrong views of life.

1.   Agreement in faith and knowledge.  This is further amplified in Ephesians 4: 13 and shows what the ministry is intended to do.

2.   Maturity of experience.  Faith and knowledge will result in ripeness of understanding.  Christian experience is one of the essential features of ministerial effort.  'Unto the perfecting of the saints for the work of ministering.'

3.   Reality of life.  Truth and life are to be the ultimate goal—character and conduct, holiness of heart and life.

As we look at this view of the ministry, do we not obtain the proper perspective by which to gauge the various elements that go to make up the ministerial life to-day?   In the light of these profound spiritual realities where can amusements come in?   In the face of the experiences of heart and life what need can be found for the technicalities of criticism?  And in view of these fundamental requirements of spiritual life and progress how subsidiary do our denominational differences become?   The more thoroughly a man will ponder these thoughts the more clearly will he come to know the paramount idea and meaning of the ministry, and in so doing he will realize the Apostolic call to 'take heed.'   (1) He is to take heed to 'himself' and his 'flock' (Acts 20: 28).  To himself on account of his flock; to his flock by care of himself.  No man set over such a charge can possibly be indifferent to the greatness and solemnity of the position. (2) And for this he will take heed to 'himself' and his 'doctrine' (1 Tim. 4. 16). Himself first, his doctrine next, his flock next. If he is right with God, and his doctrine true to God's Word, his flock will assuredly be right, and his ministry will be an increasing blessing to his people, an increasing joy to himself, and an increasing glory to God.

### Section 3. the guarantees of the ministry.

With the Dignity and Responsibility of the Ministry clearly and constantly in view, the natural and inevitable inquiry comes, 'Who is sufficient for these things?' Whence comes the ability?

### I. *The Source of Power.*

From God alone comes the power of true ministry. 'Our sufficiency is of God, Who also hath made us able ministers.'

And it was always through the Holy Spirit. As we study the New Testament we see on almost every page the prominence given to the Holy Spirit in relation to life and work for God.

### II. *The Conditions of Power.*

1. Prayer.

Our prayer must be individual and intercessory. We must pray for ourselves and for others, and this, regularly, intellectually, and faithfully.

We are in danger of being too much with men and too little with God. While we must not be ascetic we certainly must not be too social. Forbes Robinson used to say that he could do more for a man by praying for him than by talking to him. It is a searching question, how much time we spend a day in private prayer.

'Someone has asserted—I do not believe it is true—that an average Christian does not spend more than three minutes a day in secret prayer, and the average minister not more than five minutes. I do not believe it is true, but it is a good deal nearer the truth than it ought to be. A friend quoted that statement, and an older minister came and said, "You should not have done it." He said, "Try it on your-self, and come back and report." He said, "I will." But he forgot to come back, so my friend went to him and asked, "Did you try that?" He said, "I did." "What was the result?" "I thought my watch had stopped." '

Dr. S. Tyng, one of the finest clergymen in the American Episcopal Church, said:—

'I do not wish I had preached more, or visited more, but prayed.'

And as Leighton said:—

'Let prayer be not only the key that opens the day, and the lock that secures us at night, but let it be also our staff and stay through-out the whole of our daily journey, and enable us to ascend into the hill of our Lord with cheerful alacrity.'

2.   Bible Study.

This reading and study of the Bible must be at once in-tellectual and spiritual, an endeavour to get first at the mean-ing and then at the message.   It can be said without hesita-tion or fear of contradiction that ministerial weakness and, still more, ministerial unfaithfulness spring from neglect of the Bible and prayer.

There are from time to time awful tragedies in the min-istry; the complete breakdown of character which often in-volves others in ruin.   It will be found that these moral ship-wrecks have been preceded by slow decay of spiritual life. The fall of large trees in the Broad Walk, Oxford, pro-claimed rottenness long going on within, and I believe that moral spiritual decay is also traceable to neglect of private meditation of Scripture and prayer.

3.   Holy Living.

The minister's life should be consistent with his teaching. In the New Testament we have a reminder of the distinc-tion between sins and weights; things wrong and things doubtful; things essential and things unessential for life.

4.   Concentration of purpose.

The need of this is seen in the fact that no position exists which has more opportunities for laziness, or more oppor-

tunities for intellectual and social dissipation. And a man
who has been known as a 'slacker' in the College or Seminary
is more than likely to be a 'slacker' in the ministry. 'This
one thing I do' should be writ large over our study desk and
imprinted deeply on our conscience.

## III.   *The Outflow of Power.*

1.   Growth in ministerial experience.   Growth is the
great law of ministry.

'In America they have what is called the "dead line"—fifty years
of age. It is held that a minister need not look to be invited to a
new sphere if he is above fifty years of age. Mr. Moody once said
to Dr. Torrey, "Torrey, this dead line is all nonsense. The reason
they cross the dead line at fifty is because they do not study, and
keep on preaching old sermons." He said, "Torrey, if a man will keep
studying he will be better at fifty than he was at forty, and he will be
better at sixty than he was at fifty." '

2.   Progress in personal holiness.   There is constant danger of professionalism.   Our dress, gait, manner, reading,
tone, may lead to unreality and professionalism.   The minister must ever be a man if he is to be a true minister.

3.   Reality of spiritual influence.

Dr. G. S. Barrett tells us that:—

'One day, now many years ago, a friend of mine, a man of letters,
of some distinction in his day, told me that he had just been to call
on the late Samuel Martin, himself one of the saintliest ministers,
and I have never forgotten what my friend added to his announcement, "Do you know, I never leave that man's presence without feeling I could never sin again." '

Then, as Dr. Barrett asks:—

'Do we leave behind us wherever we go that aroma of saintliness which they who breathe find goodness sweeter and easier than
before? There was a tradition in the early Church that wherever
the foot of Jesus trod sweet flowers sprang up as He passed by. Are
our footsteps marked by any such fair flowers of goodness, blooming
because we have passed that way?'

In reviewing these aspects of ministry, we see as never before that the ministry of the Church is first of all, and always, one of personal power. 'Thou must thyself be true.' Lord Leighton was once addressing a company of artists at the Royal Academy. He said, 'Gentlemen, you can only put into a picture what is in yourself.' And for this there is only one way; we must live with God.

# THE WORK

*THIS section endeavours to discuss some of the most important parts of the clergyman's work. It does not pretend to be exhaustive, but only aims at dealing with the more usual aspects of ministerial service.*

## CHAPTER I

## THE PUBLIC WORSHIP OF ALMIGHTY GOD

WHILE it is impossible to touch upon every point of importance found in the course of Church services, the more outstanding features of Praise, Prayer, and Reading of the Word, together with the ordinances of Holy Communion and Baptism, may be considered as being common to all churches of every denomination.

I. *Praise.* 'O come, let us sing unto the Lord' (Psa. 95: 1) should be the first and finest attitude of praise. If the singing is 'unto the Lord,' it must not be a task left for the choir alone in the hymns and chants, but a joy to be shared by the whole congregation. 'Singing and making melody in your hearts to the Lord' may well spring forth to the lips in public worship, and from time to time the minister may point out the importance of congregational singing, invariably setting an example by joining in heartily himself.

II. *Prayer.* In liturgical services there is a danger in not '*praying*' the prayers. Familiarity inevitably tends to carelessness. Too often the prayers are *said* or *read* only, and are thus mechanical in expression. Rapidity and absence of proper emphasis can spoil the most incomparable of liturgies. So, too, in non-liturgical services, prayer is apt to become stereotyped, lacking in spontaneity and carrying a monotony of expression week after week, so that members of a church can even sometimes anticipate some of the very phrases that the pastor will use.

In the desire to make the petitions intelligible to the congregation, there is danger lest the minister shall, as someone has said, give information to the Almighty. Perhaps the most satisfactory prayers are those of the minister who shows in his praying that he has the habit of prayer in his daily life, that he is conscious of the presence of God and that he knows what communion with God means. His prayer leaves the

129

impression of an approach to God through the Holy Spirit in which the minister is as little conscious of his people's presence as is compatible with the voicing of their needs as well as supplication for the world at large.

III.  *The Scripture Reading.*  The importance of this part of the Service cannot be exaggerated, for it is a solemn responsibility to read God's own Word to the people, and it may easily be made a powerful influence for spiritual blessing. 'Faith cometh by hearing,' and if only the Scripture is read as it should be read, there is no reason why the hearing of the Word of God should not produce faith, and thereby bestow blessing.

There are three requisites for good reading, and these concern the physical, mental, and emotional aspects of our nature. The first is Distinctness, the second Intelligence, and the third Impressiveness.  All are necessary and not one can be omitted in any truly acceptable reading of the Word.  'You read as if you had no God in you,' said a French teacher of elocution to a young preacher, and the laity often have to complain bitterly of the way in which the Scriptures are read. Nothing suggests that they have been studied beforehand, while the inaccurate emphasis, wrong pronunciation, and frequent haste, tend to make God's Word either inaudible, or even worse. We must take care in our reading to be natural and free from artificialities, and yet reading is an acquired art.  'All art is nature better understood.'  Not the least element of importance in reading Scripture is the thought that even though people do not understand or appreciate our sermons, they will have had the Word of God, if we have read it as God's Word should be delivered to the people.  Many years ago an undergraduate sauntered into an Oxford Church, of which afterwards he was quite unable to remember the name.  At that time he was nearing his final examination and was feeling somewhat depressed.  As he entered the Church the second lesson was being read (Ephesians 2:), and the reader made somewhat unusual pauses as he read verse 8 thus: 'By grace ——are ye saved——through faith——and that, not of yourselves——it is the gift of God.'  The Divine Word went home to the undergraduate's heart, and led to his conversion. His name was John Charles Ryle, and in later life he became Bishop of Liverpool.

The following suggestions are offered in the hope that they may be of service towards the better rendering of this supremely important part of our time of public worship.

1. The Scripture chosen should be read thoughtfully beforehand; the New Testament Lessons in the Greek text and with a comparison of the Revised Version. No clergyman ought to assume that the passages are known because they are thought to be familiar.

2. The reading should not be too fast, and pauses should be made for the purpose of breathing. Ordinary punctuation is not as a rule sufficient for public reading; there should be what are called oratorical pauses as well. A very brief pause between the nominative and the verb enables the congregation in large Churches to grasp the subject before the verb is heard; and a slight emphasis on the verbs as the important words is also valuable.

3. All staccato reading should be carefully avoided. The verse division of the A.V. is responsible for some part of this danger.

4. Let every part be enunciated well, remembering the valuable rule for speaking and reading: 'Use your lips and spare your throat.' The voice should be maintained to the very end of the sentence and not dropped towards the close.

5. Both extremes of monotonous and dramatic reading should be avoided.

6. The five characteristics of good reading are: (*a*) Accuracy; (*b*) Distinctness; (*c*) Intelligence; (*d*) Sympathy; (*e*) Reverence.

7. The faults to be avoided are: (*a*) Indistinctness; (*b*) Rapidity; (*c*) Absence of Emphasis; (*d*) False Emphasis; (*e*) Absence of care as to pronunciation.

8. All strict pedantry with proper names should be studiously disregarded and English current usage observed as closely as possible.

9. While every Scripture demands careful study from the reader, the following passages seem to call for special care. In Genesis 1: 3, the verb 'to be' should not be empha-

sized. 'And God said, Let there be light: and there was light.' To read 'and there *was* light' gives a wrong impression. Similarly with St. John 1: 1-3; if emphasis is placed on the words 'was' and 'with,' our hearers will fail to appreciate the profound truths taught by the Apostle. The emphatic words are 'Word,' 'God,' and 'made.' No one ever dreams of emphasizing 'was' in verse 4, or in verse 6, and it is only custom that leads to a persistence in the error now mentioned. In St. Luke 14: 18-20, the three excuses should be read in such a way as to suggest that they were made quite independently. To emphasize the pronoun in the second and third would give an entirely wrong idea. In contrast to this, St. Luke 16: 5-7 requires stress on the pronouns, because all the debtors were present at the same time and were asked in turn. In St. Luke 15: 32 we must again avoid emphasizing the verb 'was.' Attention must be given from time to time in reading the A.V. to the distinction between 'that' as a conjunction and 'that' when used as a relative pronoun. St. Luke 19: 22 is a case in point. In St. Luke 19: 24, which is the emphatic word; 'hath,' or 'ten'? The Greek will solve the problem for us. In reading Isaiah 9 it seems impossible to render verse 3 according to the A.V.; the negative must surely be omitted. St. Luke 24: 25 is a well-known difficulty, which will cause both error and irreverence if the comma should happen to be made after the word 'believe.' We must read right on from the comma after 'fools' to the end of the verse.

The names of Romans 16 demand careful attention, for they are often very seriously injured in reading. For the most part it will be found that the Greek and the English pronunciations agree. It would sound curious to hear Aristobulus emphasized on the third, instead of the fourth syllable; and in spite of ordinary Shaksperian usage, Andronicus should be emphasized on the third, not the second syllable. Some of the names in the A.V. will be made clearer and more intelligible if the R.V. is compared with it. One of the worst mistakes sometimes made in reading verse 9 in the A.V. is to make Urbane a word of three syllables.

In Ephesians 4: 9, no emphasis is to be placed on the first

syllable of the word 'ascended,' because the people are not supposed to know that there is about to be a contrast between 'ascended' and 'descended.' The emphasis will come on the first syllable of 'descended,' though of course in verse 10 the first syllable of both words will be properly emphasized. In Hebrews 4: 3, if the Scripture is read from the A.V., we are perfectly justified in rendering it, 'They shall not enter into My rest,' because the English version is senseless in its literal translation of the Greek form of the Hebrew idiom. So also in Hebrews 4: 8, 'Joshua' should be substituted for 'Jesus.' The names of the stones in Revelation 21 will also need attention.

It is recorded of the late Archbishop Temple that when he had the preliminary interview with candidates for Ordination he invariably required them to read aloud to him in his study, and he always chose one passage: 2 Kings 19: 20-34. With characteristic wisdom he thereby tested the man's powers of reading, and also at the same time his intelligence. There are few passages more difficult and require more care in the due change of voice and emphasis in order to give the prophet's thought its full expression. I have often heard it read incorrectly. Verses 23 and 24 are the boast of the King of Assyria, and should be read accordingly. Then should come a pause, and verses 25-28 read in a different tone as expressive of God's answer to the boastfulness of the King. It is between verses 24 and 25 that the real crux comes, and of course the 'I' in verse 25 should have special emphasis. Then verses 29-34 should be read in yet another tone of voice, as addressed by God to His people Israel. When these three differences are clearly made the chapter becomes luminous with suggestion.

These illustrations, which are just a few out of many that could be given, will show the imperative necessity of careful study before reading the Scriptures. The greatest possible care, feeling, and reverence should be given to our reading. If only we become convinced of the power of God's Word we shall regard it as a means of grace to give the Divine thought in the clearest and best possible way.

IV.  *The Communion Service.*  Familiarity with this beautiful and solemn Service must not blind us to the fact that it calls for constant and thorough attention if it is to be conducted as it ought to be.  Inasmuch as everything depends upon the spiritual and intellectual state of the clergyman who leads the Service, no thought or prayer can be too much to give to this work of helping the people to 'worship God in spirit and in truth.'

V.  *The Baptismal Service.*  To receive into the Church of Christ those who come for baptism (whether as infants or as adults), is one of the highest privileges of the Christian minister.  People are never told in Scripture to baptise themselves, but to allow themselves to be baptised, and when the minister performs the act of Baptism he does so as God's representative.  Thus Baptism is primarily God's act towards man, not man's act towards God.  It is therefore essential that the minister should approach this sacred duty fully conscious of the solemnity of the occasion and of his responsibility both to God and to the one who is acknowledging in baptism his relationship to Jesus Christ.

# Chapter II

# PREACHING

### Section 1. the importance of preaching.[1]

THERE is a decided tendency to-day to neglect preaching. The multiplicity of church organizations demands time, thought and strength. To organize clubs, guilds, entertainments, is easier than to study for sermons. The work of the Church has become extended and secularized, with the inevitable effect of weakness in the pulpit. Added to this, there is in some quarters the consciousness that great preaching is not necessary for leadership, and as a consequence, administration is regarded as the prime essential for the minister.

There are also tendencies at work which lead to the depreciation of preaching. Other channels of instruction are thought to be of greater importance, and the platform and the press are accordingly emphasized to such an extent that, in the mind of many, preaching is no longer regarded as essential. It must be confessed, too, that in certain Episcopal quarters Ritual and Sacraments have been over-emphasized to the disparagement of preaching. With the New Testament in our hands, it is perplexing to read that 'the altar is a more sacred place than the pulpit; the function of the priest is greater than that of the preacher.' Considering that the 'altar' finds no place in the New Testament, and the Holy Communion is only mentioned twice in all the Epistles, it is certainly difficult to account for the perspective suggested by the above remarks.

There are still other tendencies which are positively hostile to preaching. The critical spirit of to-day is largely impatient

---

[1] I thankfully acknowledge my indebtedness here and elsewhere to that most valuable book *The Work of the Preacher*, by A. S. Hoyt. (MacMillan & Co.).

of teaching, and considers that it knows sufficient of itself, and has powers of its own which are adequate to all needs. Social problems, too, lead men to denounce what they regard as 'mere talking,' while the growing materialism and wealth occupy the undue attention of many people.

And yet it is simple truth to say that there can be no strong ministry, and no effective Church to-day without preaching. The Census of Church Attendance, some years ago, showed with convincing proof that churches are well attended in proportion to the vigour of the preaching. People will forgive weakness anywhere in clerical life and organization sooner than in the pulpit. If preaching should ever be regarded as 'out of date' it is pretty certain that Christianity will soon be considered in the same light, for the preached Word and the living Christ have always been closely associated. We may go so far as to say that the spiritual prosperity of any Church is mainly determined by the preaching gift of its ministry, and we make bold to affirm our conviction that the spiritual condition of the Church to-day is largely related to the neglect of preaching. When we observe the lack of interest in Church attendance, and, still more, the absence of spiritual power in Church life, we do not think it is inaccurate to describe the situation as due to the neglected gift of preaching.

Preaching is always prominently set forth in Holy Scripture. The prophets of the Old Testament were great preachers. The ministry of our Lord was very largely one of preaching and teaching, and His earthly ministry closed by a fivefold emphasis on the great commission to His disciples to go into all the world. The Apostles were pre-eminently preachers, and the preaching of St. Paul in such passages as 1 Corinthians 1, clearly emphasizes the truth of his own contention, 'Woe is me, if I preach not the Gospel.'

Church History tells the same story. Is it not the case that for the first four centuries, when preaching and teaching were emphasized, the Church was kept largely pure and strong, while with the decline of preaching came the loss of spiritual power? Preaching in the Middle Ages was a comparatively insignificant feature of Church life, but its revival in the sixteenth century by Luther and other Reformers tells its own story. The Evangelical Movement of the eighteenth century in connexion with Wesley and Whitefield, and many others, bears the same witness, while in missionary work to-day preaching and teaching occupy a prominent place. Where the spiritual life has been greatest there the preaching has been strongest, and it is not in the slightest degree inaccurate to say that wherever the priest goes up the prophet goes down, and contrariwise, where the prophet is exalted the priest is seen to be unnecessary. It has often been pointed out that Augustine was prayed for by Monica for thirty years, but the Churches did not attract him. Faustus, the philosopher, was the great magnet, till at last Augustine reached Milan and came in contact with Ambrose, the great man, the Christian, the great preacher.

Experience to-day all points in the same direction. Where preaching is emphasized and valued by the minister the people come and will come. Nothing, however able and effective in writing, will ever make up for the living voice. Not even the great cause of politics or any other element in life, will ever supplant preaching. 'Truth through personality' is the classical definition of preaching, and carries with it clear testimony to the essential need of the person as the channel of the truth. If people are ever impatient with preaching to-day, it is not with the fact, but with the sort.

The call of the present time on theological students, and on the younger clergy in particular, is to give special attention to preaching. Both in theological schools and in Church work we must make preparation for preaching a prominent feature and factor of our clerical life. We must give the best we can in matter and manner. We must work as hard as we can in order to produce the best results. No time, no strength, no thought, no effort, can be too much to devote to this duty. Even if this means the surrender of organizations, the result in the long run will not be harmful, but advantageous. It may be that we need to do less in order to do more. By transferring purely secular administration to laymen, or if we cannot obtain them, by omitting such secular methods and concentrating our attention on the spiritual element of the ministry of the Word, we shall obtain the best and most permanent results of the ministry.

There is perhaps nothing in life to compare with the joy of true preaching. What an exquisite satisfaction it gives to witness for Christ, in proclaiming His Gospel, in teaching His truth, in cheering the lonely, the sorrowing, the desolate and the afflicted, by some message from on high! Above all, is there anything in the world to compare with the profound and inspiring satisfaction of winning men and women to Christ through preaching, and of ministering to their education as we endeavour to build them up in their most holy faith? Let us be firmly convinced of, and deeply impressed with the absolute necessity, the supreme importance, the profound influence, and the great joy of preaching the Gospel. Well said the great Thomas Goodwin, 'God had only one Son, and He made Him a Minister.'

Section 2.  the nature of preaching

Homiletics is the science of which preaching is the art, and the sermon is the product. But what is a sermon? Many years ago the following definition was given in the course of a lecture on this subject:—

'An oral discourse, or address to the public mind on a religious subject, carefully prepared, with a definite object.'

This definition consists of five parts, each of which needs careful study.

1. 'A sermon is an oral discourse or address.' This means that a sermon is a speech, not a book, nor a treatise, nor an essay. No one can doubt that the extemporaneous idea is the true one. The Latin *orator* was not a reader, but a speaker, and the true idea of preaching is to combine the weight of matter in reading and writing with the ease, fluency, versatality, and animation of speech. To quote Bacon's familiar words, 'Reading makes the full man, writing the exact man, conversation the ready man.'

2. 'An oral address, to the public mind.' A sermon is not a lecture. It is an address to a mixed class, and therefore

ought not as a rule to deal with any specialty, still less with any technicality.

3. 'An oral address, to the public mind, on a religious subject.' It is not concerned with politics, or literature, or science. The sermon is essentially Christian, and is to be drawn from the Bible. A definite message should be extracted from the Scriptures. As a matter of history, the sermon is a definitely Christian institution.

4. 'An oral address, to the public mind, on a religious subject, carefully prepared.' It is a serious and dangerous fallacy that preaching is a gift rather than an art. It does not come as a chance effort. According to some people, it would seem as though sermons are made very much according to the description of Aaron's work with the people's gold. 'There came out this calf.' But we know that unless a sermon obeys the laws of art, and is the result of genuine work, it will be of no value whatever. It was the great Henry Melville who, in reply to the inquiry how many sermons a man could prepare every week, said, 'A clever man, one; an ordinary man, two; a fool as many as you like.' If our sermons are not the result of downright work, they will not be sermons at all.

5. 'An oral address to the public mind, on a religious subject, carefully prepared, with a definite object.' An essay simply presents truth for consideration, but a sermon adds to presentation the two essential elements of persuasion and action, and unless this definite object is steadily kept in view, the preacher will not provide a sermon. Preaching is God's Word to man through man, and the motto of every preacher should be, 'I have a message from God to thee.' A story is told of a tradesman who was convicted by a sermon of giving short measure to his customers, and as a result of what he heard he went home and 'burned his bushel.' This indicates the true ideal and aim of the Christian sermon.

SECTION 3. THE PREPARATION FOR THE SERMON.

'Some men prepare their sermons; other men prepare themselves.' Lyman Beecher (or his son, Henry Ward Beecher, for the story is told of both) was once asked, 'How long did it take you to prepare that sermon of this morning?' 'Forty years,' was the reply. The sermon is only properly made in proportion as the life is being enriched. A well-known American preacher has suggestively and strikingly said that it takes three men to preach a sermon; the physical man, the mental man, the spiritual man. And each of these three elements of preparation must be included and given proper attention.

The physical preparation is by no means unimportant. Eating is to the body what fuel is to the fire, and just as a fire must not be choked up with too much fuel if it is to burn brightly in a short time, so, if the physical powers are surfeited with eating just before a sermon, the preaching must necessarily suffer. Fresh air, a well-ventilated study, and regular exercise will be found invaluable in preparation for preaching. Not least, the clergyman ought to have one day's rest in seven, and as, in the very nature of his vocation, Sunday is his most strenuous and exacting day, he should make a point of setting aside, as far as possible, some other day of the week as his sabbath.

Intellectual preparation necessarily occupies a very prominet place, and by this is to be understood the exercise and training of memory, reason, and imagination. Let no preacher think that 'anything will do' for a sermon. If he is not prepared to undertake genuinely hard mental work, he has failed to realize one of the prime necessities of all preaching.

Intellectual preparation will start with a general study of the Bible; this indeed will be the paramount necessity. The preacher must be in the true sense, a 'man of one book.' This study, in so far as it is intended to minister to preaching, will include a careful consideration of the various periods, close attention to the biographies, and a constant study of the books of the Bible. Side by side with this, the preacher will make a point of studying both preaching and preachers in order to become acquainted with the best methods and at the same time to keep up his own ideals. We must not only read the best sermons and the best books on preaching, but take every opportunity of hearing the greatest preachers.

A general study of books will also form an essential feature of intellectual preparation for preaching. This will preserve the mind from falling into ruts, increase our general information and material for sermons, help in the interpretation and application of the Bible, and enable us to enter into sympathy with the men of our time and the tendencies of our age. This general study of books will include as far as possible some acquaintance with History, Science, Philosophy, Fiction, and Poetry, though of course, as temperaments vary, emphasis will be laid on one or the other of these departments of life. The value of History is that it reveals God in human affairs; the value of Science is that it will bring God before us in nature; the value of Philosophy is that it will manifest God in the process and progress of human thought; Fiction will have its great value as an expression of human character. No one can read such masterpieces of literature as those of Shakespeare, Bunyan, George Eliot, Hawthorne, Thackeray, and Dickens, without obtaining an added knowledge of that human nature with which we have to deal in sermons. Poetry will help us in particular with the expression of our thought, and a preacher who draws from such 'wells of English undefiled' as Milton, Wordsworth, and Tennyson will never lack lucidity and grace.

A study of men must also be included in our intellectual work. Truth must ever be related to life, and a knowledge of men as well as of books will be the sure preventive against mere theorizing. Some one has aptly and wisely said that 'a sermon must have heaven for its father and earth for its mother.' Once again, let it be emphasized in the strongest possible way that we need the keen and most strenuous intellectual preparation if we are to do effective service in preaching. There are far too many preachers who have been described as 'men of thoughts rather than of thought.'

Spiritual preparation might be regarded as so essential as not to require notice, and yet it is necessary to emphasize it as one of the methods of true discipline for preaching. Nothing can make up for the training of the spiritual man.

This will come about pre-eminently by the daily devotional study of the Bible, which will give freshness, force, and fragrance to our message. The man who plunges his soul in the pure stream of Bible meditation day by day will find his preaching marked by vividness and purity which will bring joy and blessing to his hearers. Indeed, it may be fearlessly said that such a devotional study of the Bible will do much to settle critical questions for the preacher himself, for when a man has fellowship with God through His Word it gives him a criterion by which to test everything in the Bible. If a man meets God in the book of Genesis, that meeting will affect every subsequent consideration of that wonderful book.

Devotional reading will also form part of our spiritual preparation, and so long as it is kept really secondary to the Bible, it can do nothing but good for us to see what God is teaching other souls, and to learn every possible lesson of His grace and love. Richard Cecil once said, 'I have a shelf in my study for tried authors; one in my mind for tried principles; and one in my heart for tried friends.' But of course this devotional study of the Bible and of other books will always be associated, and, if it may be so said, saturated with prayer. As we honour the Holy Spirit of God, Who is the real Author of the Bible, as we trust Him, as we seek Him, and as we pour out our hearts before Him, our spirits will become strong as the Word of God abides in them and we shall become 'thoroughly furnished' for the work of the ministry.

SECTION 4.   THE PREPARATION OF THE SERMON

In all suggestions for sermon work it must never be forgotten that individual experience is only valuable for comparison. Every man must be himself and follow the lines of his own temperament. At the same time it may often prove of service to compare notes with others in order to see what general lines of preparation for the sermon are followed.

1.   First, we must get our text. This will best be obtained while we are alone with our Bible. The true-hearted minister will desire to seek to know God's will for His people, and lifting up his heart in prayer and trust he will wait upon

God for the message. Nor will he ever be really disappointed
in his quest. At one time he will be led to preach from an
Old Testament topic, at another time from a New Testament
subject, whether in the Gospels or Epistles, while yet again,
the Psalms will yield their fruit to every earnest seeker. From
time to time, however, nothing from the Scriptures read and
pondered in the daily portion will impress itself upon his mind,
but in answer to continued prayer and trust something else
will be shown, and the mind directed in the right channel.
There is a profound and genuine sense of spiritual satisfaction
in the consciousness that our text has come in answer to faith
and prayer; it tends to make us confident that our message is
from God.

2. With our text ready, we have to bear in mind and apply
the simple and yet great principles of all sermon preparation.
These principles are usually stated as three in number,[1] but
perhaps it may be permissible to add one more as the final and
culminating requirement.

(a) We must 'think ourselves empty.' By this is meant
that we must take our text and proceed to ponder its meaning. Our thoughts should be jotted down as they come, on
a sheet of paper, without any attempt at arrangement, but
only with an endeavour to elicit for ourselves every aspect of
the meaning and message of the text. This effort to think
for ourselves will prove of the greatest possible value, and
whether it takes a long or short time to 'think ourselves empty,'
we ought not to approach any outside help to sermon preparation until we are conscious that to the best of our ability we
have exhausted for the time our own mental possibilities.

(b) We must 'read ourselves full.' After thinking out
for ourselves the bearings of the text, the mind is in the
proper state to approach the views of others who may have
commented, or otherwise written on the passage. The mind
that is 'empty' becomes thoroughly hungry, and the consciousness of first-hand thought of our own enables us to assimilate
in a true sense all that is within our reach in the books of
others. Let us read as widely as possible in the books and

[1] Bishop Boyd Carpenter's *Lectures on Preaching.*

magazines at our disposal, and incorporate in the work everything that is appropriate to our subject.

(c) Then we must 'write ourselves clear.' After thinking and reading it is essential to put your thoughts into proper
order, and this can only be done by writing. Since 'writing
makes the exact man,' the use of our pen in sermon preparation
will be an indispensable requirement. When we have arranged our outline and method of treatment we should write
out our sermon in full, for the very exercise of writing will
give clearness and precision to our thought. The eye is a
great help to the mind, and the very sight of what we have
written will enable us to correct our material in a way that
would be quite impossible apart from writing. These are the
three principles which are usually emphasized in all books on
sermon preparation, and it will be seen that they refer ex-
clusively to the purely intellectual aspects of the sermon. For
this reason we venture to add a fourth principle to the foregoing.

(d) We must 'pray ourselves keen.' When the intellectual work has been done, or rather, all through the process
of intellectual acquisition, our work should be steeped in
prayer, and then when the preparation is over we must commit ourselves and our work to God in order that our delivery,
when the time comes, may be 'in demonstration of the Spirit
and of power.' If a man will only observe these four principles in his preparation, he will find that they cover the entire field of need.

3.  Some words about methods seem to be required at this
point. Sermon preparation should begin early in the week. It
is injurious to ourselves, as well as wrong to our people, to
allow our week to be crowded with engagements which compel us to postpone our sermon work till almost the very end of
a busy, and, it may be, tiring week. If we begin on Monday
morning for the next Sunday we shall soon find the advantage
in a variety of ways. Then something, however little, should
be done each day. We must never forget the great intellectual law known as 'unconscious cerebration.' The subject
once started, is certain to germinate, and in ways of which we
know nothing, material will be gradually collected, and mind

and heart will be preparing themselves all through the week as we give attention to our work day by day. Then we must endeavour to discipline our mind to think distinctly and connectedly. This is easier said than done, and yet unless some effort is made we shall find our thoughts only desultory and of no practical value. Further, as we are thinking and reading, we should take every opportunity of using our pen. It it probably true to say that no great speaker has ever lived who did not make full use of his pen. Writing has a remarkable effect upon our powers of thought and reading, and no clergyman can afford to dispense with the discipline that comes thereby. As Lord Brougham himself said: —

'I should lay it down as a rule admitting of no exception, that a man will speak well in proportion as he has written much and that with equal talents he will be the finest extempore speaker, when no time for preparing is allowed, who has prepared himself most sedulously when he had an opportunity of delivering a premeditated speech.'

At the same time, our writing is not for the purpose of committing our sermon to memory. There are very few preachers who can memorize their sermons and deliver them *memoriter* with reality and directness. There is a sense in which the words are absolutely true. 'Take care of the thoughts and the words will take care of themselves.' If only we ponder and read, and read and ponder, when the time comes for us to deliver what we have prepared, mind and memory will not be found wanting.

4. It now remains for us to consider with care the essential requirements of every sermon. They seem to be four in number.

(*a*) There must be definiteness of aim. It is said of one preacher that 'he aimed at nothing and hit it every time.' A man should know with clearness and directness what he wishes to elicit from his text and deliver to his people. At every point of his preparation he should rigidly inquire of himself, What do I mean by this? What does the text teach? What do I intend to give to my people?

(*b*) There must be simplicity and precision of language. All high-flown language should be carefully avoided. Simplicity, lucidity, and preciseness are all that are required of the sermon. A man's wife should not be termed 'the partner of his joys and sorrows,' and we must carefully avoid the temptation to be original in the desire to keep clear of the hackneyed and trite. The man who wished to dispense with the familiar 'From the cradle to the grave' did not improve matters by describing life as 'from the basinette to the sepulchre.' We must do our utmost to weigh words, to seek their etymological meaning, and to cultivate familiarity with their true force. For this purpose a good etymological dictionary will prove of constant service. We must do our best to cultivate style. Perhaps for pulpit work there are no authors to compare with George Eliot and Froude, because of their simplicity, force and directness; and one of the finest models for the young clergyman is to be found in the well-known books and tracts by the late Bishop Ryle of Liverpool. It is known that he commenced his ministry in a country parish in the West of England, and determined to model himself on the great Canon Henry Melville of St. Paul's, but he soon found that the country folk were utterly unable to appreciate the rounded periods and florid language employed after the example of the eminent and eloquent Canon. And so Mr. Ryle, to use his own expression, determined to 'crucify his style.' He did so to some purpose, in view of the almost unique terseness, clearness, and force of his inimitable writings. In the course of an article in *The British Weekly* some years ago by the late Ian Maclaren, reviewing his ministry, he gave expression to the following words:—

'Had I another thirty years, I should give more earnest heed to style, and especially I would enrich my mind by daily study of its great masters, so that as a farmer quickens his soil by nitrates, one might enrich his mind by the assimilation of noble language. Nothing has degraded preaching more than tawdry appeals, in which the pathos has no passion, and the argument no force. Evangelistic preaching has seemed to us to be, as a rule, careless to a scandal and almost squalid in style, with vain repetitions of hackneyed words by way of exhortation and with incredible anecdotes by way of illustration. But I am moved at present to judge this difficult and delicate form of preaching with the utmost charity, when I review the glaring deficiency of my own style and the repeated evidence of unfinished work. Let me record my solemn conviction that in the day when he gives in his account the preacher of the Evangel will be held responsible, not only for the truth which he declares, but for the dress with which he clothed it.'

(c) There must be clearness of arrangement. The old-fashioned 'Heads' to Sermons are by no means unworthy of consideration by preachers of to-day. They help the preacher in his preparation, and they certainly help the hearer to follow point by point the various divisions of the sermon. It is quite unnecessary, as we shall see later, to announce these 'Heads' beforehand, but if they are mentioned one by one as they come, it will conduce to clearness of statement which will be undoubtedly effective. But whether we have 'Heads,' or not, there should be something like a logical arrangement of the sermon from commencement to conclusion.

(d) There must be forcefulness of application. A sermon without an application is not a sermon at all, but only an essay. Application is like the bait on the hook. We must be 'fishers of men.' A clergyman once told a friend of mine that he had laboured for eleven years in one parish without knowing of a single conversion. My friend and I knew very well that the man who made this confession was one of the ablest and most acceptable of teachers, honoured and loved by his people, and all who knew him. But, as my friend explained it, 'The fact of the matter is, he provided a splendid meal, but he did not show his people how to eat it.' In other words he was a teacher, but he did not apply his teaching and lead to immediate acceptance and obedience. Let us never fail to drive home our message and make it as personal, direct, and definite as possible.

Along these lines it may be confidently said that a general preparation of the sermon will proceed. Once again, let us fix it in our minds that no work can be too great, no labour too severe, no trouble too much, no toil too exacting, if the Christian preacher is to do his duty to his God, himself, and his people.

SECTION 5.   THE STRUCTURE OF THE SERMON.[1]

Every sermon should have a plan.  It is true that sermon outlines, or plans, are not very fashionable in the present day; they are either ignored or else very carefully disguised; and yet they possess a twofold advantage: they are good for the preacher, and certainly good for the hearers.  The preacher will be enabled to study much more intelligently if he proceeds along the lines of a carefullly worked out plan.  He will be helped to keep a proper proportion between the parts of his sermon.  His edifice will not be all porch, or otherwise out of proportion.  For extemporaneous preaching a sermon plan will be of extreme value.  Not least in importance, an outline will provide a constant exercise for the mind in construction.  For these reasons a clergyman should certainly practise the making of sermon plans and outlines.  As to hearers, no one can doubt that an outline makes a sermon intelligible and attractive.  People are able to carry away the main ideas of the preacher if they are put before them in something like outline form.  This outline should conform to the regular threefold division of every true sermon; the Introduction, the Substance, the Conclusion.

*A*.  The Introduction is very important.  Some one has remarked that 'the first five minutes of a battle are decisive.' But whether this be the case, or not, the first few seconds of a sermon are undoubtedly of the greatest importance.

1.   What should be the substance of a good Introduction? It should possess four qualities.

(*a*)   It should be arresting, in order to gain attention.  An introduction should never be too obvious, and for this reason it should be made as interesting as possible.  When a preacher commences with the hackneyed words, 'The chapter from which my text is taken,' one feels inevitably inclined to settle down to slumber.  All the best preachers make their introduction attractive and arresting.

---

[1] In this section it has only been possible to summarize (mainly from Hoyt, *The Work of Preaching*, chaps. 8 and 9) what all authorities on sermons require.

(*b*)   It should be sympathetic, in order to win the goodwill of the congregation.   One of the finest books for work among children is called *The Point of Contact,* showing the need of a teacher becoming at once *en rapport* with his juvenile hearers.   The same thing is really true in connexion with sermons, and it is of the greatest importance to win the goodwill of our audience by some point at the outset with which they will agree.

(*c*)   It should be appropriate.   The introduction must have a close connexion with what follows.   If there is no vital relation between the introduction and the substance of the sermon, what is said will not only be futile but harmful.

(*d*)   It should be short.   Sermons are sometimes weighted with too long an introduction.   The house is all portico, and people are tired before the substance of the sermon is reached. Some of us have very vivid recollections of an able and scholarly preacher whose introductions as a rule used to take at least twenty minutes.

2.   What should be the form of a good introduction? The only answer to this is that the form must be varied if it is to be good.   Sometimes it will take the form of an explanation; at other times an observation; and yet again an illustration. So long as there is variety and appropriateness to what follows we can adopt whatever form we wish.

3.   What should be the spirit of a good Introduction?   It should be at once modest and simple.   Anything approaching egotism or conscious authority in the preacher will be at once futile and fatal.

*B.*   The Substance of the sermon naturally occupies our attention after the Introduction, and this involves a due and appropriate use of the methods of analysis and synthesis. The former will be for instruction; the latter persuasion.   Both are needed and should be constantly kept in view.

1.   What is the character of a thoroughly good sermon?

(*a*)   It should possess unity.   Every part of the sermon should be connected with the rest, and our treatment should proceed step by step from the opening to the close.

(*b*)   It should be marked by progress.   We should prepare so carefully that we may be able to avoid putting into division 1 what ought to be in division 2.

(*c*)   It should possess clearness.   Whether this is done by means of divisions is a matter of opinion and choice.   If we have divisions for our sermons it will usually be found wise not to announce them beforehand, for the element of surprise is of great importance in all preaching.   If our subject happens to be specially abstract, or theological, it may well be thought necessary to announce our general treatment beforehand, but, as a rule, in our ordinary sermons each point should be announced at its proper place.

(*d*)   It should be characterized by vitality.   All the unity, progress, and clearness that our sermons reveal will count for nothing unless they are also possessed with life.   The dry bones must be clothed with flesh, the flesh must be vitalized, and the sermon made living for its purposes.

2.   What are the elements of the form of a thoroughly good sermon?   The following four elements will probably be found essential to every satisfactory sermon.

(*a*)   There will be propositions.   We must state our case, and show our people what we intend to do with our subject.

(*b*)   There will be explanations.   We must interpret, elucidate, and justify our propositions.

(*c*)   There will be observations.   We shall comment on, and apply our text in all suitable ways.

(*d*)   There will be illustrations.   There are very few sermons that will not be greatly benefited by some illustrations to let in the light and impress the subject on mind and heart.

*C.*   The Conclusion of the sermon is not the least important section of it.   Indeed, it is absolutely essential, for, as we have said, it distinguishes the sermon from the essay or the lecture.

1.   What is the character of a good Conclusion?

(*a*)   It should be short.   Let us beware of saying, 'Finally' until we are really at the close of our sermon.   When a clergyman uses this often welcome sound about twenty times before he actually closes, and when it is followed by similar remarks, like 'Lastly'; 'One word more'; 'In conclusion'; hearers are apt to get impatient and resent such an inaccurate use of language.  An American clergyman entertained a number of eminent men at dinner.  The guests were speaking in praise of a sermon the host had preached.  The preacher's young son was at the table, and one of the guests said: 'My boy, what did you think of your father's sermon?' 'I guess it was very good,' said the lad, 'but there were three mighty fine places where he could have stopped.'

(*b*)  It should be simple.  No oratorical flights are in place at the conclusion of a Christian sermon.  Young preachers are often tempted to indulge in a 'peroration,' but it should be avoided, because it will inevitably fail of the effect essential to a Christian discourse.

(*c*)  It should be pungent.  That is to say, there must be a direct, personal appeal.  Each hearer must feel the force of the words, as though the preacher were saying to him, 'Thou art the man.'

(*d*)  It should be definite.  This means that the preacher should not fail to tell his people how to do what is required by the message.  Whether it is an evangelistic, or an instructive sermon, this definite presentation of the method of realization must form part of our conclusion.

2.  What is the form of a good Conclusion?  Here again, the answer is that it may be, and ought to be varied.  Sometimes it will take the form of a recapitulation, but it is not often that a preacher can invest his recapitulation with that freshness which the subject requires.  Every review should be a *new* view, and this is not an easy task.  It is probable, therefore, that the more familiar form of application will be the prominent feature in our conclusions.  But whatever may be our methods, we must take care that there is a real, forceful, pertinent, and practical ending to our message.

As we contemplate these three parts: Introduction, Substance, Conclusion, we naturally inquire what proportion of our time and material should be given to each.  It is difficult to say, but the suggestion has been made that the Introduction should take one-fifth, the Substance three-fifths, and the Conclusion one-fifth of our time.  But we must not be slaves to any such rigidity, for from time to time we shall probably find that one-tenth for Introduction, four-fifths for Substance, and one-tenth for Conclusion will be more appropriate to our needs. The one thing essential is that there should be a fair and due proportion between these three parts, and we can test the matter by the manuscript pages of our sermons when written. If only we keep before our minds the absolute necessity of these three parts and do our utmost to make them the very best we can, our sermons will never lack appreciation on the part of our people.

## Section 6.    Scripture in relation to the sermon.[1]

As sermons are essentially a Christian institution, the Word of God is naturally prominent and important in connexion with them. The Bible often speaks of 'the Ministry of the Word,' and the Church of England Prayer Book title is 'Ministers of the Word and Sacraments,' never of the Sacraments alone. The use of the Bible is essential to the minister merely for style, illustration, and interest; but far more than this, it is essential for his message. All the great preachers have been truly Biblical preachers. No one can read a sermon of Spurgeon's without becoming aware of his intimate acquaintance with the Bible. Holy Scripture was the atmosphere in which he lived and preached. The same is true of all other pulpit giants, like Maclaren, Parker, and Liddon; they were 'mighty in the Scriptures.' No one can exaggerate the value of a prolonged study of the Bible alone for the work of Christian preaching. If the mind is saturated with such portions as the Fourth Gospel, or the Epistles to the Romans and Ephesians, or the last great section of Isaiah, the result will be nothing short of wonderful in providing thought and experience for the ministry. If our preaching is not Biblical it is certain to be thin, poor, and hesitating, but if it is made up of the Bible it is sure to be rich, strong, penetrating, and satisfying both to preacher and hearers. Preaching that is not Scriptural cannot be regarded as Christian preaching. But at once the question arises, What do we mean by Scriptural preaching? Various aspects of the subject call for attention.

[1] See Hoyt, *The Work of Preaching*, chaps. 5 and 6.

## I. *The Use of a Text.*

It is the invariable custom to employ a text as the introduction to sermons. It is a little difficult to discover the origin of the use of the term. 'Text' means 'something woven,' and we may at least apply it to suggest the importance of the message being woven with the Word of God. Shall we continue to observe this old custom of giving out our text? Almost every preacher would answer this question with a hearty affirmative. A text will give a sermon the authority of a Divine message, and this is the most important part of our work. The hearers will also thereby be helped to study the Scripture for themselves and will be enabled to recall the sermon as they give attention to the text. But perhaps the greatest value of the text lies in its effects on the minister himself. It will give definiteness to the entire sermon, keep the preacher strictly to his subject, enable him to concentrate attention on the aim of the moment, and in the course of his ministry the use of texts will afford him opportunities for providing the necessary variety in his subjects as he endeavours to bring out of his treasure things new and old. For these and other reasons it is not too much to say that the employment of a text should be continued as in every way of the greatest possible advantage to preachers and hearers.

## II. *The Choice of a Text.*

Several considerations should weigh with us in the actual selection of a passage of Scripture for our message.

1. It should be a genuine message. The text should be based on the true meaning of the passage, so far as we can derive it under the guidance of the best available scholarship. Any other use than the true exegetical meaning will need the greatest possible care. Preachers must not fail to distinguish between interpretation and application, and if our sermon does not deal with the original meaning of the passage, but is used in some secondary way, the fact should be stated and the people told what the passage really does mean in its original idea. Serious injury is likely to be done if we misuse Scripture by not giving the proper interpretation. A clergyman

once delivered a series of sermons on Popular Sins, and when he had to discuss the subject of Smoking he took as his text, 'Do thyself no harm.' It is probable that he did himself untold harm by such a deplorable misuse of the Word of God. Care should also be taken about any human words that are found recorded in the Bible, and we should ask ourselves before using such words as our text whether they are true. If the clergyman takes his text from the speeches of one of Job's friends, it is essential to discover whether the words are themselves true apart from any particular use made of them by the friends, for we remember how they were rebuked by God for giving Job a wrong impression. Of course there are words spoken by man which are true in themselves, as, for example, the words of the guards sent to apprehend our Lord: 'Never man spake like this man;' or the enemies of Christ: 'Who can forgive sins, but God only?' In such cases we are quite safe in taking the words as our text, even though Divine inspiration only concerns the accuracy of the record. On one occasion a minister took as his text the words of Satan: 'Skin for skin; yea, all that a man hath will a man give for his life'; and after announcing his text he commenced in a sensational way by saying, 'That's a lie.' It was a striking way of calling attention to the fact that not every word found in Scripture is a word of and from God.

2. It should contain a complete message. There is a real danger of using the text as a 'peg' on which to hang certain thoughts which may be used in themselves but have no real relation to the Scripture passage. A text ought not to be employed as a mere motto, or even as a point of departure. Our duty is the elucidation of the text, and we ought not to select our subject first and then ransack the Bible for a text to fit it. It is only very rarely that any clergyman need go outside the Bible for the subject of his preaching. A young minister once preached from the words, 'Nevertheless afterward,' and although he had much to say that was helpful about the discipline of life, it certainly seemed incongruous for so young a man to take so pretentious a subject and with so unsatisfactory a text. As it has been well put, we must be particularly careful not to use our text as a 'pretext.'

**3.** It should never be in any way incongruous. There must be no eccentricity, no humour, and of course nothing approaching buffoonery. Some authorities go as far as to say that there is no humour in the Bible, that the prophets and apostles were too deeply concerned with the realities of life to indulge in pleasantries. Whether this is so or not, the preacher must be particularly careful in his use of passages of Scripture for his text. Even a passage like 'Ephraim is a cake not turned' (Hos. 7: 8) will need all possible care and reverence.

**4.** It should be as suggestive and striking as possible. How wonderful is the freshness of Bushnell's sermon titles! They are sermons in themselves. Who but a genius like Bushnell would have entitled a sermon on Cyrus from Isaiah 45: 5, 'Every man's life a plan of God?' Another suggestive illustration of the same value of freshness is found in the use of the text 'See thou make all things according to the pattern showed to thee in the mount' (Heb. 8: 5).[1] No one can read Matheson's Devotional Meditations, *Moments in the Mount*, without being aware of the great helpfulness of the themes. If our text should happen to be familiar we must do our utmost to invest it with some novelty and freshness. The glorification of the obvious is one of the greatest needs of the ministry, and every man should strive to excel along this line. Perhaps the finest illustration, of investing with freshness a familiar text is found in Dr. Maclaren's great sermon on John 3: 16. (*a*) The Lake: God so loved the world.' (*b*) The River: 'He gave His only begotten Son.' (*c*) The Cup: 'that whosoever believeth.' (*d*) The Draught: 'have everlasting life.' We cannot all be Maclarens, but we ought to give our very best attention to the need of investing with newness the most familiar texts.

**5.** It should be guided by three things.

(*a*) By our past sermons. There should be as much variety as possible and the avoidance of repetition. Dr. R. W. Dale tells us that he kept lists of sermon subjects pinned up in his study, so that he might be able to see at a glance what subjects he had been taking for weeks and months past.

---

[1] Hoyt, *ut sup.*, p. 135.

(*b*) By the present needs of our people. We must consider what we believe to be their requirements, and our texts should as far as possible be such as can be divided and treated intelligently and suitably for our flocks by our own personal predilections. What grips our own spiritual life is pretty certain to impress our people, and if the Word of God is vital in our own experience it will inevitably become powerful as we proclaim its message week by week.

III. *The Interpretation of a Text.*

It is our bounden duty to find and give the proper interpretation of the text as preachers of the Word of God. This will mean study, and unless we are prepared for hard, strenuous, intellectual work we have not yet conceived the true idea of preaching. The interpretation of the text demands a knowledge of the language, whether in Hebrew or English; some acquaintance with Eastern customs so far as they are employed in the passage; and certainly an accurate knowledge of the context on both sides of the passage from which we propose to preach. For example, no one should preach on 'Lord, increase our faith' (Luke 17: 5) without careful reference to the thought of forgiveness in the context. No sermon should be preached on Nicodemus (John 3: 1) without observing the connexion in the Greek and the R.V. with chapter 2 and the special point illustrative of Nicodemus' character in the usual emphasis on the word 'man.' No preacher should dream of using 'Touch not; taste not; handle not' (Col. 2: 21) without a thorough knowledge of the situation which led to those words. To separate them from the context and use them on behalf of temperance is to do plain violence to Holy Writ. The use of the Greek will often save us from error, even though it may occasionally spoil some useful sermons. Thus, no one could possibly exalt the ordinance of preaching from 1 Cor. 1: 21, if he looked at the verse in the original.

We must also beware of spiritualizing Scripture. Teaching by types is of course legitimate and necessary, but it needs a good deal of intellectual care and not a little spiritual com-

mon sense. A preacher once had to preach on the subject of
temperance, and emphasized quite rightly the importance of
Christian people opposing and fighting the drink traffic in
every possible way, but it did not seem quite a happy use to
make of the text, 'Samuel hewed Agag in pieces before the
Lord.'

Not least of all, we must insist on verbal accuracy in our
interpretation of texts. There must be no twisting to obtain
our point, however important that point may be. Unless there
is intellectual honesty on the part of the preacher, there will
soon be intellectual disgust on the part of hearers who are
just as capable to consider the bearings of Scripture as he himself is. There is scarcely any more clamant call in the present day in connexion with preaching than for a thorough,
intellectual, genuine interpretation of the Scripture we use.

IV. *The Adherence to a Text.*

The subject should grow out of the text, and usually there
will be no difficulty in accomplishing this. To choose and
work out a subject and then prefix a text to it, is likely to
lead to the production of an essay, not a sermon. The text
should be the germ and the sermon the product. If only we
carefully expound the text, discovering its meaning, and pro-
nouncing it in its natural divisions we shall be thereby enabled
to keep closely to the text all through the sermon. It was
a sad and sorry testimony of the hearer who sarcastically remarked of his preacher that there was so little connexion between the text and the sermon that if the text had been in-
fected with fever the sermon would not have caught it. The
application as well as the subject and substance of the sermon
should be strictly based on the text. Our message is pre-
sumably the Word of God, and it must be applied to our
hearers. This will prevent us from giving them any mere
personal exhortation, still less any oratorical declamation.
When subject, substance, and application are thus kept in
close adherence to the text, we shall accomplish our purpose as
'ministers of the Word.'

When a man is called to minister to the same people week after week for several years, it goes without saying that his messages should have all possible variety. Unless this is so, intellectual and even spiritual ruts and grooves are inevitable, and both preacher and people will feel monotony. The following are some varieties of sermons that should be kept in view.

## I. *Textual.*

By this is meant a sermon that arises definitely and directly out of a single text, and if we cannot find a text to fit the topic it is probable that we shall be well advised to change the topic itself. The fulness of Scripture is such that even the longest ministry may be maintained by sermons that come from Scripture. Before using a text out of its ordinary meaning we must pay attention to the context. Thus if we should be taking Isaiah 61: 3, 'Beauty for ashes,' as a text on the sermon of the transformation of sorrow, we ought first of all to look at it and expound it in the light of Eastern customs and the circumstances of the return of the Jews from exile. And in all textual sermons we ought to endeavour to divide our texts so as to give unity and definiteness to our message. The following may be suggested as examples of textual preaching:—

Genesis 42: 21. The three elements of repentance: Conscience, 'we are verily guilty'; Memory, 'in that we saw the anguish'; Reason, 'therefore is this distress come upon us.' I remember Dr. A. T. Pierson calling my attention to this when we were travelling together from Dublin to London, and comparing notes on Bible study and sermons.

Matthew 6: 22. The Kingdom of God: What? How? Why?

Luke 19: 42. Opportunity: Given; Limited; Lost.

Acts 10: 43. The Great Offer: The One Way; The Strong Confirmation; The Simple Means.

1 Corinthians 13: 13. Faith, Hope, Love. Why all three are permanent; Why Love is supreme.

Colossians 1: 21-23. Alienation; Reconciliation; Presentation; Continuation.

Colossians 1: 27, 28. Our Message; our Methods; our Motive. Many other instances of this method will be found in those invaluable volumes of Expositions by Dr. Alexander Maclaren. The only trouble is that when we have looked at one of Maclaren's felicitous and inimitable treatments, we not only wonder why we did not see it ourselves, but we find it difficult to avoid a similar treatment when we are called upon to preach from the passage. Who that has read his sermon on Luke 22: 28 can ever forget his natural and suggestive divisions? The Lonely Christ; the Tempted Christ; the Grateful Christ.

From a different point of view Dr. Joseph Parker was equally felicitous in textual preaching, and in his *People's Bible* will be found many of his fertile suggestions. It is not everybody who would be able to avoid the incongruous in taking such a text as 'Now Sheshan had no sons, but daughters' (1 Chron. 2: 34), and deduce therefrom the great principle of compensations in life. In Dr. Parker's *Ad Clerum* there are many illustrations of his striking treatment. Thus on Job 14: 10, 'Man giveth up the ghost, and where is he?' The treatment is: (1) If he is a good man, he is where he desired to be, where he is prepared to be, and where he will remain. (2) If he is a bad man, he is where he did not desire to be, but where he is prepared to be, and where he will remain. On 1 Peter 5: 7, we are reminded of a traveller with three bundles or burdens: (1) Past Memories; (2) Present Difficulties; (3) Future Fears. All these we are to 'cast upon' the Lord. On one occasion I heard Dr. Orr give a brief address on the subject of the rich fool (Luke 12: 16-21) who, it was said, made three mistakes. (1) He mistook his body for his soul. (2) He mistook himself for God. (3) He mistook time for eternity. It is difficult to think of any more satisfactory, suggestive, and complete treatment of this passage.

Courses of Textual Sermons are also very useful from time to time. The following may be suggested as illustrations of what is meant:

Matthew 2: 1-10. The Light. (1) Sought by the Wise Men; (2) Ignored by the Jewish Authorities; (3) Opposed by Herod; (4) Welcomed by Joseph, Mary, and the Magi.

Luke 9: 57-62. The Three Temperaments. (1) Impulsive; (2) Cautious; (3) Vacillating. Or, Bunyanlike, following the suggestions of the late G. H. C. Macgregor: (1) Mr. Too-Quick; (2) Mr. Too-Slow; (3) Mr. Too-Soft.

## II. *Expository.*

On almost every hand to-day we are urged to make our sermons more expository because our people need instruction in the Word of God, but those who proffer this advice are by no means clear as to what is meant by expository preaching. Dr. Maclaren's textual preaching is essentially expository, even though it deals with one verse only, because it is thoroughly Biblical and arises immediately out of the text. But usually by expository preaching we are intended to mean the use of some passage of Scripture to be explained verse by verse and applied to our hearers. There are serious dangers for most men in attempting anything of this kind at a time of worship, as distinct from a Bible Class, because the treatment is liable to lack unity as well as to be protracted to too great a length. If inquiry be made, it will be found that there have been very few really expository preachers in the Christian Church; expository, that is, as distinct from Biblical preachers. Spurgeon was a Biblical preacher, so was Moody, but neither of them could be called an expository preacher. Maclaren is the nearest approach to a preacher who is at once Biblical and expository, and his expositions will be found to be the finest models of all expository preaching.

Three requirements should be emphasized in every endeavour to present to our people an exposition of any passage. (1) It should only concern the *salient* features. There are many details that must be resolutely omitted, lest we are too long, and lest we blur the definite impression. (2) It should mainly concern the *spiritual* meaning. Anything historical, or geographical, or oriental, must be kept resolutely subordinated to the supreme issue; it is a sermon, not a lecture. (3) It should always have a *searching* message. The application in an exposition should be emphasized and never omitted. If these three essentials are observed; only salient; mainly spiritual; always searching; there is no reason why many of us should not develop into capable and acceptable expository preachers.

Some examples of this kind of sermon may perhaps be offered.

Psalm 16: The Life of the Believer. (1) Its Commencement (*vs.* 1-4). (2) Its Course ( *vs.* 4-8). (3) Its Culmination (*vs.* 9-11).

Psalm 23. The Divine Shepherd, and Seven Reasons why 'I shall not want.' The rest of the Psalm provides the justification for the statement of *v.* 1.

Luke 7: 36-50. Simon and the Woman. (1) Simon the Sinner. (2) The Woman a Sinner. (3) Christ's Attitude to Both.

Luke 15: 11-32. The Prodigal Son. (1) The seven steps down. (2) The seven steps up.

The Prayers of St. Paul.

The Thanksgivings of St. Paul. 'Thanks be to God.'

The Doxologies of St. Paul.

III. *Biographical.*

As there is so much of human life recorded in the Bible, more than half of Holy Scripture being given to us in the form of history, the biographical element of preaching should not be overlooked. Its value is evident because of the living interest in other lives, and because human character is so vividly and faithfully depicted in Scripture that there are few lives recorded which do not provide counsels and warnings for the spiritual life. The larger biographies found in both Testaments are a perennial source of helpfulness, and no one can take such subjects as those of Abraham, or Jacob, or Elijah, or John the Baptist, without discovering a mine of wealth for intellect and heart. Not the least valuable point of these biographical sermons will be that we shall be enabled to introduce the experience and make direct personal applications to the lives of our people when they least expect them, and when they cannot charge us with introducing anything merely personal. No one who has tried this method with the suggestive help and guidance of such biographies as those by the Rev. F. B. Meyer, Dr. Alexander Whyte, or Dr. George Matheson, will ever fail to give biography a prominent place in his ministerial preaching and teaching.

The shorter biographies are equally valuable for this purpose. Even though very little is told us of many of the characters recorded, sufficient is very often found in a short space to indicate lines of thought and reveal developments of character. Thus the three chapters in which Nicodemus is mentioned lend themselves admirably to a sermon on the spiritual development of the 'ruler in Israel,' as (1) the Secret Inquirer, (2) the Timid Advocate, and (3) the Open Confessor. The passages connected with Barnabas can be easily and naturally grouped under five headings, giving to us so many aspects of his character and service. The same is true of the Mother of our Lord, whose spiritual life may be comprised in five definite periods.[1] Such a book as Dean Howson's *Companions of St. Paul*, will provide ample material for several truly helpful sermons. The one great need in all this biographical teaching is to make the men and women live over again, to show the reality of their experiences, and to bring them out of the framework of old days into living contact with modern experiences. When this is done biography will prove one of the most attractive features of the Christian ministry.

IV. *Topical.*

By topical preaching is not meant preaching that deals with 'Topics of the Day,' but subjects found in Scripture associated with various texts rather than with one only. The subjects of Scripture are almost endless, but the following may be adduced as examples of this method.

St. Paul's three Ambitions. 2 Cor. 5: 9; 1 Thess. 4: 11; Rom. 15: 20 (see Greek).

---

[1] Perhaps the author may venture to refer to his own little book, *Methods of Bible Study*, for further illustrations of these statements.

The Three Burdens. Sin (Psa. 55: 22); Service (Gal. 6: 5); Sympathy (Gal. 6: 2).

Christ's Visits to Bethany. (1) As Teacher. (2) As Sympathizer. (3) As Redeemer. (4) As Lord.

'Whatsoever ye do . . . do all.' (1) 'To the glory of God' (1 Cor. 10: 31); (2) 'In the Name of the Lord Jesus' (Col. 3: 17). (3) From the soul (Col. 3: 23; see Greek).

'Be of good cheer.' Five occasions on which this word (see Greek) was used by our Lord.

'All things are possible.' (1) With God. (2) To the believer.

'I have sinned.' Eight confessions of sin in these words; four real, four unreal.

'So.' (1) 'Loved' (John 3: 16); (2) 'Great Salvation' (Heb. 2: 3).

'Wist not.' (1) Moses. (2) Samson.

'Thorns.' (1) Ruin (Gen. 3:); (2) Redemption (Gen. 19:); (3) Restoration (Isa. 55).

Peter's Three Sleeps. (1) Unripe Experience (Transfiguration); (2) Unfaithful Life (Gethsemane); (3) Unquestioning Trust (Prison).

The Beatitudes. (1) Of the Psalms; (2) of the Gospels; (3) of the Apocalypse.

The Four Suppers. (1) Redemption (Luke 14: 16-20); (2) Communion (1 Cor. 11: 23-29); (3) Joy (Rev. 19: 9); (4) Judgment (Rev. 19: 17).

Justification in its seven aspects.

## V. *The Secret of True Scriptural Preaching.*

For all phases of preaching two requirements are absolutely essential.

1. There must be daily Bible Study. First, the Bible alone without any outside helps. Then, and then only, with all available assistance.

2. There must be daily Bible Meditation. This means that we shall read primarily for our own life. What grips us will assuredly grip our people. These two, Study and Meditation, are the secret of perennial freshness and force.

SECTION 8.   ESSENTIAL QUALITIES IN A SERMON.

Although we have discussed some of the vital requirements necessary for the preparation of the sermon, it seems
imperative to consider still more fully some of those essential
features of substance and form which go to make up the true
sermon.

### I.   *Every Preacher should have a Dominant Theme.*

Our theme is a Person rather than ideas or truth in the
abstract. It is a weakness of many a ministry that it concen-
trates attention on ideas.   Dr. Dale once confessed that for
years he had been thinking only of the truth he preached,
and not of the people to whom he was preaching. 'Christianity is Christ', and we must never forget this in our preaching.
It was the Person of Christ Who constituted the theme of
Apostolic preaching ('Whom we preach,' Col. 1: 28).   And
it was the Person of Christ as crucified (1 Cor. 2: 2), not
the Cross, but Christ crucified.   And it was also Christ as
Lord (2 Cor. 4: 5).   This great truth is found exemplified
in all the earliest preaching.   While there are various rela-
tionships between Christ and the soul, it is always the Person
of Christ, whatever may be the relationship. Philip preached
Christ (Acts 8: 5) and Jesus (Acts 8: 35).   The disciples
ceased not to teach and preach Christ (Acts 5: 42), and Paul
preached Jesus as the Messiah (Acts 17: 3).   All doctrines
and duties are to be linked to Him.   It is only thus that a sermon becomes living, personal, and not merely intellectual
and abstract.   Truth is always to be associated with Christ;
'Truth as in Jesus.'   And our ethics must always be associated
with His love, His grace, His spirit.   It is only in the presence
and power of Christ that our sermons and addresses, however
orthodox, will kindle spiritual fire in the soul.   In the fine
articles in the *Britsh Weekly,* in which Ian Maclaren reviewed
his ministry shortly after his resignation of his Liverpool
church, we read the following:—

'I now clearly see every sentence should suggest Christ, and every
sermon, even though His Name had not been mentioned nor His words
quoted, should leave the hearer at the feet of Christ.  In Christ there

is an irresistible charm; without Him the sermon may have beauty, it will not have fragrance. With Christ every one is satisfied, although men may differ widely about Christian creeds and Christian customs. After Him every human soul is feeling, and in Him alone all human souls meet. As it now appears to me, the chief effort of every sermon should be to unveil Christ, and the chief art of the preacher to conceal himself.'

## II. *Every Preacher should have a Clear Message.*

By this is meant a portion of Divine truth, selected, prepared, and delivered under the guidance and in the power of the Holy Spirit, and adapted to present needs. Unless there is some definite truth from God for those to whom we speak, the sermon will fail of its distinctive purpose. A story is related of a Scottish minister who was given to weeping during the delivery of his sermons. A visitor had been a worshipper in his church on one occasion, and observing the minister crying, inquired of a member of the congregation the cause of the tears. The whispered reply was, 'If ye was standin' up there, and had as little to say as he has, ye wid greet yersel'.' The message must be clear first of all in the preacher's mind, and then clearly expressed on the preacher's lips. Otherwise it will never be clear to the hearers.

## III. *Every Preacher should have a Definite Aim.*

Knowledge is not an end but only a means in preaching. Herein lies the difference between the essay and the sermon. We have to convince the intellct, to stir the heart, to quicken the conscience, and to move the will. Matthew Arnold's well known phrase, 'Light and leading,' aptly expresses what sermons ought to be. Sermons are intended to lead as well as to illuminate. Cicero said that the be-all and end-all of eloquence is *actio*.

What then is our aim in sermon work? It has always one or more of these three ends. (1) Salvation; personal and present; (2) Sanctification; full and constant; (3) Service; hearty and devoted. Under these three aspects of Christian teaching, perhaps the aim of every sermon can be put. They should be ever in view, and we must never rest content in ideas, however interesting, true, or important. It is recorded of a French doctor that he performed a certain surgical operation a great many times, while an English doctor had only performed it on eight occasions. The Frenchman was asked how many lives he had saved. He replied, 'None, but then the operation was so brilliant.' The Englishman saved seven out of the eight. All the brilliance of our sermons will count for nothing unless we are enabled to 'save some.' A Briton and a Boer went out shooting deer for food. The Briton took a case of cartridges with him, the Boer only took one. 'Why,' asked the Briton, 'do you only take one cartridge?' 'Because,' was the reply, 'I only want one deer.'

It is this definiteness of aim which gives point to such phrases as 'a word in season' (Isa. 50: 4); 'food in due season' (Luke 12: 42); 'present truth' (2 Peter 1: 12). In an article which appeared in the *Sunday School Chronicle* some time ago, the following words seemed to go to the heart of the problem:—

'An ignorant man may draw great draughts of spiritual strength from the higher life, when a more mentally alert man may be spiritually meagre and barren. Why? Because the mind, wholly absorbed in its ideas, is not tuned to the Infinite. The freer and humbler soul expects to meet the Saviour, is conscious of His nearness, speaks as in His presence. It is not that the full mind is any hindrance; far from that. It is the mind averted from Christ, or the mind wholly occupied in its own processes, that fails to bless.'

One point in particular may perhaps receive special notice. It has been said that there are few lives into which some shadows or sorrows have not come, and that for this reason the message of comfort, which means in the true sense of that old word, an inspiration to strength, courage, and consolation, should not be often away from our messages. To quote Ian Maclaren again:—

'The review of the past has convinced me that while preaching has various ends, the chief ought to be comfort. It is useful in its way to explain the construction of the Book of Isaiah, and to give the history of Hebrew literature, but it is better to minister the consolation of Isaiah's fifty-third chapter to the weary heart. The critical movement has not only affected students in their studies, but also preachers in their pulpits; and while I have ever pled for full liberty in criticism, and have used that liberty myself, I am free to acknowledge that I would have done more good if I had been less critical and more evangelical. And by evangelical I mean more heartening and more comforting. People are interested in an expository discourse; they are lifted by a consolatory discourse. Life we may take for granted is hard enough for every hearer, and every man is carrying his own burden. My conclusions on this point are (and I offer them with confidence to younger men) that the people appreciate literature in your style but do not desire literature for your subject, and that while they do not undervalue information on the Bible, they are ten thousand times more grateful for the inspiration of the Book, and that our preaching should be more according to the words of Isaiah, "Comfort ye, comfort ye, my people, speak ye comfortably to Jerusalem." '

## IV.   *Every Preacher should occupy a Right Attitude.*

It is very helpful to observe the various names given to the preacher in the New Testament. He is a 'herald' (1 Tim. 2: 7); an 'ambassador' (2 Cor. 5: 20); an 'evangelist' (2 Tim. 4: 5); a 'witness' (Acts 1: 8); a 'teacher' (1 Tim. 2: 7); a 'prophet' (Eph. 4: 11); and an 'encourager' (παρακαλέω, 2 Cor. 6: 1). When the Apostle uses the words, 'we beseech you,' we readily enter into his spirit as he endeavoured to present his Master to others. He also uses three words in 1 Corinthians 14: 3 which need careful study by all preachers: Consolation, Edification, Exhortation, thereby appealing respectively to the feeling, the intellect, and the will. When we gather together the aspects of truth underlying all these titles of the preacher, we realize that he should be a man of convinction, a man of sincerity, a man of sympathy, and a man of authority.

## V.   *Every Preacher should employ True Methods.*

Here again the New Testament will be our best and safest guide. When we study 'the preaching of the blessed Apostle Paul,' we cannot fail to notice the various words that he uses in connexion with his message. Thus we read of him as follows: 'Opening and alleging that it was necessary for the Messiah to suffer, and to be raised from the dead, and that this Jesus is the Messiah, Whom I proclaim to you.' 'Opening,' 'alleging,' 'proclaiming.' He expounded the Scriptures, he placed the truth carefully before them, and proclaimed the Person of his Master as the fulfillment of the Old Testament prophecies. In his work at Corinth another word is used. 'He reasoned in the synagogue every Sabbath, and persuaded Jews and Greeks (Acts 18: 4). 'Reasoning, 'persuading.' Thus he appealed to mind, heart, and will. In Rome, we are told that he preached the kingdom of God, and taught the things concerning the Lord Jesus Christ with all boldness (Acts 28: 31). 'Heralding,' 'teaching.' Here are the two aspects of the preacher's work; announcing his Master 'to them that are without,' and instructing believers in Christ. At Colosse we learn yet another method of the Apostle, for we read of him 'admonishing and teaching every man in all wisdom' (Col. 1: 28). The admonition was for warning and the teaching was for instruction; the two sides of Christian teaching. The minister must be Salt and Light.

But the finest method of all is that of the Perfect Teacher, as illustrated for us in His dealings with the Woman of Samaria. That chapter should be pondered again and again by every Christian preacher who desires to know the deepest secrets of winning the soul for Christ. We observe that our Lord took four steps towards the possession of that life. (1) He first attracted her *heart* by asking for a draught of water, and thereby predisposing her to listen without prejudice to anything else He might have to say. (2) He then arrested her *mind* by giving her food for thought as to the living water and the difference between that and the water in the well. (3) When the woman's interest was aroused, and her desire stirred to ask for the living water, our Lord made his searching appeal to her *conscience* by telling her to go and call her husband. When the woman fenced with this awkward and unwelcome inquiry, and endeavoured to divert attention to a religious custom on the merits of Jerusalem and Samaria, our Lord kept her to the point and insisted on the necessity of spiritual reality and no mere locality in worship. (4) Then at length when the poor soul was broken down, unable to make any further resistance, our Lord assured her *soul* by the present and personal revelation of Himself as the Messiah. The very truth that was hidden from the Jews and refused by our Lord to them. was given gladly to this weary, convicted sinner, who so badly needed Him and His grace. Heart, mind, conscience, soul; to these four elements of human nature every sermon should make an appeal. Probably the subject will from time to time lead to more stress being laid on one or other of the elements, but not one of them must be out of sight in any sermon that can be called really Christian.

It is not to be supposed that these five qualities—a dominant theme, a clear message, a definite aim, a right attitude, a true method—exhaust all the essential features of a sermon, but at any rate it may be fairly said that, given these requirements, God's blessing cannot fail to follow the word preached.

## SECTION 9. DELIVERY.

The intellectual and spiritual preparation of the sermon, though very important, is not everything, for the finest material will fail unless it is properly delivered. Public speech is intended to be effective, which means that it must effect something as a means to an end. What then are the elements necessary for the effective delivery of a well-prepared sermon?

1. The Spirit of the delivery needs attention, first of all. It goes without saying that the speaker should be in earnest, for without this all else counts for nothing. He should also be fearless. Nothing mars a sermon so much as a hesitating or nervous delivery, as though the preacher was not at all sure of the truth of his own words. All the great prophets of the ages have been men of courage, and they never feared the face of man as they declared the message of God.

> 'Oh! a glorious gift is prudence,
>  And they are useful friends
> Who never make beginnings
>  But where they see the ends.

> But give us now and then a man,
>   That we may crown him king,
> Who just will scorn the consequence,
>   And just will do the thing.'

But the fearlesslessness must be blended with tenderness. However courageous a man may be. his fearlessness alone may suggest severity and a disregard of the feelings of his audience. He must blend tenderness with his courage if he is to be an effective speaker.  Then with earnestness, clearness, fearlessness, and tenderness, happily harmonized and blended, he must pour over it all a spirit of trustfulness.  His message is not his own but his Master's, and he must so deliver it as to feel and let other people feel that he looks to God for the blessing and the power.

2.  The Manner of the delivery comes next, and it will be in the manner that the spirit is very largely expressed. The following elements seem essential to all true speaking:—

(*a*)  The preacher must be humble and not self-assertive.

(*b*)  He must be bright and yet not light.

(*c*)  He must be winsome without undue expression of feeling, or overflow of emotion.  Any such excess of feeling is apt to be attributed to what, for want of better words, may be described as 'gush' or 'oiliness.'

(*d*)  He must be reverent, as befitting his theme.

(*e*)  He must be natural in gesture.  Everything about his movements should be seen to be spontaneous and free, not studied and artificial.

3.  The Voice calls for special attention.

(*a*)  The utterance should of course be distinct; enunciation good, with vowels and consonants properly pronounced. The old rule cannot be too often emphasized: 'Use your lips and spare your throat.'·

(*b*)  The expression should be correct.  While it may be inevitable that the preacher should have certain indications of the locality from which he comes in the accent that he puts upon words, yet his speech should be free from all vulgarisms.

(*c*) The pitch of the preacher's voice should be varied, and he should take special care not to be too loud to be heard. If Milton can speak of that which is 'dark with excess of light,' it is only too possible for a man to speak so loudly that he cannot possibly be heard by his audience.

(*d*) The tone should of course be sympathetic, possessing and expressing a personal quality without which all the orthodox doctrine and all the literary grace will count for very little.

4. The Method of delivery is one that admits of more difference of opinion. Shall we read, or shall we speak? If the sermon is read, the manuscript ought to be thoroughly known, so that the preacher may be as free from it as possible. To this end it should be clearly written, so that there may be no hesitation in the course of reading. If the sermon is spoken rather than read, the manuscript should first of all be analyzed into notes which can be placed in the preacher's Bible, or else he should dispense with notes altogether, which he will find far the better plan. The one thing to be avoided is *memoriter* preaching, unless it be felt necessary to memorize the beginning and the ending. This method of preaching will prove burdensome to those who adopt it, and will almost certainly tend to artificiality and lifelessness, for the man will be constantly thinking of what is coming next, and be attending to his memory rather than to his message and his people. Great preachers, like Chalmers, have read their sermons, but most of the outstanding preachers favour the spoken utterance. The value of the written sermon lies in the clearness of thought, the precision of language, the balance of treatment thus afforded, together with the permanent use that can be made of the manuscript. And yet, however well a man may read his sermon, he cannot be so sensitive to the needs of the congregation, and his delivery will be hindered to some extent. Canon Liddon's method in St. Paul's was the perfection of reading, and yet hearers could not help being conscious that the sermon was being read. The advantage of the spoken sermon is that it gives ease and vigour of style, affords an opportunity of the expression of the personal element, and leaves the whole man free to bring

himself and his message to bear upon the people. And the disadvantages are that it tends to diffuseness, to occasional superficiality, to inaccuracy of speech and to disproportion of treatment. For those who think that preaching without notes is an utter impossibility, the careful study of Dr. R. S. Storr's *Preaching without Notes* may be warmly commended, while a similar work dealing almost entirely with extemporaneous preaching is *The Use of the Eyes in Preaching*, by Neville.

5. The Aim of the sermon should be kept in view all through the delivery. The preacher has a definite object and it should never be overlooked. As we have seen when considering the preparation, he is concerned not only for the presentation of truth, but for its acceptance and practical use. In the course of delivery this aim should be constantly before us.

6. The Rules of delivery are few but important. They may be summed up by saying that all speech should be in the key of 'B natural.' The speaker should be himself and his best self. There is much to be said for the old familiar advice; 'Begin low, go slow, rise higher, take fire, wax warm, sit down in a storm.' At any rate there is sufficient truth in the suggestions to enable us to see what is required. Some years ago the Dean of Canterbury, in presiding at a meeting where the speakers were limited to ten minutes each, gave them three pieces of advice which he had read in a German periodical. He first read the German and then gave his audience the terse, colloquial English rendering: 'Stand up; speak up; shut up.' Mr. W. T. Stead offered some practical counsel to public speakers which is well worth passing on :—

1. Never speak without having something to say. 2. Always sit down when you have said it. 3. Remember speech is dumb show when it is not audible. 4. Think definitely, pronounce clearly, stand naturally, and do not speak too fast. 5. Welcome articulate interruption, no matter how hostile. 6. Two things should never be lost— your temper and the thread of your discourse. 7. Remember that the eyes are as eloquent as the tongue. 8. Never hesitate to let yourself go, at the right time. 9. Never read your speech, but always

have heads of discourse handy. And never forget Cardinal Manning's words of wisdom to myself: "Be full of your subject and forget yourself." '

A layman once asked the pertinent question why most of the sermons to which he had listened had been forgotten? He attributed it to the bad delivery, because while the theology and erudition were all that was desirable, the men who spoke were so devoid of the art of public speaking as to leave their words wasted and worthless. The first duty of a preacher, he urged, is to make himself heard, and the second to be impressive and convincing. And he actually advocated the rule that every minister should pass an examination before being allowed to mount a pulpit, because 'a bad preacher will empty a Church more quickly than a good preacher will fill one.'

SECTION 10.  SERMONS TO DIFFERENT SECTIONS.

While the main principles of preaching apply to all sermons, it is useful, if not essential, that a preacher should study as carefully as possible the art of 'putting things' before particular classes and sections of his congregation. A few illustrations may indicate what is meant.

I.  *Sermons to Children.*

This is a kind of work which is well worth cultivating, however great the trouble. What should be the characteristics of a sermon to children?

1. It should be short. Fifteen minutes will be quite long enough.

2. It should be straight. The lessons should be definite and not too numerous. Perhaps two points will be ample, though one carefully stated and elaborated might be found better.

3. It should be simple. By this is to be understood that it is child-like, not childish. Language for children must necessarily be simple, or else it will fail of its purpose. We once heard a speaker warning children of from one to

twelve against 'compromising their position.' A preacher once asked a number of children to tell him the meaning of the word 'analysis.' Silence reigned supreme after the question was asked, and the preacher was compelled to give the answer himself. He said that analysis was 'synonymous with synopsis.' On another occasion, at a large Children's Service, the preacher beamed upon his young flock and said benignly that the scene before him was 'one of unparalleled sublimity.' It was soon one of unparalleled restlessness. And at yet another children's gathering the clergyman, in appealing for gifts to send Bibles to children in India, told the boys and girls that of course the Bibles would be in the 'vernacular.' It was a pity he did not himself use the 'vernacular' on that occasion.

4. It should be illustrated. The illustrations or anecdotes used for children need the greatest possible care.

(*a*) They should be true, or else parabolic. Preachers must beware of using any anecdote about which they are at all uncertain. Moral honesty is absolutely required on this point.

(*b*) The illustrations should be *ad rem*, or else they will fail of their purpose.

(*c*) They should not be overloaded with detail or else their object will be lost.

(*d*) The moral should not always be kept to the end, but either introduced elsewhere, or perhaps left to the application of the children. It is a well-known fact that children are only too quick to see the application of what is being told them. Some years a well-known Scottish preacher was addressing a large gathering of boys in Glasgow, and after telling them an interesting story, he said, 'Now boys, the moral of this is,' when a young ragamuffin cried out, 'Never mind the moral, sir, gi'e us another story.'

Object Lessons are a source of perennial interest to children. A lead pencil, a house, a penny, are but a few out of many such objects that can be utilizated to convey spiritual truths. At the same time it will need a fair amount of masculine common sense to avoid a misuse of objects for moralizing purposes.

Preachers to children cannot do better than study the sermons and addresses of those who have been specially used of God in this work. Perhaps to this day there are no volumes to compare with those books of sermons well known thirty years ago, by Dr. Richard Newton of Philadelphia. Some of us were almost brought up on such admirable books as *Rills from the Fountain of Life*, *Bible Jewels*, and many others which are full of fine illustrations and admirable methods.

## II. *Sermons to Men.*

This is a day of special services and classes for men, and there are few clergymen who do not desire to be of service to the men of their flock. A clerical friend, in arguing for the fundamental importance of work among men rather than among children had a great deal to say for himself and his position, for most assuredly if we can lay hold of the men we go far to lay hold of their children at the same time. It is only possible in our space to make a few simple suggestions on this subject, and we must refer our readers to books that deal specially with the subject. Preachers should not think that Men's Meetings always need to be addressed on the subjects of Gambling, Intemperance, and Purity. While these three subjects are important and essential there are many other topics of equal importance and definite bearing for the manhood of our land. For a long time it was my happy privilege to conduct a weekly men's service in a London parish, and there were very few Biblical subjects which could not be adapted and applied to men. We should not shrink from teaching as well as preaching, and personal appeal. Men need instruction as well as inspiration and invitation, and if the same men are in the habit of coming to a meeting week by week the need of teaching is all the more imperative. They will value it and will rejoice in the opportunity of hearing modern topics and Biblical truths put in such a way as to appeal to their intelligence.

to men (1) Thought; we must give the men something to think about. (2) Sympathy; we must express our thought
Three characteristics seem to be required in all addresses

in terms of brotherly sympathy. (3) Directness; and we must make a definite appeal to the men to accept our thought and to live it day by day. Above all, our addresses to men should invariably be concerned with the Lord Jesus Christ as a Saviour and a Master as well as a Teacher and an Example. It is all very interesting and useful to speak of the 'Ideal Man,' and to preach the Christian ethic, but men also need the Christian dynamic, and this is only possible as they receive into their heart and life a personal Saviour, a personal Friend, and a personal Lord. Once again, let it be said that work for men only will be found among the most fruitful methods of genuine service in any parish.

III. *Sermons to Boys.*

In some respects this is perhaps the hardest of all preaching, because it is so difficult to define and express what precise religious experience ought to be expected from boys. We are so apt to read back into our boyhood the spiritual experiences of maturer age, that we find it almost impossible to set due limits on what is to be regarded as the religion of boyhood. One thing is perfectly certain in all preaching to boys: we must be manly. While we are good, we must not be 'goody-goody.' Here again, it is essential to make a personal and present Christ a reality to boys, and in particular to emphasize Divine grace as a present power. We are apt to preach an ideal which they are to realize in the future when they become men, and the result of this is that we may lose them during that terribly difficult period from thirteen to seventeen, when boys as well as girls are 'where the brook and river meet.' The only way to overcome this difficulty is to lay the greatest possible stress upon the Lord Jesus Christ as the present Saviour of boyhood, and the gift of the Holy Spirit as the present and momentary secret of victory over sin, and holiness of heart and life. Mr. Arthur C. Benson has some fine suggestions in his *Upton Letters* on Preaching to Boys. He pleads for homeliness, simplicity, directness, shrewdness, and incisiveness. He thinks that holiness, saintliness, and piety are virtues which are foreign to the character of boys and the ideas often imply sanctimoniousness and hypocrisy. There is sufficient truth in this to make us very careful about our ideal and our actual holiness which we present to boys. Mr. Benson is only too correct when he deprecates for boys what he calls 'feminine religion; a religion of sainted choir boys and exemplary death-beds.' All these dangers can be avoided if Christ is a living reality to the preacher, and if the preacher is able to recommend his Master by that godliness and manliness which finds expression in that highest of all Bible descriptions, 'a man of God.'

## IV.  *Evidential Sermons.*

This class of sermon will of necessity be only occasionally preached. It appeals to very few, and many of the congregation will probably prefer not to have doubts and difficulties brought before them. Christian evidence work is usually best done in connexion with Bible and other similar classes, but from time to time evidential sermons in Church will be of use, if only to show that the preacher is in touch with the times and is not afraid of difficulties. The supreme need in every evidential sermon is to link on the subject to personal contact with the living Christ. Discussions of Christian evidences are only too apt to be merely intellectual and abstract, and while the preacher may obtain an intellectual and logical victory and convince the minds of his hearers, he may fail to lead them on to the acceptance of Christ as their Saviour.

## V.  *Pastoral Sermons.*

This aspect of preaching will necessarily form a prominent part of the work of the settled pastorate. The ministry to believers occupies an important place in the New Testament, because of the purpose of God for the life of every Christian. The ascended Lord is said to have bestowed the gifts of ministry for a very specific purpose, and when we read that purpose in the Greek we see the first importance of a pastoral ministry, 'for the perfecting of the saints, unto the work of ministering, unto the edifying of the body of Christ. (R. V.)' That is to say, ministerial gifts are in-

tended to 'perfect' or 'adjust' the saints, that they in turn may
do the work of ministering, and thereby help forward the up-
building of the Church, the Body of Christ. It will therefore always be an essential part of ministerial preaching, so
to teach and train Christians that they may become evangelists
and workers for Christ. The New Testament lays the greatest possible stress on 'edification.' Everything in the Christian
Church, Scripture, worship, sacraments, and work, is intended
in some way or other to promote 'edification.'

## VI. *Evangelistic Sermons.*

Although these have been kept to the last for fuller consideration, they are by no means least in importance, and it is
probably true to say that evangelistic sermons are never more
required than in the settled ministry of an ordinary pastorate.
During the last few years it would seem as though God has
been teaching His people to depend less and less upon special
Mission Services, and to make more and more of the ordinary
ministry for the purpose of evangelization. While it is possibly too much to say that every minister should be his own
evangelist, since spiritual gifts are diverse and distinct in the
New Testament, there is sufficient truth in the statement to
lead every clergyman to ask himself how far he has endeavoured not only to build up the Body of Christ, but to 'do
the work of an evangelist.' Some time ago a friend told me
that he had been for nearly a year in regular attendance at an
Evangelical Church where the preaching to Christians was
everything that could be desired, spiritual, strong, fresh, and
Biblical; and yet during the whole of that period he had
never once heard a sermon to the unconverted, or any appeal
to the hearers to accept Christ. And yet there must be in
every congregation a large number of people who have never
yet really accepted Christ for themselves. They have been
brought up as regular Church-goers, they are interested in
Christian truth, and all the while they may be without a personal share in spiritual blessings. It is for such as these that
evangelistic sermons should from time to time be attempted.
What are some of the elements of ordinary evangelistic
work?

1.   A clergyman should not fail to teach what our fore-fathers called the three R's: Ruin by the Fall; Redemption by the Blood; Regeneration by the Spirit.   If these notes are lacking in our preaching we shall never be evangelists.

2.   We must not hesitate to divide our people into two classes: the Saved and the Unsaved.   It is not for us to go beyond this and differentiate, but we must insist upon the fact that in every congregation these two classes are represented, and, as such, are known to God.

3.   We must take care to offer Christ for present accept-ance.   It is unwise, and may even be dangerous, to advise peo-ple to 'go home and think about it.'   Moody once did this in Chicago, and that very night the great fire burst out.   The people never had the opportunity of coming back to hear him the next Sunday, and he himself said that from that time for-ward he never advised people to go home and think about it. We must press Christ upon our hearers for present accept-ance.

4.   Whenever we feel led to have after-meetings we must beware of any stereotyped plan.   Let us trust the Holy Spirit more than we do sometimes, and let us believe more firmly in the power of the Spirit to bless and use the Word preached. Variety of method in the conduct of after-meetings is es-sential.

(a) Sometimes while people are on their knees we may give them the opportunity for silently surrendering to Christ, and then after a moment or two of silence close the meeting.

(b) We may lead them verbally and audibly in prayer, as appropriate to our theme; and then after a moment's pause bring the gathering to a conclusion.

(c) Sometimes, though perhaps very occasionally, we may give an invitation to people to stand, or to raise the right arm as an indication of their wish and willingness to accept Christ. But this method, as it is the most common, is perhaps the least trustworthy, because the people who ought to stand often do not do so.

(d) I have personally found one method of great value as a change.   It is the suggestion that the people should take with the preacher the following steps, on each of which a few words of comment and appeal, as they are kneeling, should be made. (1) I must; (2) I can; (3) I may; (4) I will; (5) I do.

These are but bare suggestions, such as can alone be included in our present space. But they may serve to show the supreme importance of these phases of ministerial work. Dr. A. T. Pierson's admirable book, *Evangelistic Work*, should be pondered by all who wish to 'do the work of an evangelist.' And some words which were uttered not long ago deserve to be written in letters of gold over every preacher's desk: 'Preaching which is not evangelistic will soon cease to be evangelical.'

### SECTION 11. MATERIALS FOR SERMONS.

It has become proverbial that we cannot make bricks without straw, and all the foregoing references to preparation and delivery have necessarily presupposed the provision, possession and use of adequate materials for the work of the pulpit. It is to the acquisition and preservation of these materials that we must now address ourselves.

### I. *Materials Gathered.*

What are the main channels through which a clergyman may fairly expect to obtain the necessary materials for use in sermons?

1. First, and most important of all must come his own study of the Bible. Nothing can make up for this, whether we think of intellectual consistency or spiritual force. Dr. Maclaren once told a gathering that he owed everything to his study day by day of a chapter in the Hebrew and a chapter in the Greek. No ministerial life can ever be satisfactory, and no ministerial work will ever be properly performed unless there is this constant, definite, first-hand, thorough study of the Bible. Our methods of study will vary from time to time, but it will prove useful to have some system and order year by year. If, for instance, on our return from our summer holiday we determine to take up some book of the Bible,

whether Old or New Testament, and give it all the attention in our power, we shall soon find how it will enrich our mind, widen our outlook, and stimulate our spiritual life. The greatest and most acceptable preachers of all ages have been men who through personal study have become 'mighty in the Scriptures.'

2. A study of the best Commentaries will prove fruitful in connexion with sermons. One of these should always be on hand. Emphasis is laid on the 'best,' which means those that help us to understand most thoroughly the text of our Bible. Who that has worked through a volume of Lightfoot, or Westcott, or Plummer, or Swete, or Armitage Robinson, or Vaughan, or Ellicott, will ever feel other than profoundly thankful for the ripe scholarship and deep experience which enable the student to see the force of word, and tense, and phrase, and to get at the very heart of the Divine meaning? Any one of these Commentaries, with their minute, accurate exegesis, is an education to a clergyman.

3. The best books of theology should also receive attention. As a rule, dogmatic theology is thought to be uncommonly dry, uninteresting, and abstract, but this cannot be said of some of our modern works on the subject. It is impossible to do more than mention a few by way of illustration, but it would be possible to feel deeply sorry for the man who found no interest in Denney's *Death of Christ,* and *Studies in Theology;* Dale's *Christian Doctrine;* Liddon's *Divinity of Our Lord;* W. N. Clarke's *Outlines of Christian Theology;* W. A. Brown's *Christian Theology in Outline;* and not least, Litton's two great works, *Introduction to Dogmatic Theology,* and *The Church of Christ.* Such books as these will put iron into our convictions as well as give freshness to our theological outlook. We are not to be supposed to endorse everything that may be found in these books. They are only mentioned as illustrations of what can be read and should be read by every clergyman.

4. The best books of devotion will occupy an important part in our ministerial life. Sermons, as we have seen, can never be wholly intellectual. 'It is the heart that makes the theologian,' and it is the heart that will make the preacher.

By 'best' in relation to devotion, we mean books that will suggest thought as well as stimulate to meditation. It is a great mistake to think there is any incompatibility between earnest thought and earnest devotion. Books like those of the late Dr. George Matheson will show what is meant. We shall probably find ourselves disagreeing with Matheson's interpretations again and again, but they compel us to think, and this is a great virtue in any book. An author of an equally helpful kind, and always true to the cardinal points of New Testament teaching, is the Rev. W. M. Clow, whose *The Cross in Christian Experience*, *The Secret of the Lord* and, *The Day of the Cross*, will rejoice and inspire the heart of every one who reads them.

5. The best volumes of sermons must not be overlooked. Of course there is danger here, especially if a man has an assimilative mind and a retentive memory, but he must resist the temptation to incorporate unduly, because of the absolute necessity of studying the finest possible models of sermon work. For this, I put Alexander Maclaren high above every one else, past and present. For a combination of gifts; exegetical insight, homiletical power, spiritual insight, illustrative fertility, and literary grace, I do not know of any preacher to equal him. Not far short of Maclaren is Dr. J. H. Jowett, any of whose volumes will be found abundantly helpful to preachers. From another point of view, the volumes by Dr. W. L. Watkinson will be found truly helpful for their suggestive thought, their acute analysis, and above all for their wealth of apt illustration. I took the trouble once to make an index of all the illustrations in one of Dr. Watkinson's books, and was astonished to find how much space was needed for it. Dr. Joseph Parker and Bishop Phillips Brooks will also prove a mine of wealth to the preacher, nor will it be time wasted to give attention to some of the more important of the Puritans, like Howe, Owen, and Goodwin. Even though their style may be regarded as heavy, their insight into Divine truth and their marvellous facility for homiletic analysis cannot help being of value to a preacher. Dr. Alexander Whyte is never tired of speaking of Thomas Goodwin as still our greatest commentator on St. Paul. Vol-

umes of sermons, though helpful to read, are not as a rule so useful in providing materials of expository and homiletic suggestion. But of course every man will naturally favour this or that preacher, according to his own mental and spiritual temperament. The names now mentioned are simply offered as the testimony of one who has found their work abundantly helpful to mind and heart.

6. Books of sermon outlines will, if studied, have to be used with the greatest possible care. It is always valuable to see how another man treats his subject, but intellectual honesty must be kept constantly in view, or else we shall have to preface some of our sermons, or some of our sermon outlines with: 'Alas! Master, for it was borrowed.'

It is believed that by means of these channels every preacher will be able to provide himself with ample material for all the sermons of the longest ministry. Once again let it be said that the first of these channels, the personal study of the Bible, must be kept paramount, and every other method made strictly subservient to it.

## II. *Materials Stored.*

It is one thing to amass materials, it is quite another to keep them in so convenient a form that we may be able to avail ourselves of their help even after some period of time. Many a man has read, and noted what he has read, and yet has not been able at the 'psychological moment' to find the material through a lack of method or system for storing the results of his reading. What then are we to do? The following suggestions are made as the result of a good deal of personal experience and not a little outlay of money in order to arrive at some practical results. If only beginners are warned against the mistakes and failures of the writer, the suggestions will not have been in vain.

1. A minister should index his books. This at first may seem somewhat remote from the present subject, but in reality it has a definite and practical bearing on it. The card-index system is in every way the best, and even though a man may only have a few books there is no reason why he should not

commence the work of indexing at once. A few cards with a small tray to hold them will suffice for a start. The books should be indexed under three heads, Author, Title, and Subject; and there is no reason why all three should not be kept together in one tray in alphabetical order. The use of the guide cards will help to find readily what is required. The young clergyman who is only just commencing his library should not think this work of indexing unnecessary until he obtain a larger number of books. If he commences the work at once, and then adds to it as his books increase, it will be no labour, and the results will prove their value all through his ministry.

2.   Then he should commence a series of cards on which he enters under the appropriate texts anything that he may read from time to time. This series of cards should be kept in Bible order, and as anything is read it should be placed on the cards. In process of time it will be found that everything a man has in his study will be available for reference by means of this index. Thus, if he feels led, say, to preach on the subject of Genesis 28, or any verse in that chapter, he turns to his card under Genesis, and the whole available material will be found ready for reference. It is impossible to exaggerate the importance of this method of recording the results of our reading and study.

3.   A notebook for extracts is also very necessary. There are books and magazines belonging to other people which we read from time to time, and from these we are often desirous of making extracts. In the old days this was done by means of a familiar book known as the *Index Rerum,* which was a manuscript book divided up according to the letters of the alphabet, with so many pages assigned to each letter, but this does not prove convenient, for the simple yet adequate reason that it is impossible to say beforehand precisely how many pages will be required for a particular letter. The result is that in many cases we have too many pages for one letter and too few for another. The only possible note-book for these extracts is one which has an alphabetical index in front, and then pages which are, or can be, numbered. The result is that if we read anything on Temperance, we can put it on

page 1, and then index it under T, and if afterwards we read anything on the Atonement we can put it on page 2, so long as we index it under A.

4. The question of newspaper cuttings is one of the greatest problems of a clergyman's life. After putting several methods to the test and rejecting them for one or other reasons, the conclusion has been forced upon me that the only real way to preserve these helps in a conveniently available form is by means of what is known as the Envelope system. A number of large-sized manilla envelopes should be obtained, and the subject of the cutting put outside. If these envelopes are kept in alphabetical order, and from time to time a fuller and more detailed index is made of subjects which allow of various departments, or aspects, it will be found that the cuttings are ready for use, as they are in no other system.

5. The preservation of sermons which are reported in newspapers is also of value. From time to time our weekly papers and monthly magazines contain sermons by leading preachers which are not always available afterwards in book form, and many a suggestion for study and preaching will be found in this way. The best method of preserving is again the envelope system, or else by means of cardboard boxes with springs for holding the papers as in a file. These envelopes, or boxes, should be arranged in the order of the books of the Bible, for this will be found in every way the easiest and most convenient plan for reference.

6. The preservation of pamphlets is also not to be disregarded. There is much material available to-day in booklet and pamphlet form which will be of true service to a clergyman.

7. It is difficult to describe the method of storing which we have purposely left to the last. From time to time in our reading and study we have suggestions both of texts and subjects for sermons. What are we to do with them? By some preachers these hints are recorded in commonplace books which are looked over from time to time, added to, and then in due course used. But the trouble is that there is no system in the paging of such a book, and an important topic may easily be overlooked and lost. We have therefore found

again by definite experience that the best way of preserving this material is by using a filing cabinet containing pieces of glossy manilla paper, 9 inches by 5, indexed in the order of the books of the Bible. When ever an idea or a subject presents itself, one of these pieces of paper is taken, the notes jotted down, and the paper inserted in the proper place under the text which it is proposed to treat. These papers can be looked over from time to time, and as the result of that process known as 'unconscious cerebration,' the materials can be added to and developed. Then when the time comes for a sermon to be prepared on any of the topics, the rough paper is naturally torn up, because there is no further use for it. This provides against the trouble and inconvenience of having a note-book in which the pages still remain, even after the material is used. Sometimes this method of storing sermon-material is called the 'stock pot.' In certain housekeeping arrangements we believe that such a receptacle is of the greatest importance, and the additions to it go to provide the foundation of the soups that are served from day to day. A clergyman will find these notes a veritable 'stock-pot,' for they will hold him in good stead on many an occasion when he finds his mental powers tending to droop, and in need of some fillip from other days and other men.

### Section 12.   open-air preaching.

No one can question the splendid possibilities of open-air preaching. It affords an occasion of testimony for Christ to many who never enter a place of worship. Every Church should make the most of this opportunity by suspending indoor week-evening meetings during the summer months. There might easily be at least three open-air meetings each week; one on Sunday, and two on the week-day evenings. To those who are responsible for the management of open-air work the following considerations may be commended.

### I. *Carefulness.*

All the arrangements should be thought out and planned with care. The music should if possible be a special feature, though it should never be forgotten that many open-air gatherings are held without much, if any, singing. Still, when singing is available there is no doubt as to the value of the help; and while the music is never elaborate it should always be good. The accompanist should know his tune-book thoroughly, and the choir, even though small, should be as efficient as it can be made. A platform (not a chair) for the speaker should be used if practicable; it gives a vantage ground that will prove distinctly helpful. An arrangement can be made for utilizing the platform as a box for the harmonium and hymn books.

## II. *Thoroughness.*

It is fatal to think that anything will do for open-air speaking. On the contrary the very best is absolutely essential. Those who are called upon to speak at these meetings should be urged to prepare thoroughly, and to give the people that which is really worth hearing. A definite message of God's truth well steeped with the elements of reason and persuasion should characterize every open-air address. Of course a simple personal testimony to the grace of God is quite different. If any workers should be found to have rambled on without any special point in their address, they should not be asked to speak again unless they are willing to put some preparation into their messages.

## III. *Shortness.*

All prayers should be short. Passages of Scripture read should be short, addresses should be brief, and hymns should not be too prolonged. Twelve or fifteen minutes will be found enough for an address as a rule, because it is not so easy to hold an audience in the open air as indoors. The best speakers are always the shortest, and those who have the least to say generally take the longest time to say it.

## IV. *Naturalness.*

As a rule, it will be found helpful not to announce the text as though it were a sermon, but instead to plunge in at once by some illustration or incident.  Indeed, it will be wise to make the address as unlike an ordinary sermon as possible. The speaker should not shout, but allow his voice to sound at the usual pitch.  Penetration, not volume, is what is really required.  Of course the speaker will have to dispense with all notes and deliver his message purely extemporary.  Anything else would be fatal, for the attention of the audience would not be held.

## V.  *Definiteness.*

The one aim of open-air work is to win men for Christ, and everything must be strictly subordinated to this purpose. Speakers should not range from North to South, still less endeavour to give the Christian system of doctrine complete in one address.  One point driven home, or at most two points, will usually be found enough.  The arrow must be sent home, pointed, barbed, and ready for use by the Holy Spirit.

## VI.  *Earnestness.*

A speaker in the open air should be cheerful and yet serious, with no attempt at cheap wit, or unworthy humour.  If a man feels led to preach on the dark side of God's truth, and refer to the future consequences of sin, he must pray to be faithful without being stern, to appeal rather than to denounce, to be loving and not hard.  The issues at stake are so serious that a man needs much grace and wisdom from on high to say the right thing in the right way.

## VII.  *Tactfulness.*

There is scarcely any form of Christian work in which the leader needs 'sanctified common sense' so much and so often as in open-air preaching.  When the crowd has gathered it is not wise to continue the singing of a hymn, but to stop at once and go on with the preaching.  If the crowd should show any indication of moving the speaker should be ready to close at once, ready with his application to drive home the message immediately.  If any opposition should arise it will need to be dealt with wisely and firmly. Ordinarily, however, it will be found in every way wise to ask the objecter to speak privately after the meeting in order that the point raised may be discussed. Workers should not be allowed to do anything in the way of tract distribution or personal appeal during an address. All this should be done either during the singing of a hymn, if opportunity affords, or, still better, at the close of a meeting, after the benediction has been pronounced. The choice of tracts and books demands a good deal of wisdom lest inappropriate, and therefore ineffective, literature should be given.

These hints will probably be endorsed by all who have had experience of open-air work. and it only remains to be said that together with these suggestions the open-air preacher should seek to be filled with the spirit of trustfulness, believing that his Master's Word shall not return void.

## SECTION 13. SOME GENERAL COUNSELS.

It is of course quite impossible to cover in our present space the whole field of sermon work, and the reader must necessarily be referred to authorities on preaching for a complete treatment of this pre-eminently important subject. But there are a few considerations that still remain to be noticed by way of conclusion.

### I. *The Use of Illustrations.*

No one doubts for an instant the supreme value of 'letting in the light,' illustrating our sermons. Sometimes the illustrations may be in the form of similes to adorn our style, but for the most part they will be incidents or other forms of illustration for the purpose of explanation and persuasion. The value of an illustration will lie in the following fourfold characteristic: (*a*) It must be clear; (*b*) it must be telling; (*c*) it must be attractive; (*d*) it must be brief. The illustration must be to the point, or else it will do harm rather than good. If we favour the use of anecdotes we must take care that our stories are true, and speaking of anecdotes, it would be worth while avoiding that which is hackneyed, and keeping as closely as possible to that which is fresh and suggestive. An interesting article appeared some time ago in a religious paper entitled 'S.D.W.S.P.I.,' with a sub-title, 'A Sorely Needed Society.' The meaning of the initials was 'A Society for Doing Without Some Pulpit Illustrations.' The article recorded a conversation held between a number of preachers, and one after another gave his opinion as to the illustrations that might be allowed a rest from use. Among them was the story of a gentleman who was engaging a coachman, and asked all the applicants how near they could drive to a precipice close to his house; the story of Havelock on London Bridge; the Dutch boy who stuffed his hand into a hole in the dyke; the incident of Napoleon and the English drummer boy; of George Washington and his axe; of Michael Angelo and the marble block, were cited as examples of illustrations to be avoided. Hackneyed quotations were also referred to. Longfellow's 'Psalm of Life'; Browning's 'God's in His heaven'; Tennyson's 'Flower in the crannied wall'; Bailey's 'We live in days, not years'; Lowell's 'Truth for ever on the scaffold.' Ministers who have been in the Holy Land were to be warned that there are some advantages in *not* having visited Palestine, and allusions to pictures like 'Diana or Christ' or 'The Doctor' were thought to be somewhat too familiar for use at present. No one can question the value of these suggestions, and it is to be hoped that every clergyman will constitute himself a member of this very valuable Society.

Literature will of course provide many illustrations for sermons, so also will fiction, history, and science. One of the most striking features in the sermons of Dr. W. L. Watkinson is the marvellous fertility and felicity of his scientific illustrations. Dr. Jowett and Dr. Maclaren are scarcely inferior in this respect. Illustrations must always be kept strictly subsidiary to their purpose. Some one has well said, 'Don't construct your ornament, but ornament your construction.'

Illustrations are best gathered by reading and by cultivating our powers of observation. We may occasionally find it dangers in such a plan, and by far the best way is to keep our eyes and ears open and make our own compilation. One thing necessary to buy books of illustrations, but there are obvious is certain, that our people will often remember our sermons by some illustration which we have been enabled to include in it.

## II. *Preaching old Sermons.*

This is a question that comes up in ministerial life from time to time. There is no reason why old sermons should not be blessed quite frequently. George Whitefield used to say that he never felt satisfied with a sermon until he had preached it about twenty times. But we must be particularly careful to prepare them over again and let them pass through the alembic of our present experience. It may be advisable to burn our old sermons every ten years for fear we should be tempted to preach the man and his experience of ten years ago. Bishop Whittaker of Philadelphia once told of a young clergyman whose pastoral charge had fallen to him out in the thinly populated end of a Western State:—

'Riding the circuit of his tiny churches, he never imagined that the auditors of one town ever sat under him in another, and so he had been delivering everywhere the same sermon, and it seemed to take well; just how well that preacher never guessed until one Sunday he was stopped at the church door by an old negro. "Pardon me, suh, fer a moment," he said, with a respectful bow. "I jus' wan' to say that I suttinly have enjoyed dat sermon. De fust time I heard it, suh, I liked it, and de secon' time I liked it better, an' as I been follerin' you around' hit jus' keep growin' on me like. Now, suh, I'se sorter in de preachin' business my own se'f an' it jus' occurred to me dat you gwine to wear out dat sermon some fine day, an' den I wants to buy it. When you get ready to sell it, suh, I stan' to give you fifty cents." '

## III. *Plagiarism.*

This is one of the perennial problems of the pulpit, and it must be confessed that the position is one of genuine difficulty. We must preach, and we ought to read, and yet we are warned of plagiarism, and so we fear to read. Our work presses upon us, our body is weary, our mind is dull, we call spirits from the vasty deep, but they do not come. What then are we to do? If we use other men's materials improperly we are despised and thenceforward always suspected, and yet if we fail to use the work of others we and our people will be all the poorer. How are we to define plagiarism? It has been defined as the adaptation of other material without any attempt at mental assimilation. Originality is thought that has not been conceived by any one else, and this is of course quite out of the question and impossible for ordinary preachers. True originality in preaching is really a new presentation of old thoughts so as to show our own work. There is nothing finer in a preacher than his ability to 'glorify the obvious,' and to give at least some freshness to familiar truths. How, then, is a man to use the material of other men properly so as to avoid plagiarism and at the same time to provide himself and his people with all possible intellectual nutriment?

1.   We must think hard and long before reading. It is only by and after the exercise of our mind that we are enabled properly to approach the minds of others. There is probably far too much reading to-day and far too little thinking.

2.   We must think out fully all that we read. There is not enough *independent* thinking at the present time. But if we read, pencil in hand, ready to criticise and discuss at every point, we shall make the most out of the books at our disposal.

3.   Above everything else, we must keep mind and heart close to the Bible for devotional purposes. This is the secret of perennial freshness, for a man who puts the Bible first, and steadily maintains his quiet time day by day for personal, direct meditation will not only possess in himself a fount of real interest for his people but will thereby be enabled to make the best and truest use of all that he reads. Whenever there is any phrase or sentence that comes direct from another mind we must of course acknowledge it, and we must also take care not to allow our sermons to be a mere cento of quotations from other authors, strung together by our own effort.

IV.   *The Power of Interesting through Preaching.*

Some one has given a brief description of the three types of preachers. 'There are some whom you *cannot* listen to; there are some whom you *can* listen to; there are some whom you *must* listen to.' Sermons should 'grip' their audiences, and in order to do this they must be characterized by the three essential features of all acceptable speech: *placere, docere, movere.* A young preacher once asked an older man how he could interest his people. The reply was 'Give them something to interest them.' But in order to do this the preacher must himself be interested in his subject. The very word 'interest' seems to suggest the secret: '*inter-esse,*' that is, there must be something 'between' the preacher and his hearers. He must get in touch with them. The famous John Gregg, Bishop of Cork, said, 'First, throw the subject into yourself, next throw yourself into the subject, and then throw yourself and the subject into your hearers.'

But the question still remains as to how this is to be done, and the answer is that it is probably more personal and moral than anything else. The better the man the better the preacher, and no personal development, whether intellectual, social, or moral, will come amiss. (1) There must be more labor in thinking out our subject. No work ought to be regarded as too great, no trouble too severe for the pulpit. (2) There must be more courage in speaking out our subject. The man must be faithful whether people hear, or whether they forbear. (3) There must be more earnestness in living out the subject. The life as well as the lips must speak, and lest any one should feel that this is impossible it should never be forgotten that what is known as personal magnetism is not a gift, but a grace.

## V. *The Deepest Secret of All.*

As we draw these considerations to a close it is impossible to avoid repeating and emphasizing the truth that the most important factor of everything is the man behind the sermon. 'Thou must thyself be true, if thou the truth wouldst teach.' St. Paul told Timothy to take heed to himself before he spoke of taking heed to the doctrine. Some one has truly said that 'a sermon gets to be a sermon, and not an essay or lecture, by being made and delivered in the power of the Holy Ghost.' Sir William Robertson Nicoll was preaching some time ago on this subject, and urged his hearers who had the work of preaching and teaching not to go forth until they were clothed with the power of the Holy Ghost, saying, that 'we cannot deliver the saving message with converting power unless we are clothed. Some shining robe must cover our poor, weak, frail personalities':—

'Study is needed, preparation is needed, but when all is said and done it is this clothing, this robe of light that we must seek first, and without which we can do nothing. Have you not known it to be so again and again? You have listened to famous men, and to what are called great sermons, and they have not touched you. You have heard broken words from those whose natural gifts were small, and you will never forget them even in the new country. Why? Because they were spoken in the power of the Holy Ghost.'

To the same end are the words of a well-known Professor who, in addressing the students of the Bible Teachers' Training School in New York some time ago, spoke as follows:—

'The future sphere of the pulpit is along the line of devotional inspiration, to elevate the spiritual part of man to a dominant position in his life, to make his religion not occasional but constant. This can be done only by men in the pulpit who have so entered into the spirit of the Gospel that it clothes them with ambassadorial rank and makes them able to speak with regal authority. Such men can be found only among those who stand close to the Bible and whose allegiance to that Book is based upon a knowledge of its contents more profound than anything which intellectual astuteness can discover.'

For all this we must have our times of retirement and solitude. If we are to come forth with power we must have what the old Puritans used to call the spirit of 'recollectedness,' the habit of communion with God. In spite of its familiarity we will dare to call renewed attention to the story of Christmas Evans, the great Welsh preacher, whose absence in the vestry after the time for commencing the service was a great perplexity, until some one went to the door, and heard him pleading with God, 'I will not let Thee go, except Thou bless me.' In a few moments he came forth clothed with power, and preached in demonstration of the Holy Spirit of God. A seer is one who sees, and it is the man of spiritual vision who will do the true work of preaching. 'Solitude is the mother-country of the strong,' and we shall never be strong preachers unless we take time to wait upon God. Then we shall go to the pulpit, and our heart's desire and earnest prayer will be:—

> ' When telling of Thy salvation free,
> Let all absorbing thoughts of Thee
> My mind and soul engross.
> And when all hearts are bowed and stirred
> Beneath the influence of Thy Word,
> Hide me behind Thy Cross.'

CHAPTER III

# THE RECEPTION OF CHURCH MEMBERS

### SECTION 1. INTRODUCTION.

THE occasions for receiving new members into the Church of Christ provide one of the finest, if not the very finest opportunity afforded to the minister for personal dealing with individual souls. For the most part, the age of the candidates is in our favor, because they are usually at an impressionable time of life. In the Church of England and the Episcopal Churches of America, it is continually found that the rite of Confirmation, (administered as it is to those who have reached the years of discretion as the fulfillment of the vows taken for them in infant baptism), provides an occasion of almost incomparable value for individual work and personal contact. Other Churches frequently testify to the value of a similar opportunity with the young people who come forward to join the Church. Be it ours to realize the splendid possibilities of our position and to make the best use we can of them.

We shall do this, first of all, by making sure of our own personal life. Unless the pastor is spiritually fit for the training of his candidates the whole preparation will suffer. There is scarcely any occasion when he needs to be more 'thoroughly furnished' for the work of getting into the closest possible touch with individual souls on behalf of Christ. Another way of making the most of this time is by remembering that the preparation must be very much more than instruction. It must extend to inspiration, for we must ever keep in view the definite object of personal influence. Its crowning purpose is the genuine personal contact of the soul with Christ as Saviour and Master.

## SECTION 2.   THE PREPARATION.

The approach of the season for receiving new members will naturally be introduced by announcements in Church, together with a sermon on the spiritual meaning and importance of the rite.   At the close of this sermon an invitation should be given to candidates to send in their names, and arrangements be made for the meeting of the class.   The length of the preparation may be determined by the discretion of the minister.

In the conduct of the classes care should be taken to make them definitely spiritual and personal.   They should lead up to decision each time, whatever the subject may be.   A hymn to open is helpful, if found practicable.   The duration of the meeting should not be longer than forty-five minutes, and the gathering should be as bright and hearty as possible.   The minister should be at the door at the close, to shake hands with the candidates as they leave.   He should invite inquiries on any points arising out of his teaching, and, above everything, he should put his very best into this work of preparation, the best that his mind and heart can produce.   He will never regret it; he will always thank God for the time and strength given to this important part of his ministry.

At the time of application for Church membership, there will most naturally be found an opportunity for a private interview between pastor and candidate.   This need not be long, and should close with definite personal prayer.   It is so easy to use the occasion for a very frank, personal talk. and this in almost every case will prove spiritually fruitful, if there is faithfulness on the part of the minister with a view to decision for Christ.   He will not be unduly encouraged or elated if some of his candidates are quick to respond to his inquiries and appeals, nor unduly discouraged or disappointed should they show a need of further effort on their behalf.

A spirit of expectation should be encouraged and cultivated at the last meeting of the class and the significance of the approaching service impressed as deeply as possible on the candidates.   If the preparation has been earnest, thorough, and detailed, the truths of the Christian life will be very real to them, and they will look upon the occasion as a blessed opportunity of entering into the fulness of fellowship with Christ and His Church.

It is of the greatest spiritual value to make as much as possible of the first administration of the Holy Communion after the reception of new members. In many Churches it is the custom for both services to be included in the morning worship of a particular Sabbath, and for the new members to join with the rest of the congregation in partaking of the sacrament. Thus, the occasion may be made one of special blessing to the entire Church.

A useful practice pursued by many ministers is, as soon as possible after the service, to write to each of the new members a friendly pastoral letter of welcome, urging them to faithfulness in church attendance and co-operation in the various departments of religious activity. A definite interest in Sunday School, young people's society, choir, or other organization may be suggested, and the letter may close with a personal message of spiritual counsel or encouragement.

## Section 3. an outline of teaching.

Two main ideas must ever be kept in view; instruction and impression. Perhaps the greatest need of all is the endeavour to invest old truths with something like freshness of treatment for the young life that comes before us.

The main lines of preparation may be suggested as follows:—

I. *The Meaning of Church Membership.*

1. Show that at baptism we were designated, or dedicated to, and introduced into, the privileges and opportunities of the Christian community after prayer and sponsorial promises to teach what personal Christianity really means. Baptism may be illustrated by the soldier's enlistment, and then, after the necessary training and discipline, uniting with the Church may be likened to his putting on his uniform, when he confesses Whose, and what he is.

2. Uniting with the Church implies that we have been taught this, that we realize its meaning and intend to follow it for ourselves.

3. The Christian life may be summed up in two ways. (*a*) 'I give myself to God' (Josh. 24: 15; 1 Kings 18: 21; Matt. 6: 24; 2 Cor. 6: 14-16). (*b*) 'God gives Himself to me' (Luke 11: 9-13; John 14: 14, 16, 26; Phil. 4: 13, 19).

4. Nothing less than this is personal Christianity, and it must be faced clearly. Then, when we are right with Christ, we enter into a true relation to Christians.

## II. *The Christian Life: Its Divine Side.*

Three blessings are offered.

1. Forgiveness and life. Sin separates, Christ unites (John 5: 24; John 15: 5; 1 John 1: 7).

2. Grace and strength. Arising out of the former blessing (John 1: 12; Gal. 3: 26; 2 Cor. 6: 17, 18; Eph. 3: 14-16).

3. Protection and preservation. Present grace and future glory (Eph. 1: 13, 14; Phil. 4: 19; John 14: 2, 3; 2 Cor. 5: 1; 1 Pet. 1: 4).

Observe the completeness of these blessings, covering past, present and future. All possible circumstances are provided for.

All these are ours because of God's love. The three circles of love: (*a*) the world (John 3: 16; (*b*) the Church (Eph. 5: 25; (*c*) the individual (Gal. 2: 20).

All become ours when we receive Jesus Christ as our personal Saviour and Lord. In Him all gifts and blessings are included.

Dwell wholly in this lesson on the Divine side and not at all on the human. This will encourage and inspire. Give Isaiah 41: 10 as a motto.

## III. *The Christian Life: Its Human Side.*

Now comes the question: How are these three gifts to be enjoyed as our own? The answer is, By Repentance, Trust, and Obedience.

### (1)  *Repentance.*

We are to renounce everything that is sinful, or liable to lead to sin.  Three special enemies:

(*a*) The enemy above us, the author of all evil, who tempts directly by suggestion, especially to unbelief and pride (Gen. 3: 1-5; Jas. 4: 7; 1 Pet. 5: 9).  Note that all Bible temptations of Satan are against believers, not against people of the world.  Satan has no need to tempt *them*.  This should keep us from discouragement when we are tempted by him.

(*b*) The enemy around us.  Everything evil, or likely to lead to it, in persons and things around us.  We have no difficulty about what is actually evil; only about what is doubtful.  How are we to know what is 'worldly'?  One test will settle almost everything: either, What would Jesus have done? or, still better, What would He wish me to do (Rom. 12: 2; 1 John 2: 15-17)?

(*c*) The enemy within us, the flesh.  Everything in our own hearts, thoughts, and desires.  Distinguish carefully between temptation and sin.  We cannot prevent thoughts coming, but we can prevent them staying.  Luther wrote to his own son that we cannot prevent the birds from flying around our heads, but we can prevent them from building their nests in our hair (Rom. 8: 5-8; Gal. 5: 17-21).  On this occasion, but only quite generally, make pointed reference or allusions to sins of the flesh.

Place strong emphasis on the true meaning of repentance, that it is not penitence, or sorrow for sin, but the forsaking of sin.  This is the key to the Christian position.  Without repentance, no blessings of Christ are possible.

### (2)  *Trust.*

1.  The particular points of Christian belief are found in the Bible as a whole and yet are summarized conveniently in the Apostles Creed.

(*a*) Three parts: belief in God the Father, the Son, and the Holy Ghost.  Dwell upon all these sections without undue detail.

(*b*) Words to be explained: 'holy,' 'quick,' 'Catholic Church,' 'Communion of Saints.'

2.  Belief is not everything that is required.  From belief

of facts, we have to ascend to trust in a Person. Not belief in facts. about God only, but trust in God Himself (Heb. 11: 3, 6; Acts 15: 31; Jas. 2: 19; John 1: 12).

3.  Emphasize the necessity of personal trust: faith is found essential in every department of life.  So in religion, it is the only answer to God's revelation if there is any connection between Him and man.

(3)  *Obedience.*

1.  What is obedience?  The expression and proof of our repentance and trust.

2.  What is the standard of obedience?  The Bible as the Word of God.

3.  What is the summary of that standard?  The Ten Commandments.

(*a*)  Observe the outline: God and others.

(*b*)  Note the completeness: covering thoughts, words, and deeds in relation to God and our neighbour.

4.  What is the motive of obedience? Redemption.

IV.  *The Christian's Need of Grace.*

(1)  *Prayer.*

1.  What prayer is.  Trustfully telling God what we need, and asking Him for it according to His will.  Illustrations of prayer: the telegraph, telephone, microphone.

2.  Encouragements to prayer: (*a*) the promises in the Bible; (*b*) examples of men and women of prayer.

3.  Times for prayer: (*a*) regular; (*b*) stated.

4.  Ejaculatory prayer.  Prayer that 'darts' up to God like an arrow.  Illustrations from the Bible: e. g. 'Lord, save me;' 'Lord, help me.'

5.  The model prayer: the Lord's Prayer, with its (*a*) three petitions for God's glory; (*b*) three (or four) petitions for our needs.

In all our instruction on prayer make the matter quite simple, easy and natural, as the expression of our spiritual life.

(2)  *The Bible.*

1.  The Bible as a means of grace covers everything, since grace rests upon Divine revelation.

2. The uniqueness of the Bible. It is the only Book revealing (*a*) God's love; (*b*) deliverance from sin.

3. This is due to Christ the Living Word as (*a*) God's revelation; (*b*) God's power.

4. To be read primarily for ourselves and not for others: see the examples, promises, warnings, precepts, hopes. 'What saith my Lord unto His servant?'

5. To be read with prayer. Prayer and the Bible are the two sides of communion. Our talking to God and God talking to us.

6. To be read with definite personal application to our own needs day by day. This is the meaning of meditation.

7. To be read daily. Food is needed regularly for the body, and this is the food for the soul. Even five minutes will suffice, if we cannot spare more. Quality, not quantity, is to be insisted on.

8. This method of daily personal Bible meditation is the supreme safeguard against all backsliding. The Bible is the mirror in which we see ourselves (Jas. 1: 23-25), the water to cleanse ourselves (Eph. 5: 26, 27), and the food to strengthen ourselves (Jer. 15: 16).

9. The value of regular systematic reading in connexion with a Bible Union or other definite plan of study.

10. In all this teaching on the Bible, try as far as possible to make it novel and fresh in treatment.

(3)   *The Holy Communion in Scripture.*

1. The teaching must be positive, not negative; spiritual and devotional, and not at all controversial.

2. The leading ideas from the New Testament: (*a*) a Remembrance; (*b*) a Picture; (*c*) a Promise. Distinguish between *knowing* and *remembering*. We cannot remember if we do not know, and we cannot 'do this in remembrance' unless we know Christ as our personal Saviour.

3. In the New Testament observe the various aspects of Christ's work expressed in the Lord's Supper: Christ for us; in us; with us; coming.

4. Two points in regard to the Lord's Supper: (*a*) What it is: a remembrance of Calvary and of its spiritual benefits; (*b*) What it does: strengthens and refreshes.

5. In all this teaching on Holy Communion, endeavour to fix the minds of the candidates on Him, not on it. Point out that the relation between the sign and the thing signified is one of parallelism, not of identity. There are two givers: the Lord and the minister; two receivers: the body and the soul; two methods: the mouth and faith. When we approach with a true and living faith the two acts are simultaneous; the Lord gives His grace as the clergyman gives the elements, so that we can eat and drink the elements *in* faith, and at the same time we feed on Christ *by* faith.

V. *After Uniting with the Church: What?*

1. Either just before, or preferably just after, the special first Communion, an address should be given, showing of what is to be expected from the new members.

2. The Christian life must first be emphasized: (*a*) on its human side of consistency; (*b*) on its Divine side of grace sufficient for every need.

3. Christian service must then be taught: (*a*) a general witness of the life; (*b*) some definite form of Christian work in connexion with the Church.

4. Once again the endeavour should be made to put the new life at once brightly, earnestly, and definitely before the new members.

It has of course been impossible to do more than give the barest suggestion for this work. But it is only right before passing away from the subject to emphasize afresh in the plainest way the unspeakable privilege and great responsibility of this opportunity of coming so closely in contact with the spiritual needs of the young people of our Church and parish. The man who undertakes this work in the right spirit will often feel overwhelmed as he contemplates the solemn possibilities, and yet will find his heart rejoicing again and again in the indication of God's gracious blessing resting upon his prayerful efforts.

## Chapter IV

## VISITATION.

THERE is no doubt that visitation, when properly
carried out, is closely related to a minister's preaching.
It acts and reacts on what he says. Intercourse with
his people will enrich his preaching, making it real, practical,
sympathetic, and alive. The life of the preacher in the week
will either deepen or remove the impression of the sermon. His
people will naturally want to see and know whether he is the
same in and out of the pulpit. It is also in many cases more
likely that they will come to hear a man whom they meet in
the week. There is a constant danger of a minister coming
under the category of the Scottish pastor who was said to be
on week-days 'invisible,' and on Sundays 'incomprehensible.'
But this is not to deny the necessity of allowing exceptional
men like Spurgeon, Beecher, and Talmage to exercise their
great preaching gifts apart from pastoral work.

It must never be forgotten that the old adage, 'a house-
going parson makes a church-going people,' is only a half-
truth, and sometimes not that. There are many parsons who
are 'house-going' who do not thereby get hold of people for
their church. The other half of the truth is, 'A preaching
parson makes a church-keeping people.' If it should be said
that 'a visiting parson makes a fat church,' it is equally true
that a 'visiting pastor often makes a lean pulpit.' If there is
to be a choice, people will much more readily excuse poor
visiting than poor preaching, and it is imperative that our
pulpit work should not be allowed to suffer even from pastoral visitation.

The relation of preaching and visiting is of course a difficult one in regard to the time and strength required. While
what has been said about the value of visiting in enriching
the pastor is perfectly true, there is another side which must
not be forgotten. If a man spends his time in visiting to such

an extent that his time in his study suffers, he will experience an intellectual and a spiritual deadness when he comes to prepare his sermon which will inevitably affect the reality of his preaching. A man who visits morning, noon, and night, will find himself at the end of the week physically fagged, and intellectually unfit to brace himself for the effort required to prepare a proper sermon. He will then have to fall back upon helps, hints, and scraps from other sources, which will inevitably do moral and spiritual harm to himself and his people. The man who is to preach acceptably must never allow anything, even pastoral visitation, to interfere with those hours which should be given religiously to the work of study. Some time ago the letters of the late Dr. Marcus Dods were published, in which it was seen that during an early pastorate he devoted himself specially to the work of visiting. And yet as an acute thinker, the Rev. Arthur Hoyle, in the *Methodist Recorder*, well pointed out, if Dods had continued that type of ministry he would never have written his important works. Mr. Hoyle also remarks that if a man feels called upon to give himself to the work of visiting he cannot be expected to do proper justice to his study work.

'The love of his books will go from him, and at the end of ten or fifteen years he will be done for. We shall never have great teachers, great preachers, that way. Such an one may have a great experience of the people; he may be loved and honoured, he may have done more work than some others who have taken another line—on all that I say nothing at all; but it is as sure as anything can be, that if he has not his times of meditation, and of prayer, his lonely wrestlings with the truth, and his feeling after God, he will be nothing accounted of when he stands forth, and he will have nothing to say to the man who has a grave problem or a desolating burden.'

If we keep the New Testament proportion in view we shall find that the emphasis is laid upon preaching and teaching, and everything else must be regarded as secondary. The proclamation of the Gospel to sinner and to saint is the supreme work of the ministry, and as it demands strenuous preparation of spirit, soul, mind, and body, it is obvious that nothing must be allowed to weaken it. But if visitation is kept strictly subordinated to preaching, it will prove one of the most un-

failing opportunities of ministering to those who are familiar
to the preacher, whose life he knows, whose interests he ap-
preciates, whose joys and sorrows are his own, and whose life
in Christ is his constant thought and prayer.

The primary aim of all our visitation must be spiritual and
not merely social. Of course the social element must enter
into it, but it certainly must not predominate. The intercourse
contemplated between a clergyman and his people is almost
wholly spiritual, and is intended to be constantly directed
towards definite spiritual objects. Mere social visiting can
be very easily overdone. It is very easy to multiply visits,
with no spiritual gain unless the clergy have a clear idea and
a steady resolve. A clergyman once said that his people would
do anything for him except come to church, and it is worth
while remembering the words of a practical layman who remarked that, 'If the parson spent less time in the houses and
more time in the study, it would be better for the people.'
The character of our visiting is a real test of spirituality,
and there is an almost constant risk of a clergyman losing his
spiritual power by excessive social visitation. Our work is
mainly and primarily that of teaching spiritual truths and
ministering spiritual realities, and anything that tends to rob
our life of spiritual force is to be guarded against and avoided.
Of course this does not mean that we shall necessarily feel it
incumbent to offer prayer or read the Scripture every time we
visit, but our message and our work ought never to be far
away. It is significant that the people soon notice if a clergyman comes again and again without speaking some spiritual
word. Our visiting may fail either from being made too
official, assuming the position of a priest or spiritual director,
or else by being made too social, adopting the attitude of 'a
good fellow' only. We need to blend the true elements of
the pastor and the friend in all our social efforts on behalf of
our flock.

For visiting the men of our congregation the evening is
of course absolutely essential, and three characteristics of
dealing with them must be constantly kept in view. We must
be manly, brotherly, and godly. This is only another way
of saying once again that the key of our life must be 'Be

natural.' A Professor of Pastoral Theology once asked a question of his class in an examination paper, How can clergy get the closest in touch with working men? As he invited the students to be frank in their replies, one of the men put on his paper, 'By being less of the priest and more of the man.' We must try to get into touch with the interests of our men. Dr. W. M. Taylor tells a fine story of Edward Irving and an infidel shoemaker. Patent leather had then been recently invented, and as Irving's father was a tanner he himself knew all about this new product. When he called upon the shoemaker and endeavoured to engage him in conversation, the first question was, 'What do you know about leather?' Then, as he discovered that Irving did know about leather, he remarked, 'You are a decent sort of fellow, do you preach?' The very next Sunday the infidel was at Irving's church, and when others present wondered at his being there and asked the reason, the shoemaker replied, 'He is a sensible man, he kens aboot leather.'

Interest in the children will also prove fruitful in work among the men, and any kindness we can show to them will prove a sure way to the father's heart. If at all possible, we ought to work up to a Men's Meeting, or a Men's Discussional Bible Class, to show them that the church and its gatherings are for them, and to let them see that their manhood will find its complete realization only in fellowship with Christ and His people. We ought to have an especial eye for young men, as we do our visiting, and we shall find that the work will prove infinitely more fruitful than a succession of meetings where perhaps we are only called upon to preside or to 'make a few remarks.'

Then again, an occasional meeting for the men of the church or congregation after dinner at the parsonage will be found useful. An ordinary invitation card may be sent announcing a meeting, when some leading man, clerical or lay, might be asked to introduce some general topic of spiritual interest. This would be followed by discussion, and in due course the gathering would be closed with a brief word of prayer. This kind of meeting has proved on several occasions a useful opportunity for the men of the congregation to get to know one another, to come in contact with their pastor and also to obtain some spiritual influence from a meeting such as has been suggested. Of course there are obvious difficulties in the way of arrangement, but these are to be faced and met as effectively as possible.

In a public address, General Booth, founder of the Salvation Army, remarked that there are certain people who cannot be reached by a spiritual influence except through their circumstances, and he added that this is one of the reasons for the success of his Army. When a sick woman, unable to attend to her children and perform her household duties, receives practical help from a Salvation Army sister, she is the readier, on her recovery, to appear at the meetings and receive a spiritual message to her already touched heart. So, too, visitation by the minister at the homes of the bereaved is a rare opportunity. Hearts are then softened and will be further drawn out by the minister's sympathy and prayer. Here, if anywhere, is the occasion for making a clear distinction between 'pity' and 'sympathy.' Pity is feeling *for* a person; sympathy is feeling *with* him. Moody tells the story of taking his little daughter with him when he went to visit a woman who had lost her own little child by drowning. Moody offered prayer and expressed his sympathy in a sincere way, and yet there did not seem to be much power in it. As he went back, and they were walking along the river-side where the accident had taken place, his little girl said, 'Father, suppose it had been me.' This went like a dagger to Moody's heart, and he turned back and went to the woman with sympathy this time, not with pity, and spoke and prayed with her, and then cried with her in her trouble. No one can estimate the value of loving, Christ-like visitation at the time of bereavement.

The aged will also call for and repay all the attention that we can give them. Let us make much of these Fathers and Mothers in Israel. There are some clergy whose thought seems to be only for the young. Let us take care of the old as well. They will repay us by their prayers, and our ministry will be all the more fruitful as we try to smooth their pathway and cheer them along with the assurance that 'at evening time it shall be light.'

Every Church has its sick cases to be visited, and these give a wonderful opportunity not only of benefit to the ailing but often of use to the pastor, in enabling him to obtain a better knowledge of the family, its cares, sorrows, and joys. If the sick case is that of a man it will be found to be a rare opportunity of influencing him for Christ. If the children are sick let us make the opportunity of taking them flowers, or pictures. In all this we must work as closely as possible with the doctor and the nurse, and we must not mind going again and again, if for any reason we cannot get in when we pay an ordinary call. For hospital visiting it will be found advisable to avoid going on visiting day. A clergyman can gain an entrance at any time, but the friends of the sick person can only visit on the proper days, and it is a pity to rob them of the only chance they have of getting their full time with their sick friend.

In every parish some chronic cases will be found, and it is imperative that a list of these should be kept in order that a regular visit may be made, whether weekly or monthly. We must never forget that these invalids are shut off from Church privileges, and will be only too glad of a visit from the clergyman. It goes without saying that we must be cheery and look on the bright side of things. Who can ever forget the story of that 'Great-heart' Phillips Brooks nursing the baby in the tenement house while he sent the poor tired mother for a little change and breath of fresh air? We may not all be able to do this, but the principle is obvious. Scripture and prayer are quite easy with the 'shut ins' for they will naturally expect us to minister to them in things spiritual. Very often we may pass on some thoughts or the outlines of a Sunday sermon, and if we can possibly do so, it will be found of immense help to sing some hymn. I have the most vivid recollection of visiting during the early days of my ministry a poor, crippled, helpless young fellow who was able to play the concertina, and the hymns we sang together were as great a joy to me as they were to him. Of course with such cases we shall offer prayer. Chronic sickness is a golden opportunity not to be let slip, and we must either set apart one afternoon for this work, or else in some way take great care that our visits are paid with regularity and fair frequency. We shall find among these poor constant sufferers some of our warmest supporters who are 'helping together by prayer.'

Sudden calls to death-beds are occasions that test very severely a young minister's spiritual life. He may often find himself at the bedside of one of whom he knows nothing. What is he to do? It will never do harm, and it will always do good, to make the Atonement as prominent as possible. He must be faithful at all costs, and, as far as he can, he must probe the conscience and find out any sin. But if for any reason all this is impossible, he may rest assured that the quiet, simple, clear, positive statement of the Atoning Sacrifice for personal acceptance by faith will do its own work, and God's Word will not return to Him void.

If the dying man or woman is a Christian it will be found useful to emphasize the promises of God. Physical weakness often leads to spiritual depression and fear, and the earnest Christian may be tempted by Satan to question and doubt his own acceptance of Christ. This is the time for dwelling upon the positive Divine aspects of truth, and especially upon the 'everlasting covenant ordered in all things and sure.' The teaching of such passages as Romans 8: 28-30 and Hebrews 6: 13-20 will come as balm to the soul, as we lovingly and earnestly show them that 'God is faithful.'

Sometimes a request is made for a little handbook suited to the needs of parochial visitors, and it is difficult to suggest anything of the kind. A useful little compilation was available some years ago, called *The Visitor's Book of Texts*, by Dr. Andrew A. Bonar, but now this is only to be had second-hand. It is far more satisfactory, however, for every visitor gradually to make his own list of suitable Scripture passages, for there is nothing like the school of experience to learn what is needed for particular cases. He will certainly need such Psalms as 23; 27; 46; 65; 103; and 130; such chapters of Isaiah as 12; 53; and 55; such chapters of the Fourth Gospel as 3; 4; 14; 15; 16; such chapters of the Epistles as Romans 8; 1 Corinthians 15; 1 Thessalonians 4; with the last two chapters of the Revelation. It will be surprising if these are not used pretty freely and frequently. Then again, the use of hymns in visiting will be found of great value, especially by reason of the power of old associations. Familiar hymns, like 'Jesus, Lover of my soul,' 'Rock of Ages,' 'How sweet the Name of Jesus sounds,' 'Abide with me,' and others, will be most welcome at sick beds and for use with the dying. Very, very often the old words will recall thoughts and places which will enable the clergyman to send home his message. A clergyman was summoned to a tenement house in New York some years ago to the death-bed of a Scotswoman. After trying several methods in vain without obtaining the slightest response, at last he thought of the Scottish version of the twenty-third Psalm, and repeated,—

> The Lord's my Shepherd, I'll not want,
> He makes me down to lie
> In pastures green; He leadeth me,
> The quiet waters by.

At once the woman opened her eyes, and said 'I learned that as a bairn in Scotland'; and it proved the channel of spiritual blessing to her soul.

In the course of reading I came across a prayer appropriate to pastoral visitation, and it seemed so spiritually suggestive I ventured to get it printed on a card for distribution among theological students and younger clergy. I subjoin the prayer in the hope that it may thereby find a still wider field of usefulness:—

Grant, Lord, I pray, that this day I may be made the messenger of Thy mercy to many. Open in my nature deep springs of love and sympathy and understanding, that when I meet with those who are in deep waters, deep may answer unto deep. Bring me into the divine peace, and let me walk this day in the light of Thy countenance, that all the influences of my person and presence may make for helpfulness. Give me Thy comfort for the sorrowful, Thy cheer for the glad, Thy love for the lonely, Thy riches for the poor, Thy peace for the anxious. May children find me childlike, and the strenuous find me courageous, and the aged find me trustful. So use me, I pray, as to quicken life with the sense of its spiritual complement, where every valley is exalted and every mountain brought low. In Christ. Amen.

## CHAPTER V

# SUNDAY SCHOOLS AND BIBLE CLASS WORK.

### SECTION 1. SUNDAY SCHOOLS.

WORK among children will always occupy an important place in the thought and interests of a minister's life. A Scottish shepherd was once asked how he was able to produce so fine a breed of sheep, and he answered, 'By taking care of the lambs.'

It is of course important that the minister should become imbued with a strong conviction of the value and importance of Sunday School work, for apart from such convictions very little will be done. It is a great mistake to think that 'anything will do' for Sunday Schools, and it is this attitude that leads many people to describe as 'Sunday School' something that stands for what is essentially weak, poor, and almost worthless.

The purpose of Sunday School work should be regarded as that of personal influence rather than education. A good deal of unfair criticism is directed against Sunday Schools because they do not teach and instruct, though a little thought should suggest that something like one hour a week, with many influences working in the opposite direction, would not be regarded by any educationist as adequate to the work of instruction. Let us by all means provide the very best intellectual opportunities we can obtain, but when everything has been said, Sunday School work will be largely that of personal impression and inspiration rather than that which is purely intellectual and educative.

A minister's association with Sunday Schools will necessarily take a variety of forms. First of all, he will endeavour to visit his Sunday Schools regularly, and see for himself what is going on. Superintendents and teachers will be glad to

213

have him open or close sessions of the school, and to get in touch with the actual work. Then he will make a special point of knowing the Sunday School teachers and doing his utmost to work for them and with them.

In some Churches a Teachers' Training Class has proved an important adjunct to Sunday School work. Such a class is useful in directing the teachers to the best available helps, while the wide reading of the minister or other leader should supplement them. The special denominational papers containing Sunday School lesson material, or such a weekly paper as *The Sunday School Times* of Philadelphia, will do their part in aiding both the leader of this preparation class and the teachers. The class also gives an opportunity for the discussion of those questions which arise in the minds of all who would teach with faithfulness and true understanding. To it can be brought also the questions and problems of scholars who 'want to know.'

Where a competent layman is not available to act as Superintendent of the Sunday School it may be necessary for the minister to undertake this work himself. While it will mean a great deal of time and a large amount of hard work, time and labour will be well spent on so valuable an aid to the work of the Church.

The elder scholars may be formed into Bible classes, and if separate rooms are available it will be all the better for teachers and scholars during the presentation of the lesson. These classes will, however, naturally be regarded as an integral part of the Sunday School as all gather together for the opening and closing exercises. Such Bible classes often result in a large proportion of the young people being retained in the congregation during those trying years of growth and development.

The Children's Sermon is an indispensable and fruitful feature in many Churches. Apart from the value of the five-minute address on some subject appropriate to the little ones, with the use, it may be, of an object-lesson, the attendance at church for a part of the service forms a connecting link between the Sunday School and congregation, so that later on children naturally remain for the whole service. This important sermonette takes time and trouble in preparation, and for some pastors it is not easy to adapt themselves to the mental capacity of young children. Yet, with the study of books of simple addresses to the young, there will usually come an ease of expression as experience is gained. It is often found, moreover, that the adults are reached by the child-like messages with their simple illustrations and pointed truths, so skilfully applied as to be inferred rather than dogmatically stated. A children's hymn may be sung before the address, and one of a more congregational nature afterwards, during the last verse of which the children leave the front of the church to go home or to join their parents in the pews.

## Section 2.  bible classes.

Among the many departments of work that of Bible Classes stands pre-eminent. Such classes provide a fine opportunity for positive teaching, as well as for free, frank discussion among those who often wish to know about points raised in sermons which obviously cannot be discussed in church. Bible classes also have a real importance in connexion with the minister's reading, for if he is responsible for teaching or conducting a class he is compelled to study in preparation for it. Then again, Bible classes will do much to keep the methods of work on spiritual lines, for with strong Bible work there will be scarcely any room for mere ephemeral work.

### A. *Men's Classes.*

A clerical friend of mine was never tired of emphasizing the special importance of work among men as likely to be more fruitful than anything else, because when the men are won the wives and children will almost always be influenced. There is a great deal of force in this contention. In any case, a men's Bible class will prove of great value and spiritual blessing.

A preliminary step in organizing this work is that of advertising the meetings. In commencing the class it is well to start punctually and close on the hour. The men ought to be able to depend upon this at subsequent meetings. The gatherings should be made as hearty as possible by a greeting at the opening and a handshake at the close.

It is very important to work through a committee of men themselves. This committee, consisting of some of the earnest members, will undertake a great deal of the work of organization.

The leader in charge should make a point of preparing with the utmost thoroughness for this work, putting his very best into it, and sparing no time or trouble to make himself efficient and proficient.

The subjects of the Class should be varied as much as possible. Sometimes a course may be given on some book, or part of a book of the Bible. Genesis, Joshua, the Fourth Gospel, and Acts, lend themselves particularly to this method. At any time a series of biographical studies will be interesting. The characters of the Old Testament are of perennial fascination. Yet again, a series of topics dealing with current difficulties and problems: Why we believe in God; in Christ; in the Bible; in the Church.

Opportunity should be given for discussion at these Classes, care being taken to keep it as pertinent as possible, but the fact that discussion is invited will prove of great service in letting it be known that difficulties are not shirked.

The visitation of the men in their homes during the evenings of the week will prove of material assistance and support to the class.

A social gathering, occasionally, on a week evening, especially at the opening of an autumn season, or the commencement of a New Year will be useful, care being taken that the items given are in strict harmony with the character and purpose of the Bible class.

B. *Women's Classes.*

A great deal that has been said about method for organizing men's classes applies equally as well here. In some churches several classes for women could be organized and may be led by the minister's wife or any capable women of the congregation. Different churches have different needs for such classes. Sometimes a class is provided for the young unmarried women who have attained the age when Sunday School is considered 'too juvenile.' One for the married women may also be arranged, in which their particular needs and problems may be met and discussed. But whether one class or several be organized, clear, definite teaching along Biblical lines is an absolute essential and needs constant emphasis. A consecrated, womanly leader, ready with sympathy, instruction and helpfulness, will do much to create an abiding influence.

Bible classes should not be mere talks or addresses. As Dr. H. Clay Trumbull has well said, telling is not teaching, for teaching is 'causing another to learn.' This thought should be borne in mind in all Bible class effort. Whatever be the subject of the class we must never forget that it is intended for definite, thorough instruction in the Scriptures.

## Chapter VI

## FOREIGN MISSIONS

IT ought to go without saying that Foreign Missions should occupy a prominent, not to say predominant place in every ministry. In some respects they constitute a test of a clergyman's own spiritual life, because they show whether or not he has the genuine missionary spirit. It is an almost universal experience that there is no contradiction or incompatibility between interest in Home Missions and interest in Foreign Missions. The distinction thus drawn is merely one of convenience, because in the sight of God there can be no 'Home' or 'Foreign' work. 'All souls are mine' is the Old Testament word, and 'Go ye into all the world' is the New Testament counterpart. It has been well and truly said that our great problem is not so much the 'non-Church-going,' as the 'non-going Church,' and it will probably be found in almost every instance that the extent and power of missionary work in a parish will depend largely on the clergyman's own attitude to God's great work of world-wide evangelization. It is unspeakably sad to contemplate the fact that there are still Churches where little or nothing seems to be done for Foreign Missions. It would be interesting, and perhaps spiritually significant, to discover what is collected each year in such churches for 'Church Expenses,' and how these expenses are made up. We happen to know two or three churches where one-tenth of every collection is devoted to the work of Foreign Missions, and we have yet to learn that these churches suffer financially or spiritually by putting God's greatest enterprise first. Let every minister therefore settle it in his own heart that if missionary work is not of much interest to him he should carefully scrutinize his own spiritual life in the light of God's Word and in the power of the Holy Spirit.

Assuming that a minister enters upon his work with a keen desire to do all in his power to further the work of world-wide evangelization, the question will often arise as to the best methods of exercising influence and bringing his people to see the claim of the world in the sight of God. What then can such a clergyman do? The following suggestions are made as the result of reading, experience, and consultation with those who are being blessed of God in the furtherance of this work.

1. First and foremost, the clergyman should study the New Testament principles of Missions in order to see what God thinks of them and where He places them. In particular, he will concentrate on our Lord's teaching during the Great Forty Days, and will find that in the five records in Holy Scripture world-wide missions formed the main theme of our Lord's conversations with His disciples. As part of this teaching, he will observe that our Lord places three great truths on an absolute level of equality and importance: the absolute necessity of the death of the Messiah; the absolute necessity of His resurrection; and the equally absolute necessity of repentance and remission being preached in His Name among all nations( Luke 24: 46, 47). This passage alone with its solemn threefold emphasis on 'It is necessary' ought to be sufficient to show the place that Missions occupied in the mind of the Risen Christ, and therefore the place that they should occupy in the heart and life of all His servants. The more a clergyman ponders the great realities of the New Testament concerning the work of Christ for the whole world, the more he will find his heart, and mind, and conscience stirred to do God's will.

2. Missionary reading will also prove abundantly fruitful. Missionary magazines often contain material of permanent value, and every minister will wish to have one of the best in circulation among his people. A Magazine Secretary who will undertake to receive subscriptions and push the sale of missionary literature will prove a help to the work. Serious reading is not only available on missionary topics, but is imperatively the duty of all who wish to do the very best for

themselves and their people in spreading the Gospel throughout the world. There may have been a time when missionary literature was dry and uninteresting, but if so, that day has gone never to return. Works on Missions in the present day merit the attention of the world's greatest thinkers, and no clergyman can regard himself as well informed if he does not know something at least of what is being written on this great topic.

3. Definite missionary study as well as general missionary reading should find a place in a clergyman's life. There are text books now published year by year which will provide a man ample material for a winter's study of some great Mission Field. Different denominations in their guilds and societies often take up the study of a recent missionary publication by forming groups for reading and comment. An enthusiastic leader, keen for missionary work, can be of tremendous value in introducing such books and in preparation for a group meeting.

It is only in recent years that we have heard of 'The Science of Missions,' for up to a comparatively short time ago no one thought of collecting, combining, and commenting on the data of missionary work. But to-day authorities in various branches of the Christian Church are generalizing on these facts and are producing results which make Christian Missions a much more intellectual reality than ever before. To this survey the Christian minister can contribute much by his interest in and study of missionary principles, missionary facts, and missionary possibilities. And in particular, his personal sympathy with and advocacy of missions will be deepened and strengthened in proportion to the thoroughness he can give to the study of the various missionary fields and problems.

4. Individual private prayer will naturally form an important part of a clergyman's work for Missions. A prayer cycle of some missionary society will give intelligent guidance day by day, as we endeavour to make our missionary intercession more definite and real. Our reading will influence our prayer, and our prayer will react in turn upon our reading.

5. A Missionary Prayer Meeting will of course be included in the parish organization. It may be monthly, or if convenient, even oftener. The ordinary Church Prayer Meeting might be given a special missionary turn on the first or some other gathering of the month. There may not be many people to attend such a meeting, but of its spiritual fruitfulness there can be no question.

6. Missionary meetings of various kinds will naturally be in a minister's mind to bring together the keen, earnest missionary workers, and these gatherings can be varied from time to time in quite a number of ways. Sales of Work on behalf of Missions are also useful, and of course they will be entirely free of all the unworthy and impossible methods usually associated with bazaars. A quiet Sale of Work undertaken by those who often have no opportunity of giving money to the cause will do nothing but good. An All-Day Working Party for Medical Missions, when bandages have been rolled and native garments made, has also proved of real service in many parishes.

7. Sermons from time to time by missionaries will also be considered, though it may not always be useless to ask our honoured brethren to give accounts of their work instead of preaching ordinary sermons. There is nothing that a congregation as a rule finds more interesting than a clear account at first-hand from those who have had personal experience of missionary work.

8. From time to time during the year missionary sermons should be preached by the pastor himself, calling attention to the work, and perhaps giving information. It may be found wise not to announce it beforehand lest people who are not interested in Missions may be conspicuous by their absence, and instead of an ordinary sermon dealing with missionary principles some Mission Field might be taken, and the salient points of the history and methods dealt with in the form of an address, or sermon. Such sermons might well be given at least once a quarter, taking morning and evening in turn. These opportunities would be as useful to the clergyman as to his people in leading him to study afresh the missionary problem, and obtain information of missionary work. No

one could 'get up' the story of a particular field or an outstanding missionary without becoming interested himself, and passing on the interest to others.

9. Medical Missions should not be overlooked because of God's wonderful blessing resting upon this twofold effort on behalf of Christ.

10. In several churches Missionary pictures cut out from current magazines are put upon a green baize-covered board, which hangs in the church porch. A notice at the foot of the board would also inform the reader where the magazines could be obtained. The interest in Missions will often be deepened by such a simple effort. This board can be put in charge of either the Magazine Secretary, or other helper. It may be suggested that very often the energies of the young people can be utilised in such small tasks for the Church, thereby engendering a real interest in its work as well as increasing their sense of responsibility.

11. If the parish has sent out any missionaries into the field it would be of great value to have a board in the church or chapel with their names, dates, and location. Nothing could well minister more to real fellowship in work than this constant reminder of those who had been 'sent forth' in the Master's Name.

12. The clergyman must ever be on the lookout for likely candidates for missionary work, young men and young women, and he should help them along after they are found. Many a candidate would be greatly assisted by the loving sympathetic efforts of a clergyman to give some lessons in Scripture, or even a little guidance in the Greek Testament.

13. Work among children must necessarily be given a prominent place in the support of Missions. A Mission Circle or similar organization may be formed for the purpose of interesting children in Missions. Then, with missionary addresses in Sunday School, together with the distribution of a children's missionary paper, the attention and interest of boys and girls will be awakened and deepened.

14. Last, but not least, let no church forget the Jews. 'To the Jew first' is a great New Testament principle, and it has its modern applications. As a rule, it will be found

that the keenest Bible students in a church are those who are interested in Jewish missionary work, and although it may not be a popular form of missionary effort, it will repay the attention that can be given to it. It is a mistake to call the Jews 'God's Ancient People,' for they are still His people, 'beloved for the fathers' sake.'

There are other methods that will doubtless commend themselves to different ministers in different circumstances. But perhaps enough has been said to show how true it is that almost everything in a parish with regard to Missions will depend upon the spiritual keenness of the clergyman himself.

## CHAPTER VII

# THE PRAYER MEETING

THE Prayer Meeting has been described as 'the big wheel of the Church,' a phrase which well indicates the necessity and importance of this part of church work. No other service can possibly take its place, and unless there is a regular Prayer Meeting, church work will never be as strong as it might, and ought to be.

The meeting should be held weekly and be made the center of intercession for the Church and parish. No other parochial or personal engagement should be allowed to interfere with it.

Very much will depend upon the conductor of the Prayer Meeting, for like everything else, the personal element bulks largely in a meeting of this kind. Perhaps a few suggestions may be found helpful by way of comparison.

1. The time as a rule should be one hour, and never longer. Punctuality in commencing and closing will be found useful in several ways. People ought to know that a Prayer Meeting arranged for eight o'clock commences at that hour, and it will be a great convenience if they get to realize that it closes at nine, or at least 9:15.

2. The hymn book used at Prayer Meetings should be of a devotional type, one which includes hymns of consecration. Missionary hymns may well find a place in this service, as the prayers will naturally be concerned with the spread of the Gospel in heathen lands.

3. A brief address should as a rule be included, with special emphasis on its brevity! The address should be based on Scripture, and devotional rather than purely exegetical in order to give point to the prayers that are to follow. It is a widespread and false conception that a Prayer Meeting is a place for instruction, and if the leader is imbued with this fallacy, and reads a long passage of Scripture and expounds

it at length, he will do more than anything else to kill the Meeting. Out of one hour, not more than ten minutes should be given to the address. Prayer Meetings are not for instruction; they are for the purpose of worshipping God in prayer, and praise, and testimony.

4. As a rule, the leader will himself open the meeting with prayer, or else get some one on whom he can depend to strike the right spiritual keynote of the gathering.

5. After the address the meeting will naturally be thrown open for prayer, emphasis being laid on the two essential requirements for public prayer: brevity and distinctness. If those present 'make long prayers,' or speak indistinctly, or with head bowed to the floor, the meeting will be injured. But if brevity and clearness are assured, the freedom of prayer will be in every way helpful.

6. Variety is one great secret of a good Prayer Meeting. The leader should invite 'sentence prayers.' Sometimes a number of prayers of one sentence, following immediately on one another will prove a most helpful feature. These sentence prayers will help the people to pray definitely for one thing, and will also enable some to open their mouths for the first time in public prayer who would not feel capable at the outset of praying at greater length.

7. Occasionally the leader will find it helpful while the people are kneeling to start a devotional chorus. The singing will prove another element of variety and help to maintain the tone of the meeting.

8. Subjects of prayer should be invited from time to time and requests will be sent in which can be brought before God during the meeting.

9. The conductor must not feel concerned, still less troubled, if there are silences from time to time in the meeting. God often speaks through our silences, and if people for any reason do not feel led to offer prayer, the meeting can still wait upon God in quietness and feel assured of His presence and blessing. The Society of Friends may err in one direction, but let not us as Church people make the mistake of erring in the other.

10. One Prayer Meeting a month, at least, should be devoted to missionary topics unless there is a separate Missionary Prayer Meeting. At such a gathering special subjects will be announced dealing with various aspects of the Mission Field, including intercession for any members of the congregation who are at work abroad, or missionaries in whom the Church has a special interest.

Once again let it be said with all possible emphasis that no Church ought to regard itself as properly equipped for the spiritual work that it has to do unless it has a weekly Prayer Meeting.

# CHAPTER VIII

## PERSONAL WORK.

### SECTION 1. ITS PLACE

*INDIVIDUAL WORK FOR INDIVIDUALS* is the title of a valuable and important book. It suggests what should never be forgotten in the Christian life, that work for Christ is pre-eminently individual and personal. Evangelism in the New Testament is essentially of this character. The first two who became disciples of Christ were led to him by the personal testimony of John the Baptist. The intercourse of our Lord and His disciples was primarily individual and personal. And although on the Day of Pentecost St. Peter preached to a large crowd, yet very soon in the record of the Acts we find instance after instance of personal efforts at soul winning. Even St. Paul with his greatness as a preacher and an administrator was first of all a personal worker, and his services at Philippi, Corinth, and Ephesus illustrate this particular aspect of Christian work.

If this is true of Christian workers in general, it is specially true of the Christian minister, for whatever else he may do, he must never lose sight of the duty of personal witnessing. No parochial organization can make up for this, and no sermons or classes, however important, can take its place. It is one of the sure marks of the true spiritual servant of God, that he will hold himself in readiness to use opportunities of witnessing for his Master and winning men to the Kingdom of God. This will not mean spiritual bondage or a compulsion under all circumstances to do this kind of work; on the contrary, it will be but the natural expression of his own loyalty to Christ and his desire to make known what is so precious and powerful in his own life.

### SECTION 2. SOME COUNSELS.

The first essential for personal work is the reality of our

own life with God. As personal dealing means the winning of individual souls for Christ, or the helping of individuals who are in Christ, it naturally follows that almost everything will depend upon the spiritual qualifications of the worker. The typical instance of personal work for Christ is found in the story of Philip and the Eunuch, and it illustrates some of the essential requirements of the personal worker.

1.   Spirituality.   How quick Philip was to see the duty laid upon him by the Holy Spirit, and how responsive he was to the call of God to go towards the eunuch.

2.   Faithfulness.   Without any hesitation he went forward, influenced by loyalty to the call of God to do personal work.   This is the true Christian aggressiveness which is so striking a feature of all New Testament evangelism.

3.   Tactfulness.   There is a beautiful point in the original Greek of the first words addressed by Philip to the eunuch. As they appear in the English version they almost suggest abruptness: 'Do you understand what you are reading?'   But as Philip actually spoke the words, they are prefaced with an exquisite bit of spiritual wisdom, as though he took up the eunuch at a point in the reading which he heard as he drew near: 'Quite so, but do you understand it?'   Aggressiveness which is not blended with tact will often do more harm than good.   The spirit in which we do Christian work counts for a very great deal.   Manner as well as matter must always be considered.

4.   Definiteness.   Philip was content with nothing short of personal contact between the eunuch and Christ.   Taking the Word read, Philip led the eunuch to the Incarnate and Exalted Word.   This is personal work, bringing the soul face to face with Jesus Christ and leading as thoroughly as possible to personal decision.

Arising out of our life with God will come a gradual experience of the needs of the human heart and of the best ways of dealing with spiritual difficulties.   The deeper and fuller our experience the greater will be the help that we can render.   The true minister will provide and welcome every opportunity for doing personal work, and in so doing his own spiritual experience of the needs of men will become deepened and strengthened. Pastoral visiting will often be a great opportunity for this personal effort, and for the constant increase of spiritual insight and experience.

As a great help, the personal worker will be only too glad to compare notes with others who have had far greater experience than himself. An old book, but one well worthy of constant attention by all clergymen, is *A Pastor's Sketches*, by Spencer, an American clergyman of a former generation. The knowledge of the human heart and the ways of dealing with individuals revealed in this book will be a constant help and guide to soul-winners. Another book on the same general lines is *Methods of Soul-Winning*, by another experienced American pastor, Dr. H. C. Mabie; while the book already referred to, *Individual Work for Individuals*, by Dr. H. Clay Trumbull, used in connexion with the companion book by his son, C. G. Trumbull, *Taking Men Alive*, will be of immense help in the study of ways of working. Of course it must never be forgotten that the personal equation rules everything, and no laws and methods can be laid down. Each man must find out his own work and do it in his own way, and if only he places himself at God's disposal day by day, seeking for opportunities, and then for grace to use them, he will quickly realize that personal work is one of the most blessed opportunities of making full proof of his ministry.

CHAPTER IX

## SOME PROBLEMS

FROM time to time questions and problems arise in a clergyman's experience which are not easily settled, and it is often useful to compare experiences. A few of these problems may be considered by way of illustration.

### SECTION 1.  ON TAKING UP NEW WORK.

When a minister comes to a church, whether as newly ordained, or from another charge, much will depend upon the way he sets out to work during his first weeks.  It will be found wise, if not essential, first of all, to pick up the threads of his predecessor's work, and continue for some little time at least the methods already in existence.  Only afterwards should he initiate plans of his own when he has been able to gauge the situation aright.  He will find it particularly helpful to give attention to the members of the paid staff of the church, and elicit their sympathy while he shows the same to them.  They will prove his best friends if only they are enabled to see that he intends to be friendly and closely associated with them.

When a man enters a new sphere the difficulty is of course much greater in regard to the work of the parish, because he is at once responsible for what goes on.  A wise pastor has suggested that the new man should begin by feeding the flock, because, as it is well known, a man can do anything with sheep if first he feeds them.  But to commence by exhortation, still more by anything like lecturing, would probably result in the people not readily entering into sympathetic fellowship with their new pastor.  With regard to changes which are generally thought to be inevitable on the advent of a new minister, there are two methods possible.  The man may decide at once on what changes he feels necessary and make

230

them, or he may avoid instituting any changes until he has become known and trusted by his new people. The latter is by far the wiser and more Christian method. One thing at any rate should be avoided if the man wishes to glorify God and be the means of spiritual help. He should not make changes gradually, and almost weekly, for some time after his arrival. There is nothing more trying and irritating to worshippers than to find some new method or practice nearly every Sunday they come to Church. It makes them wonder what will be the next change, and how many more are likely to come. Suspicions are easily aroused and not so easily laid, while if the clergyman shows himself to be a man of God, one who loves his Saviour, his Bible, and God's people, it will be found that the congregation will respond to him and rally round him in connexion with the work. A newcomer should never forget old worshippers and valued workers. In these days when we are so apt to reverence anything that is called 'up-to-date,' we are liable to forget that the Church ought to be comprehensive in both directions. While rightly giving attention to the needs of the young, we should not forget the needs of the old, especially those who have been the chief supporters of the Church. It is doubtless difficult to harmonize the claims of both parties, but we do not believe that the task is insuperable if faced in the spirit of Christ and with an earnest desire to work for the best interests of all in the congregation. There is a very real danger in upsetting all that has been distinctive of a predecessor. A well-known American clergyman has pointedly said that a new minister should 'enter into' the labours of his predecessor, not 'stamp on' them. Every man must have his own way, and it is more than probable that our predecessors were not quite so inefficient or old-fashioned as we are inclined to think. At any rate we are certain that a new incumbent will show his spiritual fitness for pastoral work if he pays careful respect to the past, gives sympathetic consideration to the needs of the old, tried, spiritual members of his flock, and endeavours to bring all classes of needs together in a desire and a determination so to live and work that the worship may be 'in spirit and in truth.'

## Section 2.  relationship to neighboring churches.

We have already considered this subject to some extent, and it must suffice to add one or two general remarks of a practical kind which may prove of service in the intercourse of parochial life. It goes without saying that a minister should always be friendly and perfectly courteous to the pastors of neighboring churches, and if he can find out, by his reading, why they hold different religious views to his, it will help him to enter into their feelings and spiritual position. This attitude will give him sympathy in meeting with them as occasion arises. It is often possible to unite in social work of various kinds, such as welfare, hospital, and prison activities. United services on national occasions such as Armistice Day may be held in churches alternately each year. Evangelistic meetings, addressed by a special preacher of ability and experience, can be the occasion for united effort, while union services arranged for the visit of some well-known Bible teacher will be found a source of great blessing. These and many other attempts at true union of heart and mind will occur to the minister who is anxious to show a kindly Christian spirit, even while he recognizes differences of opinion on certain points, realising that men of other denominations are just as conscientious in their position as he is in his.

## Section 3.  in reference to the other sex.

Circumstances in parish work frequently lead to the clergyman necessarily being very much thrown into association with lady workers, and this suggests the need of the greatest possible care and circumspection. Both in his pastoral visiting, as we have already seen, and also in connexion with various Church organizations, it is essential that the clergyman should maintain his true position, not merely as a clergyman, but in particular as a Christian man, a man of God. Anything approaching lightness on the part of the clergyman is to be deprecated, while of course, to use the word 'flirtation,' as it often is used in relation to a Christian minister, is to speak of that which is nothing short of deplorable and disgraceful.

Almost without knowing it, the clergyman may easily be led into difficult situations, and for this reason it is essential that he should maintain a life of fellowship with God that will enable him to 'walk circumspectly,' and to give no occasion of stumbling lest the ministry be blamed. As we have already pointed out in other connexions, the great word of the Apostle Paul in writing to Timothy, 'gravity,' is the key to the situation. When a man realizes who and what he is as a minister of Christ, it will enable him to walk carefully and accurately under all circumstances. Difficulties with the other sex may easily be brought about without any fault on the part of the clergyman himself. Human nature is human nature whether it refers to women or men. It is recorded of a Curate that he came to his Rector and said that he wished to leave. He was asked why, and was evidently reluctant to say. 'Is it the stipend?' said the Rector. 'No,' was the reply. 'Has it to do with the work or the climate, or the surroundings?' 'No.' 'Do tell me, then.' 'Well, it's Miss Brown, I really cannot endure her any longer.' 'My dear fellow,' said the wise Rector, 'do you not know that Miss Brown lives in every parish?' Whatever the cause or difficulty may be, there is perhaps no part of a man's life in which it is more essential that he should 'watch and pray.' The young unmarried minister often finds himself in circumstances of real difficulty, although he is simply and faithfully going about his Master's work. But prayer for the guidance and grace of the Holy Spirit will not be in vain, and wisdom will be given according to need under all circumstances. If a man will take care of his character God will take care of his reputation. If a man keeps right with God he can go anywhere and do anything that falls within his duty.

## Section 4.   different social grades.

In many a church it is a serious problem how to bring and keep together the Christian people of different social standing. There is a tendency on the part of the rich or the better educated to avoid association with other members. This may be done quite unconsciously, or it may arise from a lack of interest or a feeling that they have nothing in common. There is an equally strong feeling on the part of those less favoured that the Church is not for them, but only for the well-to-do and leisured. These distinctions frequently make it difficult for the minister to thread his way through the mazes and do justice to everyone. But it is here that the minister can, by example and precept, be truly helpful to the cause of unity in his flock. First and foremost he should lay the greatest possible stress on the fundamental principles of the Gospel: 'Ye are all one in Christ Jesus,' and he should preach in season and out of season that 'in Christ Jesus there is neither Jew nor Greek, there is neither bond nor free, there is neither male nor female.' He will be able to do this very definitely, and perhaps best of all in connexion with the Holy Communion; that Sacrament of unity has its very clear and blessed social aspect which should from time to time be emphasized. It should also be comparatively easy for the minister to suggest ways in which these social gulfs may be most satisfactorily though unobtrusively bridged. This will need all the tact and thoughtfulness of which he is capable, but he will be amply rewarded when his congregation can sing with truth:

> 'Our fears, our hopes, our aims are one,
> Our comforts and our cares.'

Of course it is impossible to avoid recognising facts in regard to various social grades, but there is no reason whatever for the clergyman, of all men, to accentuate these. His duty is to accept things as he finds them, and bring to bear upon them the first principles of the Gospel of Christ, and if he himself knows by personal experience the full reality of New Testament liberty in the Gospel, he will endeavour to emphasize those eternal truths which are necessary for all.

### SECTION 5.   THE GREATEST PROBLEM OF ALL.

As we draw these considerations to a conclusions it must be evident to every reader that the most important matter connected with the ministry is the man himself. This is indeed the greatest problem of all. Almost everything in the ministry is connected with the personal factor, and calls for the expression of the clergyman's life, and if only this is right, it may be said without much hesitation or qualification that everything else will be right also. It has often been remarked how soon and how certainly people discover whether a man is in earnest. People are very sympathetic with a beginner, and they will give him plenty of opportunity to show himself a man, but it will not be very long before they will take his measure and decide as to his reality and power. It may be said without any fear of contradiction that the average judgment of a congregation concerning their clergyman can as a rule be safely trusted. At a closing address when some young men were leaving a Theological College the Principal said to them, 'Gentlemen, you are now regarded, and you will be for some time regarded, by your congregations as young men of promise, but the time will come when they will expect you to be young men of performance.' In a book of *Hints to Parsons,* the following pointed but true remarks are found:

'You may pretend very skilfully, but you will not deceive them long; and really this makes four-fifths (or shall we say nine-tenths?) of the secret of gaining an influence over them. If you are a humbug, nobody will tell you so, they will, perhaps, like you well enough, they won't grumble, but they will simply care less about God, the fire will grow cold, religion will go on dying in the parish.'

And the longer a man stays in a field the severer will be the test. At first he will obtain a good measure of popularity, but afterwards, when the novelty has worn off, and people have become accustomed to his expressions in teaching, and his methods of work, the call is great for the maintenance of spirituality of life. The prime necessity in Christian work is the ability to 'continue.' 'So Daniel continued.' 'Wherefore having obtained help of God, I continued.' In these words the Apostle gives us the secret: 'Having obtained help of God.' It will be only by the grace of God that a man will find his ministry continuing to grow in freshness and force as long as he remains in the parish. But when the life is true to God, when the grace of God fills the heart, when the Spirit of God controls the life, then indeed does the greatest problem of all find its solution, and the man continues 'strong in the grace that is in Christ Jesus.'

Life is largely made up of activity, and the ministry finds itself engaged on a multifarious variety of work; 'the trivial round, the common task.' At times brain and body are apt to stagger under the load, and we are tempted to succumb under the pressure of the burden. Then it is that our simplifying and unifying factor comes in with blessedness and power, and we begin to realize that everything is to be done for Christ. No task that comes can possibly be outside His ken or sphere. No work that is really our duty can fail to be accomplished if done unto Him. 'For Christ' is the talisman that opens every door. 'In Christ' is the guarantee of grace sufficient for every task. As George Herbert says:—

> 'Teach me, my God and King,
>   In all things Thee to see;
> And what I do in anything,
>   To do it unto Thee.

> 'A servant with this clause,
>   Makes drudgery Divine;
> Who sweeps a room as for Thy laws,
>   Makes that and th' action fine.'

'Drudgery divine.' This is only possible when we do everything for Christ, when He is the motive, the inspiration, the joy, the power of service.

'To me to live is Christ.' Receiving everything from Christ. Seeing everything in Christ. Doing everything for Christ. This is life in its simplicity, sufficency, and satisfaction. This is ministry in peace, power, and progress. Away from this is unrest, dissatisfaction, emptiness, weariness, powerlessness. Apart from this is disappointment, depression, discontent, despondency, and despair. But when Christ is our life, ministry becomes a privilege, a joy, a delight; an ever-deepening experience, an ever-heightening glory to God. So let us sum up all by saying that for life and ministry Christ is always necessary, Christ is always available, Christ is always sufficient.

> 'Yea, through life, death, through sorrow and through sinning,
>   He shall suffice me, for He hath sufficed,
> Christ is the end, for Christ was the beginning,
>   Christ the beginning, and the end is Christ.'